Ethnography as Risky Business

Ethnography as Risky Business

Field Research in Violent and Sensitive Contexts

Edited by Kees Koonings, Dirk Kruijt, and Dennis Rodgers

LEXINGTON BOOKS
Lanham • Boulder • New York • London

Published by Lexington Books
An imprint of The Rowman & Littlefield Publishing Group, Inc.
4501 Forbes Boulevard, Suite 200, Lanham, Maryland 20706
www.rowman.com

6 Tinworth Street, London SE11 5AL

British Library Cataloguing in Publication Information Available

Library of Congress Cataloging-in-Publication Data

Names: : Koonings, Kees, editor. | Kruijt, Dirk, editor. | Rodgers, Dennis, editor.
Title: Ethnography as risky business : field research in violent and sensitive contexts / edited by Kees Koonings, Dirk Kruijt, and Dennis Rodgers.
Description: Lanham, Maryland : Lexington Books, 2019. | Includes bibliographical references and index.
Identifiers: LCCN 2019006096 (print) | LCCN 2019007440 (ebook) | ISBN 9781498598446 (electronic) | ISBN 9781498598439 (cloth : alk. paper)
Subjects: LCSH: Ethnology--Fieldwork. | Ethnology--Moral and ethical aspects. | Anthropological ethics. | Ethnology--Latin America.
Classification: LCC GN346 (ebook) | LCC GN346 .E87 2019 (print) | DDC 305.8001--dc23
LC record available at https://lccn.loc.gov/2019006096

Printed in the United States of America

Contents

Acknowledgments

All books are collective endeavours that stand on the shoulders of giants. This one is no different, insofar as its contents are the product of a process of intergenerational collaboration that has taken place over several decades, as explained in the Introduction. At the same time, this volume also explicitly draws inspiration from the foundational work regarding ethnographic endeavours in dangerous and uncertain contexts by a number of previous scholars, including most notably Nancy Howell, Carolyn Nordstrom, Tony Robben, Jeff Sluka, Christopher Kovats-Bernat, and Daniel Goldstein.

Its practical genesis however lies in a symposium that took place in Utrecht, the Netherlands, in June 2014 as part of the festivities around the 50th anniversary of Utrecht University's Faculty of Social and Behavioural Sciences. The editors would like to thank the latter for providing the funding that enabled it. They also want to thank the symposium participants who contributed to this volume for their patience, as well as Palgrave for granting permission to reprint the chapter by Monique Sonnevelt, and last but not least, Nicolette Amstutz and Jessica Tepper at Lexington Books, for their enthusiasm and support for this project.

Note on anonymity of research participants and informed consent

All chapters, with the exception of the Introduction, are reflections on fieldwork conducted on sensitive themes in settings and among people that required meticulous protection of participating individuals, groups, communities, and places. Therefore, in every chapter interlocutors, informants, or research participants have been rendered anonymous, either by not naming them—nor the specifics of their position or locality—or by using pseudonyms. All interviews and conversations have been conducted on the basis of verbal informed consent. In each case anonymity and confidentiality have been guaranteed by the researcher.

Introduction

Ethnography as "Risky Business"

Kees Koonings, Dirk Kruijt, and Dennis Rodgers

BACKGROUND

This book celebrates 25 years of ethnographic research on violence and social order conducted by successive generations of doctoral researchers in the Department of Anthropology at Utrecht University (The Netherlands) under the academic guidance of Dirk Kruijt, in close collaboration with Kees Koonings.[1] Apart from numerous doctoral dissertations,[2] among which those written by contributors to this book, this programme yielded academic monographs and edited volumes dedicated to problems of social and political violence, militarism, armed actors, and the state, as well as numerous individual journal articles and book chapters. Several of these have constituted important interventions in contemporary debates, including in particular the 1999 edited volume *Societies of Fear*, which was one of the first studies of post-Cold War Latin American violence.

This book brings together papers first presented at a symposium organised by the Department of Anthropology in June 2014 as part of the festivities for the 50th anniversary of the Utrecht University's Faculty of Social and Behavioural Sciences. The symposium brought together twelve members of this research group, as well as Dennis Rodgers, a long-time "friend" of the group whose own work has been much inspired by it. In his keynote talk at the symposium he particularly emphasized the exceptional density of quality and the common ethnographic approach shared by the group that echoed the famous US "Chicago School of Sociology," and how a number of the major scholars working on issues of violence around the world — but perhaps most particularly in Latin America — have been in conversation with Dirk Kruijt, Kees Koonings, and their students for over a decade.

The group's ethnographic research tradition has long-standing roots. Kruijt and Koonings have been influenced during the course of their own education by interdisciplinary approaches where macro and micro perspectives come together. These approaches combine a historical-sociological analysis of long-term social processes and problems with the scrutiny of daily experiences and memories using ethnographic methods from anthropology to construct deep knowledge and familiarity with a local situation, based on in-depth interviews with key persons and participatory observation carried out longitudinally. At the same time, they have always had a (silent) preference for the urban environment, and its stark and revealing contrasts between the very rich and the very poor, the very powerful and the defenceless, and the excesses of power and dominance. This is partly because their endeavours towards understanding the why, the who, the when, and the where, have always been undertaken with an eye to recommending change and transformation, a tradition which they derive from a Marxian heritage, the literary tradition of engaged "naturalism," the European sociographic orientation, and long-term engagement with policy relevance for civil society, governments and international organizations.

Of the Marxian scholars, it was not just overall visions of political economy that were influential, but also their *virtuoso* analysis of "real" class conflicts and confrontations, including in particular Karl Marx's *Eighteenth Brumaire and the Civil War in France*, which in many ways provides a clear template for political sociology. The naturalist literary tradition represented by authors like Emile Zola and George Orwell, both brilliant authors and activists with an advocacy approach, was also influential. Zola did research, preparing the many volumes of his Rougon Macquart Family history, by patient observation and interviews, many times *in situ*, and used his notebooks as the base of the romanticized reality. Orwell immersed himself in the position of the vagrants and destitutes in his *Down and Out in London and Paris* (1933), as observant living with a miner's family in *The Road to Wigan Pier* (1937), and participated as combatant before writing his *Homage to Catalonia* (1938). Both Zola and Orwell used a research style that in academic terminology is known as the sociographic method, while at the same time writing it up in a clear and readable manner.

Kruijt and Koonings also count two major works of German and Dutch sociography as major influences. Firstly, Marie Jahoda, Paul Lazarsfeld, and Hans Zeisel's (1933) study of the unemployed in the Austrian village of Marienthal, and secondly, Gerald Kruijer's (1951) study of desperation and hunger among the population of Amsterdam during the famine winter of 1944-1945 under the Nazi occupation. The former, in particular, is a highly original piece of work due to its systematic use of qualitative and quantitative data, diaries, structured and unstructured interviews, participant observations, but also in its development of typologies and middle-range theories about the consequences of unemployment (as such, it echoed William Thomas and Florian Znaniecki's famous *The Polish Peasant in Europe and America*, discussed further below). Contrarily to much of the literature at the time, Jahoda et al. did not observe the inevitable rise of a revolutionary ethos, but rather a downfall to resignation and apathy. This kind of analysis would be followed in later decades by other influential research such as Oscar Lewis's study on the culture of poverty in Mexico (1959), Janice Perlman's book about slum dwellers in Rio de Janeiro (1976), or William Julius Wilson's work on the urban underclass (1987).

Since, initially at least, the Utrecht research was strongly oriented towards Latin America and the Caribbean, major sources of inspiration were also found in Latin American structuralism and the neo-Marxian historical sociology of the dependency school that is perhaps most paradigmatically represented by the work of Fernando Henrique Cardoso and Enzo Faletto (1979). This led directly to a sustained engagement in field research by Kruijt during the 1970s and 1980s on issues such as labour relations, industrialization, entrepreneurialism, military reformism, urban informality, and civil war, much of it in collaboration with the late Menno Vellinga. Indeed, building on the latter's pioneering work on urban class conflict in Mexico (Vellinga 1979), Kruijt and Vellinga's (1979) joint research on class and labour relations in Peru was in many ways foundational for Latin American Studies in the Netherlands (Baud 2002).

The Latin American connection was strengthened by the collaboration with Edelberto Torres-Rivas, the founding father of Central American historical sociology and political science. Torres-Rivas was secretary-general of FLACSO[3] during the late 1980s and early 1990s, and became the Prince Bernhard visiting professor at Utrecht University in 1994. He was also the key note speaker at the "Societies of Fear" conference organised by Kruijt and Koonings at Utrecht University the following year (see Koonings and Kruijt 1999). Another important collaborator was the late Carlos Ivan Degregori, who pioneered ethnographic work on migration, urban informality and the armed conflict between the state and the Maoist guerrilla of Shining Path in Peru. Degregori was a visiting scholar in Utrecht in 2004, and in 2005 he was awarded a doctoral degree by the University for his seminal work. Torres-Rivas and Degregori were moreover respectively the leading authors of the Guatemalan and Peruvian Truth Commission reports.

All these sources of inspiration led to the creation and consolidation of the research program on social exclusion, political conflict, collective violence, peace, and reconstruction when Kruijt took up his chair in Development Studies at Utrecht University in 1993. Although multidisciplinary, this was firmly grounded in Anthropology, and all of the projects conducted under the program's aegis share this discipline's strong qualitative fieldwork approach in which ethnographic methods figure prominently.[4] Perhaps not surprisingly, two and half decades of sustained research have not only led to numerous important empirical studies, but also significant accumulated wisdom concerning the ethnographic method that is at the core of the Utrecht research approach, more specifically in relation to the advantages, benefits, dilemmas, and pitfalls regarding its deployment in relation to studying issues of violence.

THE ETHNOGRAPHIC APPROACH IN QUALITATIVE RESEARCH

Ethnography as a methodology denotes a particular research technique that is principally based on "participant observation fieldwork." This is perhaps best explained backwards. "Fieldwork" is a spatial practice; it involves carrying out research in uncontrolled physical locations often referred to as "the field," in contrast to "the laboratory," for example. There are different interpretations of what constitutes "the field," but these generally all assume that fieldwork will involve some form of spatial mobility—a researcher goes somewhere which is not their usual location—i.e., a desk in an office—in order to do research. This research is carried out in a particular way, through "participant observation." This is a process of simultaneous participating and observing everyday life, whereby researchers immerse themselves in people's daily lives, watching, listening, asking questions and recording actions, discourses, and routines. In other words, ethnography is a research methodology that aims to study people in their own time and space.

Rather than seeking to perform artificial experiments or administer pre-determined surveys or questionnaires, ethnography is an inherently inductive research method, and involves understanding social life as it is encountered rather than as it is expected to be.[5] This means that ethnography generates intrinsically dynamic data, permitting causal process-tracing instead of the uni-dimensional correlations that are a hallmark of much contemporary quantitative social research. Hence, ethnography allows us to understand how and why social life unfolds as it does in its uniquely complex manner, and permits sophisticated and original theorising. Ethnography moreover produces fundamentally embedded data, promoting an understanding of settings that apprehends them not just as contexts but rather as the central focus of analysis.

Few methodological approaches can arguably provide as fine-grained and nuanced a picture of life as the ethnographic. To a considerable extent, this is due to the experiential nature of the research approach. Traditionally, ethnographers go and live with the inhabitants of a given group, community or society, generally for prolonged periods of time. The aim is to be able to engage directly and systematically in people's daily lives, to achieve in-depth, intense interaction. The logic behind this immersion is to normatively participate in everyday activities and observe events and people in their everyday context. The Mexican anthropologist Renato Rosaldo (1989, cited in Clifford 1996, 5) famously qualified this as "deep hanging out." This allows researchers to gain a certain intimacy of a situation, a sense of empathy with a social environment, attaining what sociologist Max Weber called "verstehen" (interpretative understanding).

Ever since its early roots in the pioneering work of Lewis Morgan, and subsequently Franz Boas in the US and Bronislaw Malinowski in the UK, ethnography has been seen as the "crown jewel" of social and cultural anthropology. The founding fathers of ethnography, in particular Malinowski, established the consecrated practice of participant observation. Malinowski not only went to observe, but also to participate. He learnt the Trobrian language, recorded what people said, observed what they did, but also took part in daily village life, fishing, farming, and so on. He beautifully and extensively recorded the result of his fieldwork in a number of now classic anthropological works such as *Argonauts of the Western Pacific* (1922) or *Coral Gardens and their Magic* (1935). He subsequently trained and inspired whole generations of eminent UK anthropologists, the most famous of which was perhaps Edward Evan Evans-Pritchard, best known for his classic 1940 eponymous ethnography of the Nuer of Sudan.

Despite the impressive development of the ethnographic method since its inception—enhancing its scope and sophistication tremendously, as we will discuss below—its so-called classical frame established by the pioneers still stands largely uncontested (Hammersley and Atkinson 2007, 3ff). The ethnographer seeks engagement with "natural" social conditions, relations and interactions. For this to be possible, prolonged and sustained presence in the field, or rather, among and with the population or group under study, is indispensable. The core condition to be established in the field is that magical, ephemeral quality called "rapport": the trust-based set of relationships and interactions between ethnographer and informants/participants (in the research) deemed fundamental for obtaining "valid" and "reliable" data.

Although we acknowledge the inherently problematic nature of such positivist terms for an epistemology that is fundamentally interpretative and inherently reflexive, it is important to underline at this point the profoundly empirical quality at the heart of ethnographic research. Ethnographers always search for the holy grail of "real life." Successful conduct of ethnographic fieldwork puts high demands on the endurance, perseverance and social skills of the fieldworker. This, as we will argue below, makes ethnography a very personal and often emotional endeavour, apart from the intricacies of interpretation and reflexion that shape its scientific quality.

Another way to represent ethnography is to see it as a journey through time, space and permanently shifting forms of engagements. If we apply this idea to conventional notions of ethnography, the essence of ethnographic "knowing" is often portrayed as the transformation of the researcher from an absolute stranger into an intimate outsider. In the course of this journey the ethnographic researcher engages with local frames (dubbed "emic") that she/he uses to transfer from local meaning to universal scholarly understanding, the "etic" of the trade. In other words, the ethnographer has the "ability to get inside and understand other individual agents, groups and communities, to comprehend local loyalties and systems of knowledge" (Graeber 2002, 1222). Through being culturally sensitive, the ethnographer is uniquely placed to perform this and to work it into theory through procedures such as thick description and grounded theory, the "ethno-narrative from actors in the field" providing "theoretical clues" (Tavory and Timmermans 2009, 244).

Much of this epistemic is of course based on Clifford Geertz's (1973) well-known ideas on the ethnographic interpretation of culture. But our reading of Geertz opens the possibility of a more complex and critical understanding of the ethnographic episteme. Anthropology as a discipline is based on an interpretive theoretical approach to culture; culture is seen as webs of significance and their interpretation as a strategy to come to cultural understanding, "in search of meaning" (Geertz 1973, 5). Geertz and many anthropological ethnographers influenced by him have adapted Gilbert Ryle's concept of "thick description" to work their field with the intent to arrive at conceptually informed empirical categories: "this fact—that what we call our data are really our own constructions of other people's constructions of what they and their compatriots are up to" (Geertz 1973, 9).

Geertz rejected the idea that this is just an exercise in cultural decoding, because this would imply that culture is either seen as essentialist or reified, or reduced to alien or hidden cognitive schemata that have to be penetrated and translated by the ethnographic method. This would presuppose a separation between the culture as a mysterious yet knowable object and the ethnographer as a seeker of external understanding. Often, we suggest, this assumption leads to ethnographic work that is heavy with neologism and hazy concepts that guises as "thick description" or maybe even as grounded theory, but has lost any connection with the original analytical intention. This is not what interpretive ethnography is about. Rather, we argue that what Geertz contends is that since culture has to be public in order to be practiced, ethnography is the effort to establish a shared humanity through engagement and joint reflexivity without which culture as co-constructed, public understanding of meaning cannot be grasped.

Although this may sound opaque, such a position has a number of intriguing implications that transpire in the research presented in this book. First, ethnographic research is impossible without taking fully into account the role of the fieldworker in co-creating the areas of understanding. We follow Geertz's notion that ethnographic research first and foremost involves ethnographers "finding their feet," which makes it "an unnerving business" and a fundamentally "personal experience" (Geertz 1973, 13). Hence, not only is the reflexive positioning of the ethnographer crucial for gauging the reach and limits of the method, but the personal quality of ethnographic fieldwork and interpretation also cannot and should not be obscured. Indeed, we feel that this must be made explicit as much as possible, precisely to strengthen intersubjectivity and to counter any suggestion that ethnographic "evidence" is "anecdotal" rather than "scientific."

Second, and very much related to this first point, the ontological separation between the ethnographic researcher and the studied "Other" is meaningless. In fact, that would be an obstacle to interpretation in just the same way as its radical—and ideal-typical—opposite, "going native." And third, the notion of pure or objective science as the ideal remit of anthropology-as-science (as opposed to the often-used misnomer of "applied anthropology" as somehow based on opportunistic concessions to money or power) is misguided. Rather, we sympathize with multiple shades of "public" (Lassiter 2005), "engaged" (Low and Merry 2010) or even "militant" anthropology (Scheper-Hughes 1995) in which the scholarly value of research is enhanced by its critical affinity with practical concerns, value positions, or societal commitment.

A final aspect of ethnographic research, related to the preceding reflections, is that as a methodology and as an epistemic it is not bound to a single discipline, namely (social or cultural) anthropology. The social sciences in their broadest sense—that is, including economics—can clearly benefit from ethnographic understanding. Indeed, this idea goes back to the original program of the famous Chicago School of Sociology—aptly dubbed the "Chicago ethnographers" by Ulf Hannerz (1980)—in the 1920s. This research group saw ethnography as a uniquely suited strategy for systematically researching the complex and changing context of a world that was increasingly urbanizing (Bulmer 1984; Jones and Rodgers 2016). Drawing on Thomas and Znaniecki's (1918-20) pioneering use of personal documents such as life histories, letters and diaries as a means of engaging with the lived experience of urban contexts, Robert Park—the founding figure of the Chicago School of Sociology—sought to continue and elaborate this vision while promoting studies about almost every aspect of the "natural urban habitat." This included a program of research into the differentiation between urban neighbourhoods, ethnic and class divisions, the very rich and the destitute, ghettos and gangs, slums and the upper-class districts, deviants and drug users, delinquents and sex workers, migrants and established elites. As he famously told his students:

> You have been told to go grubbing in the library, thereby accumulating a mass of notes and a liberal coating of grime. You have been told to choose problems wherever you can find musty stacks of routine records based on trivial schedules prepared by tired bureaucrats and filled out by reluctant applicants for aid or fussy do-gooders or indifferent clerks. This is called "getting your hands dirty in real research."

> Those who thus counsel you are wise and honourable; the reasons they
> offer are of great value. But one more thing is needful: first-hand obser-
> vation. Go and sit in the lounges of the luxury hotels and on the door-
> steps of flophouses; sit on the Gold Coast settees and on the slum
> shakedowns; sit in Orchestra Hall and in the Star and Garter burlesque.
> In short, . . . go get the seat of your pants dirty in real research. (cited in
> McKinney 1966, 71).

Of course, the distinction between sociology, anthropology and political
sciences was not as rigid as it has (unfortunately) become in the last
decades of the twentieth and the two first decades of the present century
(Jones and Rodgers 2016). Still, the Chicago School of Sociology's powerful legacy of ethnography as both a methodology and an epistemology
that easily crosses, or even ignores, conventional boundaries between the
disciplines of social science is useful to remind us of its enduring power
and scope, and this interdisciplinary lineage is one to which the Utrecht
program subscribes. The basic underlying epistemological assumption of
all the associated researchers has always been the same, even if approaches have differed: interpretation based on personal involvement,
engagement and reflexivity. At the same time, however, a range of different dilemmas and issues have been raised over the past two decades and
a half, as the next section discusses.

REFLECTIONS ON CURRENT ETHNOGRAPHIC DILEMMAS

This is not the place to attempt a comprehensive review of the current
state of affairs regarding ethnography, a number of which have been
published by a range of scholars over the years (e.g., Atkinson et al. 1999;
Hammersley 1992; Madison 2012; Robben and Sluka 2007). Rather, in this
section we wish to highlight a number of issues that have often come to
the fore of the ethnographies in this volume. The themes that follow are
by no means unique, and may of course be encountered in any kind of
ethnographic research, but we draw attention to them in order to highlight what we believe to be significant contributions to furthering our
methodological and epistemological understanding of the ethnographic
endeavour.

A first observation is that ethnography has always been an extremely
dynamic field. While its evolutionary moments from classic to modern to
linguistic and postmodern have been noted (Denzin and Lincoln 1994),
there is arguably no really "pure" ethnographic tradition *per se*. In many
ways, though, the multiplicity of the ethnographic methods and epis-
temes mirrors the flexibility and creativity demanded from ethnographic
practitioners themselves. As Atkinson, Coffey and Delamont (1999, 469)
argue, there has always been a dialectical tension between orthodoxy (or
normal science) and experimentation within the ethnographic field, cap-

tured by the "methodological ferment" that is often inherently associated with the empirical practice of ethnography. Certainly, the researchers writing in this volume have all experienced significant moments of innovation, both willing and unwilling, in their ethnographic research, pushing the boundaries of their methodological approaches in a range of diverse and often unusual ways. In this volume, Glebbeek's formally undergoing Guatemalan Police basic training, or Toll's involvement as a peace negotiator in the Colombian transitional justice process that she studied, stand out as particularly good examples of this experimentation.

Second, the construction of meaning through ethnographic interpretation is predicated on shared reflexivity between the "researched" and the researcher. One does not have to engage in participatory or "action" research to accept that the ethnographic rendering of research results essentially comes out of sustained conversations between researcher and researched and their respective "scripts." This is more than the "double hermeneutics" Giddens (1984, 284) talks about; rather than the (re-)interpretation of interpretation, understanding and meaning is negotiated. In this exercise the ethnographer of course leads, but interlocutors are not only the research participants but also often the publics reached with writing, lecturing, debating and other forms of transmission. In other words, the positioning of the ethnographic researcher is crucial. Not only does this imply that the duality of objectivity/neutrality versus engagement/activism is rather moot, it also means that the presence and persona of the field researcher, and her/his roles and identities, co-shape the dynamics of fieldwork, interpretation and writing and cannot be separated from the insights and knowledge that are eventually claimed. This is something that can be especially complicated in certain circumstances, as the chapters by Denissen, on her ethnography of grass roots politics in Khartoum while she was posted there as an accredited Dutch diplomat, Koonings on his research on conflict and peace in Colombia carried out through a combination of consultancy assignments and "autonomous" fieldwork stints, Kruijt on his research on Peruvian and Central American revolutionaries carried out while working for Dutch aid in these countries, or Sprenkels, about his study of former revolutionary comrades in arms in El Salvador, highlight very well.

A third issue, one that directly flows from the previous point, is the importance of notions like Self, Other, encounters and emotions within ethnographic work. These are all closely and permanently connected and shaped continuously through the various "textbook" steps of ethnographic fieldwork. Hammersley and Atkinson (2007) discuss these steps and the choices and challenges involved under the headers of "access" and "field relations" in terms of managing the "relational self" in the field. Although useful because of its pragmatism, their review of issues such as the self-representation of the ethnographer, overt versus covert researcher roles, finding and dealing with gatekeepers and sponsors, impression management, establishing mutuality, and even manipulating "ascribed" personal characteristics such as gender, is strongly transactional and instrumental (cf. Huggins and Glebbeek 2009a). They state that ethnography implies a "wide-ranging and subtle process of manoeuvring oneself into a *position from which the necessary data can be collected*." (Hammersley and Atkinson 2007, 62, emphasis added). Yet the research presented in this book shows that ethnography often moves beyond such negotiated instrumentality; trust and rapport are relational qualities that can only be managed to a limited degree. This then feeds into much of what they call the "strains and stresses of fieldwork" (Hammersley and Atkinson 2007, 89). Self-doubt, insecurity, anxiety, fear, and emotion are part and parcel of every ethnographic experience (Diphoorn 2013; Hume 2007), and these should be recognised as qualities of ethnographic work rather than obscured as partial truths, self-deceptions, and even "lies" (see Fine 1993). Certainly, the contributions by Diphoorn and van Roekel highlight in different ways the deeply formative impact of emotions on the ethnographic experience, both methodologically and epistemologically.

A fourth dilemma is provided by the profound transformations undergone by the objects, settings and scales of ethnographic research. Of course, nobody believes any longer in anthropology being the science of the remote and located alterity of human society and culture. Concomitantly, ethnography cannot be reduced to the toolbox for opening up these others' black boxes, as we already argued. Especially in the so-called Western world (Europe, North America, Latin America), ethnography has been building a strong legacy of looking at the diversity and complexity of urban hierarchical and exclusionary modernity. In recent decades, the new dynamics of globalization, the post-colonial debate, the prominence of movement and flow, and the discovery of digital social space have contributed to a reformulation of the remit of ethnography (Comaroff and Comaroff 2003). Apart from what geographers call "multi-scalar" connections (Brenner 1999) and its implications for multi-sited and virtual field research, it may even mean the disappearance of the "other" as an ontological category (see also Mosse 2006). This articulation of scales, flows and objects redefines the challenge of ethnography in new and surprising ways, as the chapters by Sánchez Meertens highlighting how his experience growing up in conflict-affected Colombia impacted on his research in conflict-affected Sri Lanka, and Remijnse's exploration of her continued interaction with those she researched after finishing her PhD, describe well.

Fifth, we are forced to rethink the problem of "engagement." If ethnography is a methodology based on interpersonal engagement, social science founded on this methodology has a challenging time upholding the myth of neutrality, or the idea of being impartial as a condition for scientific rigour. This is of course not a recent insight. The classical founders of social science (including political economy) were quite aware of the political and moral implications of their science. After World War II critical theory in its many (fashionable) guises, such as neo-Marxism, dependency and world system theory, and more recently the post-colonial debate, sought to engage and emancipate the people "without history" (Wolf 1990), the voiceless, the disempowered, the subaltern (Nash 2007; Kruijt and Vellinga 1979; Spivak 1988; Roy 2011). Since ethnography seeks intimate understanding, it therefore can and should care and be socially and politically engaged. This by no means implies a one-track agenda or political correctness, and certainly does not lead to discarding the ethnographic vocation of critical autonomy vis-à-vis the human experience it studies. But as the chapters by van der Borgh on the politics of aid in post-war El Salvador, or by Simon Thomas on the ambiguities surrounding his research on indigenous disputes in Ecuador, both highlight, such an approach can raise significant dilemmas.

Having said that, engagement takes many different forms; often it is implicitly reflected in the choice of subjects and narratives; often it is explicitly claimed in work that seeks to contribute to an agenda for "public anthropology" of awareness raising and denouncing injustice, oppression or violations (Sanford 2003; Manz 2005). Even more explicit is the use of ethnography in "participatory" or "action" social research, research designs that seek to include the researched as stakeholders in the research process or pursue a combination of ethnographic research and advocacy/activist roles, such as Scheper-Hughes's (1995) "militant ethnography." A variety of this is what Baud and Rutten (2004) call the work of "popular intellectuals," scholars and academics that bring their scientific expertise and research findings to the fore to advance agendas of groups or movements to which they "belong." Here we approach the seminal post-colonial problem of representing the "subaltern." Is it possible, even for engaged or partisan scholars, to know and give voice to subaltern subjects (Spivak 1988); if so, what are the limits of ethnographic engagement, especially when representatives of the subaltern are entering the profession with a clearly political agenda? A related problem is how to ethnographically research the non-subaltern (the elites, the powerful, the exploiters, the violators, the criminal, the perpetrators)? How to give voice to their experience? For what purpose? Understanding or denouncing? Here it is important to not only resist the siren song of "ethnographic seduction" (Robben 1996) but also, paradoxically, to maintain an "outside the box" capacity to avoid all too easy canons of right and wrong (or moral high grounds) provided by specific cultural and moral repertoires. But this is by no means easy, as the chapters by Rasch on the way that she was inevitably classified in certain ways by the people she studied, or Wiegink, on having to navigate the politics of representation of former counter-revolutionary combatants in Mozambique, illustrate well.

A last point we want to briefly raise is that of the sensitive, not-taken-for-granted quality of the ethical aspects of ethnographic research. At a time when universities—especially in the U.S. and the UK, but more recently also in countries such as the Netherlands or Denmark—seek to strengthen their policies—or rather, discipline discourse and the desired public effect thereof—regarding what is now called "ethical integrity," this dilemma has been cast into new and increasingly controversial moulds. Although almost thirty years ago Philippe Bourgois (1990, 45) famously criticized what he called the "rigid, righteous" conception of an anthropological ethics that prioritized "intra-disciplinary purity" and ignored critical "societal concerns" such as "human rights violations" and "the political economy of exploitation," there has been an increasing tendency within academia over the past decade to try to promote notions and standards of "one size fits all" ethics and integrity in research that are highly apolitical. Yet this push towards a depoliticized notion of ethics is in fact clearly political if it steers academic research away from such large questions of power and inequality.[6] The ethics of ethnographic research cannot be disengaged from the real predicaments of those being researched.

The fact that this is always highly subjective makes the ethics of ethnography extremely complex. On the one hand, one can adopt a radical strategy of "militant" or "enraged" ethnographic research as advocated by Nancy Scheper-Hughes (2004), who resorted to intrinsically ethically debatable practices such as covertly assuming fake roles and identities to penetrate the dark labyrinths of worldwide illegal organ trafficking, a course of action she defends as necessary to expose the violent nature of such practices that are taken for granted in the sanitized corridors of the First-World medical profession (see also Scheper-Hughes 1995). On the other hand, we can simply also recognise the inherently "messy" nature of ethnographic research, and accept that its ethics are inevitably always "situational" (Rodgers 2007; Verhallen 2016). Such an approach fits better with the requirements of the ethnographic method than strictly protocolled ethics—such as those of the American Anthropological Association (AAA), for example—and allow for a realistic flexibility in the way that research is carried out. Having said this, what is clear is that certain circumstances heighten the dilemmas and ambiguities surrounding the ethics of ethnographic research, including in particular situations of violence and conflict, as the next section considers in more detail.

ETHNOGRAPHIC RESEARCH IN VIOLENT AND SENSITIVE CONTEXTS

If we recap what we have argued so far, we propose that ethnography is an inherently rewarding but at the same time "risky" research methodol-

ogy: "high risk, high gain." It is fraught with uncertainties, practical obstacles, challenges and pitfalls. Ethnographic researchers are unsure (or
cannot and should not know beforehand) how it will work out and with
what results. Because ethnographic research is relational and interactive
it cannot be dissociated from the social process that is studied nor from
the personal positions of all agents involved (including the ethnographer). This book engages with most of the above themes. We now want
to consider the added particularity that most of the researchers in the
Utrecht program have engaged in research in conflict or post-conflict
situations. This means that they always encountered insecurity, violence
and fear as social condition (Lubkemann 2008; Richards 2005), more often
than not against a background of what some call "structural" and "cultural" violence: inequality, exclusion, stigmatization.

A relatively young but quickly expanding literature has been dealing
with the methodological, practical, and ethical implications and consequences of this particular type of ethnographic field. It had to be invented
from the ground up. In the early 1990s, Jeff Sluka (1990; 1995) called
attention to the consequences of violence and war for conducting ethnographic research, building on Nancy Howell's (1988) more general survey of the "hazards of fieldwork" (as reported by North American
anthropologists). Carolyn Nordstrom and Tony Robben (1995) subsequently published a pioneering and landmark volume, *Fieldwork under
Fire*, which explored how violence and war as lived experiences were
intertwined with their ethnographic understanding. They argued that
"the ontics of violence . . . and the epistemology of violence . . . are not
separate," and that this had profound implications, not only for pragmatic ethnographic concerns such as the safety of researchers and informants
but also for the question of ethnographic "narration" and "authenticity,"
or in other words, giving voice to whom, by whom, how, and why (Robben and Nordstrom 1995, 4, 10-11). This epistemological quandary was
echoed by Carol Greenhouse, Elizabeth Mertz and Kay Warren (2002) in
their volume on *Ethnography in Unstable Places*, while more methodological and practical concerns about ethnographic fieldwork in violent and
dangerous places were subsequently treated in a more grounded way by
Christopher Kovats-Bernat (2002), Rodgers (2007), Daniel Goldstein
(2014), and Sluka (2015), among others.

Kovats-Bernat (2002) sets forth a number of pragmatic recommendations for "fieldwork amidst violence and terror" inspired by his own
research on the lives of Haitian street children during the 1990s. His
overall point boils down to his observation that, in dangerous fields,

> (...) methodology is defined . . . as an elastic, incorporative, integrative,
> and malleable practice. It should be informed by the shifting social
> complexities unique to unstable field sites and should depend on a
> level of investigative flexibility on the part of the ethnographer who

cannot always be expected to work in safety and security. . . . On a practical level, these strategies of study should involve a careful deter- mination of how best to approach a research field fraught with peril and tactics for reducing the likelihood that the anthropologist (or infor- mants) will be shot or arrested while doing so. (Kovats-Bernat 2002, 210).

Although his focus is predominantly on the problems of averting person- al safety risks to the field researcher and to ensure data protection, Ko- vats-Bernat (2002, 2013-2015) does come up with a timely critique of for- malized codes for research ethics and professional conduct (such as pro- vided by AAA). Instead he proposes a "localized ethic" that works with a permanent monitoring of the evolving dynamics of the dangerous field and the navigational knowledge held by local protagonists, including informants.

Rodgers's (2007; see also this volume) longitudinal research on the embedded dynamics of gangs in Managua, Nicaragua, represents a par- ticularly poignant case of how these risks unfold as part of the ethnogra- phy of violence. He adds to the situated idea of localized ethics the notion of the "violence of ethnography" which not only refers to the safety of the ethnographer and her or his informants but also to the possibility of being close to, if not participating, in violent episodes and "illicit" activ- ities. His experiences with gang anthropology show that it is not just the ethnographer who chooses their field, the field also may impose itself upon the ethnographer. His account of the initiation rites to which he was subjected by the gang of the Nicaraguan *barrio* he worked in illustrates how this can happen, but at the same time, how by building a particular- ly strong rapport, and consolidating an engagement with, a youth gang took him clearly beyond the established or known boundaries of "re- sponsible" ethnographic fieldwork, as defined by putatively "objective" ethical standards. Rodgers uses the term "involuntary anthropology" to describe his ethnographic choices, noting how his actions started off as a strategy for self-protection but evolved into a research design for getting to grips with the ambient chronic violence by living it. In his case, situa- tional ethics within a particularly risky ethnography not only informed protective practices but also the shifting boundaries of morally defend- able violent conduct in the field.

In a more didactic vein, Sluka (2015) offers a range of general recom- mendations to managing ethnographic research in violent and dangerous settings. Risks to be taken into account by the ethnographer include not only the protection of self, participant and data, but also being aware of the perception others in the field hold of the position and intent of the researcher (including, for example, whether he or she is a "spy"), the problem of being partisan or neutral, and the related risk of being tar- geted by stakeholders in violence or conflicts (including the formal au- thorities). Ultimately, though, Sluka concludes that "managing danger in fieldwork should be viewed as a dialogic *ongoing process* based on an *ethical relationship* with research participants, which requires recognizing the shifting nature of danger and risk" (Sluka 2015, 120, emphasis in original). It is very much this kind of more processual and situated approach to ethical ethnographic research in violent and sensitive contexts that emerges from the body of work produced by the contributors to this volume, as the next concluding section explores.

RISKY ETHNOGRAPHY AS SITUATED ETHICAL RESEARCH

All of the researchers in this volume have, at some point or another, encountered critical issues, faced dilemmas, and suffered setbacks during the course of their fieldwork. One of the strengths of the group, however, has been its extensive internal communication, even across generations. This produced an accumulated collective wisdom and pool of experiences that have been invaluable in permitting the sustained successful production of ethnographic research over the course of two and a half decades. This volume is in many ways a first attempt at bringing some of these insights together. In line with our suspicion of strict protocols and "one size fits all" solutions, it does not attempt to formally synthesize or extract specific insights, but rather offers a collection of experiences and reflections in the hope that these will provide inspiration to others when they develop their own situated ethical approaches.

Having said this, the contributors' exploration of ethnography as an inherently risky research strategy, particularly in violent and sensitive contexts, has brought a number of key methodologically and epistemologically issues to the fore. First, risky ethnography complicates the access to and movement in the field and poses considerable challenges for establishing trust and rapport with research participants. The second point is directly related to this. Protection is a crucial concern. We argue that the protection of participants and data takes precedence over the protection of the ethnographer-self because the latter has consciously taken the decision to engage in risky research, even in the case of involuntary anthropology. Protective concerns range from personal security and careful storage and use of data to strict guarantees of confidentiality and enhanced sensitivity regarding modes of interference in the lives and relations of the research population.

A third set of concerns has to do with the problem of manipulation of positionality and identity in the field. Researchers and participants always have agendas but in dangerous and sensitive settings these may become increasingly pressing. Informants may resort to ethnographic "seduction" (Robben 1996), may expect aid brokering from the researcher or may seek to convey political legitimation through participation in ethnographic research. The ethnographer, in turn, has to reflect and act upon the questions of engagement, partisanship, neutrality or complicity. Fourth, risky ethnography enhances the impact of usual fieldwork stressors and will always sharpen the edge of emotions such as fear, grief or doubt that come along with personal and relational research on the nature and consequences of conflict, violence, and danger. In all cases, risky ethnography has a profound impact on the self of the researcher, through discomfort, dreams, doubts, shame, fear, and sometimes trauma—both in and out of the field. Finally, risky ethnography requires careful post-fieldwork procedures, especially in data management and in writing up.

Risky ethnography often entails limitations with respect to disclosure of information by informants. This may have to do with the narrating of memories that are politically or morally charged or with the constraints imposed by privacy considerations. All researchers faced questions about how to deal with confidential, secret or sensitive information. In some of the research addressing politics and policy interventions was particularly complicated when a trade-off between short term practice—such as diplomacy or consultancy—and long term academic research had to be found. Overall, though, we endorse the position of situational and localized ethics to guide ethnographic research as a reflective and navigational enterprise, rather than adherence to strict codes of ethical conduct within the profession.

These aspects of risky ethnography, of doing qualitative social scientific research in dangerous fields and on sensitive subjects, appear in different ways in all chapters in this book. But all contributions set forth the stakes of the research subject and setting shaped by conflict, violence, hostility, and distrust. Researchers and informants facing these stakes meet, in varying ways, surveillance, monitoring, suspicion or aggression by authorities, armed actors, and other power players. In particular, all the research projects we discuss show a diversity of violent or contentious political actors set in practices (or at least recent legacies) of suspicion, infiltration, dissidence, paranoia, and double or triple agendas. The complexity of establishing and negotiating access to the field and the research subjects and of defining multiple and always shifting roles within the research setting also transpires in the problem of the personal identity of the ethnographer—and this whether in terms of gender, political alignment, or professional multiplicity—being also a diplomat, consultant, or policy practitioner—as well as generational or ethnic and racial differences.

It is however perhaps in an epistemological sense that the contributions to this book make their most important collective point. The practice of risky ethnography involves a constant patrolling of moral frontiers that has to balance the necessary intimacy of ethnographic work with an understanding and engagement with broader social issues. It brings to the fore in a visceral and immediate manner the necessity for an engaged social science, one where the actors of the social realities that researchers encounter, investigate, and describe, are not just seen as "data points" situated in broader social structures, but as full partners in the co-production of knowledge. It is this that is ultimately the greatest potential gain of carrying out "risky ethnography," the pay-off of a situated ethics that constitutes ethnography not just as being about studying the world, but very much about being in the world.

REFERENCES

Atkinson, P., A. Coffey, and S. Delamont. 1999. "Ethnography, Post, Past, and Present." *Journal of Contemporary Ethnography* 28, no. 5: 460-471.

Banck, G. and K. Koonings, eds. 1988. *Social Change in Contemporary Brazil. Politics, Class and Culture in a Decade of Transition.* Amsterdam: CEDLA (Latin America Studies 43).

Baud, M. 2002. "Latin American and Caribbean studies in the Netherlands." *European Review of Latin American and Caribbean Studies/ Revista Europea de Estudios Latinoamericanos y del Caribe* 72, (April): 139-160.

Baud, M., and R. Rutten, eds. 2004. *Popular Intellectuals and Social Movements: Framing Protest in Asia, Africa, and Latin America.* Cambridge: Cambridge University Press (International Review of Social History 49, suppl. 12).

Bourgois, P. 1990. "Confronting Anthropological Ethics: Ethnographic Lessons from Central America." *Journal of Peace Research* 27, no. 1: 43-54.

Brenner, N. 1999, "Globalisation as Reterritorialisation: The Re-scaling of Urban Governance in the European Union." *Urban Studies* 36, no. 3: 431-451.

Bulmer, M. 1984. *The Chicago School of Sociology. Institutionalization, Diversity, and the Rise of Sociological Research.* Chicago and London: The University of Chicago Press.

Cardoso, F. H. and E. Faletto. 1979. *Dependency and Development in Latin America.* Berkeley: University of California Press.

Clifford, J. 1996. "Anthropology and/as Travel." *Etnofoor* 9, no. 2: 5-15.

Comaroff, J., and J. Comaroff. 2003. "Ethnography on an Awkward Scale. Postcolonial Anthropology and the Violence of Abstraction." *Ethnography* 4, no. 2: 147-179.

Denzin, N. K., and Y. Lincoln. 1994. *Handbook of Qualitative Research.* London: Sage.

Evans-Pritchard, E. E. 1967 [1940]. *The Nuer: A Description of the Modes of Livelihood and Political Institutions of a Nilotic People.* Oxford: Clarendon Press.

Fine, G. A. 1993. "Ten Lies of Ethnography: Moral Dilemmas of Field Research." *Journal of Contemporary Ethnography* 22, no. 3: 267-294.

Fox, K. 2004. *Watching the English: The Hidden Rules of English Behaviour.* London: Hodder.

Geertz, C. 2000 [1973]. *The Interpretation of Cultures.* New York: Basic Books.

Giddens, A. 1984. *The Constitution of Society.* Cambridge: Polity Press.

Goldstein, D. 2014. "Qualitative Research in Dangerous Places: Becoming an 'Ethnographer' of Violence and Personal Safety." New York: Social Science Research Council (DSD Working Papers on Research Security: No. 1). http://webarchive.ssrc.org/working-papers/DSD_ResearchSecurity_01_Goldstein.pdf.

Graeber, D. 2002. "The Anthropology of Globalization (with Notes on Neomedievalism, and the End of the Chinese Model of the Nation-State)." *American Anthropologist* 104, no. 4: 1222-1227.

Greenhouse, C. J. 2002. "Introduction: Altered States, Altered Lives." In *Ethnography in Unstable Places. Everyday Lives in Contexts of Dramatic Political Change,* edited by J. C. Greenhouse, E. Mertz, and K. B. Warren, 1-36. Durham: Duke University Press.

Greenhouse, J. C., E. Mertz, and K. B. Warren, eds. *Ethnography in Unstable Places. Everyday Lives in Contexts of Dramatic Political Change.* Durham: Duke University Press.

Hammersley, M. 1992. *What's Wrong with Ethnography?* London: Routledge.

Hammersley, M., and P. Atkinson. 2007. *Ethnography. Principles in Practice.* London: Routledge (third edition).

Hannerz, U. 1980. *Exploring the City.* New York: Columbia University Press.

Howell, N. 1988. "Health and Safety in the Fieldwork of North American Anthropologists." *Current Anthropology* 29, no. 5: 80-87.

Hume, M. 2007. "Unpicking the Threads: Emotion as Central to the Theory and Practice of Researching Violence." *Womens Studies International Forum* 30, no. 2: 147-157.

Jahoda, M., P. Lazarsfeld, and H. Zeisel. 1975 [1933]. *Die Arbeitslosen von Marienthal. Ein soziographischer Versuch über die Wirkungen langandauernder Arbeitslosigkeit.* Frankfurt am Main: Suhrkamp Verlag.

Jones, G. A. and D. Rodgers. 2016. "Standing on the Shoulders of Giants? Anthropology and the City." *Etnofoor* 28, no. 2: 13-32.

Koonings, K. and D. Kruijt, eds. 1999. *Societies of Fear. The Legacy of Civil War, Violence, And Terror in Latin America.* London: Zed Books.

Kovats-Bernat, J. C. 2002. "Negotiating Dangerous Fields: Pragmatic Strategies for Fieldwork amid Violence and Terror." *American Anthropologist* 104, no. 1: 208-222.

Kruijer, G. 1951. *Sociale desorganisatie: Amsterdam tijdens de Hongerwinter.* Meppel: J. A. Boom en Zoon.

Kruijt, D., and M. L. Vellinga. 1979. *Labor Relations and Multinational Corporations: The Cerro de Pasco Corporation in Peru (1902-1974).* Assen: Van Gorcum.

Lassiter, L. 2005. "Collaborative Ethnography and Public Anthropology." *Current Anthropology* 46, no. 1: 83-106.

Lewis, O. 1959. *Five Families: Mexican Case Studies in the Culture of Poverty.* New York: Basic Books.

Low, S. M., and S. E. Merry. 2010. "Engaged Anthropology: Diversity and Dilemmas. An Introduction to Supplement 2." *Current Anthropology* 51, supplement 2: S203-S226.

Lubkemann, S. 2008. *Culture in Chaos. An Anthropology of the Social Conditions in War.* Chicago: The University of Chicago Press.

Madison, D. S. 2012. *Critical Ethnography. Methods, Ethics, and Performance.* Los Angeles: Sage (second edition).

Malinowski, B. 1922. *Argonauts of the Western Pacific: An Account of Native Enterprise and Adventure in the Archipelagos of Melanesian New Guinea.* London: Routledge.

Malinowski, B. 1935. *Coral Gardens and their Magic: A Study of the Methods of Tilling the Soil and of Agricultural Rites in the Trobriand Islands.* London: Allen & Unwin.

Manz, B. 2005. *Paradise in Ashes. A Guatemalan Story of Courage, Terror, and Hope.* Berkeley: University of California Press.

Massey, D. S. 1987. "The Ethnosurvey in Theory and Practice." *International Migration Review* 21, no 4: 1498-1522.

McKinney, J. C. 1966. *Constructive Typology and Social Theory.* New York: Meredith Publishing Company.

Mosse, D. 2006. "Anti-Social Anthropology? Objectivity, Objection, and the Ethnography of Public Policy and Professional Communities." *Journal of the Royal Anthropological Institute,* 12, no. 4: 935–956.

Nash, J. 2007 [1976]. "Ethnology in a Revolutionary Setting." In *Ethnographic Fieldwork. An Anthropological Reader,* edited by A.C.G.M. Robben and J. A. Sluka, 223-233. Oxford: Blackwell.

Nordstrom, C., and A.C.G.M. Robben, eds. 1995. *Fieldwork under fire: Contemporary Studies of Violence and Survival.* Berkeley: University of California Press.

Pansters, W.G., ed. 2012a. *Violence, Coercion, and State-Making in Twentieth-Century Mexico: The Other Half of the Centaur.* Stanford: Stanford University Press.

Perlman, J. 1976. *The Myth of Marginality. Urban Poverty and Politics in Rio de Janeiro.* Berkeley: University of California Press, 1976.

Richards, P., ed. 2005. *No Peace No War. An Anthropology of Contemporary Armed Conflicts.* Athens/Oxford: Ohio University Press/James Curry.

Robben, A.C.G.M. 1996. "Ethnographic Seduction, Transference, and Resistance in Dialogues about Terror and Violence in Argentina." *Ethos* 24, no. 1: 71-106.

Robben, A.C.G.M., and C. Nordstrom. 1995. "Introduction: The anthropology and Ethnography of Violence and Sociopolitical Conflict." In *Fieldwork Under Fire: Contemporary Studies of Violence and Survival,* edited by C. Nordstrom and A.C.G.M. Robben, 1-23. Berkeley: University of California Pres.

Robben, A.C.G.M., and J. A. Sluka, eds. 2007. *Ethnographic Fieldwork. An Anthropological Reader.* Oxford: Blackwell.

Rodgers, D. 2007. "Joining the Gang and Becoming a *broder*: The Violence of Ethnography in Contemporary Nicaragua." *Bulletin of Latin American Research* 27, no. 4: 444-61.

Rosaldo, R. 1989. *Culture and Truth. The Remaking of Social Analysis.* Boston: Beacon Press.

Roy, A. 2011 "Slumdog cities: Rethinking Subaltern Urbanism." *International Journal of Urban and Regional Research* 35, no. 2: 223-238.

Sanford, V. 2003. *Buried Secrets. Truth and Human Rights in Guatemala.* New York: Pagrave MacMillan.

Scheper-Hughes, N. 1995. "he Primacy of the Ethical: Propositions for a Militant Anthropology." *Current Anthropology* 36(3): 409-440.

Scheper-Hughes, N. 2004. "Parts unknown: undercover ethnography of the organs-trafficking underworld." *Ethnography* 5(1): 29-73.

Sluka, J.A. 1990. "Participant Observation in Violent Social Contexts" *Human Organization* 49 (2): 114-126.

Sluka, J. A. 1995. "Reflections on managing danger in fieldwork: Dangerous anthropology in Belfast.: In *Fieldwork Under Fire: Contemporary Studies of Violence and Survival,* edited by A. C. G. M. Robben and C. Nordstrom, 276-294. Berkeley: University of California Press.

Sluka, J. A. 2015. "Managing Danger in Fieldwork with Perpetrators of Political Violence and State Terror." *Conflict and Society: Advances in Research* 1: 109–124.

Spivak, G. 1988. "Can the Subaltern Speak?" In *Marxism and the Interpretation of Culture,* edited by C. Nelson and L. Grossberg, 271-316. Urbana-Champaign: University of Illinois Press.

Tavory, I. and S. Timmermans. 2009. "Two Cases of Ethnography. Grounded Theory and the Extended Case Method." *Ethnography* 10, no. 3: 243-263.

Thomas, W. I. and F. Znaniecki. 1918-20. *The Polish Peasant in Europe and America* (5 vols). Boston: Richard G. Badger.

Vellinga, M. 1979. *Economic development and the dynamics of class: Industrialization, power and control in Monterrey, Mexico.* Assen: Van Gorcum.

Verhallen, T. 2016. "Tuning to the Dance of Ethnography: Ethics during Situated Fieldwork in Single-Mother Child Protection Families." *Current Anthropology* 57, no. 4: 452-473.

Wilson, W. J. 1987. *The Truly Disadvantaged : The Inner City, the Underclass and Public Policy.* Chicago: University of Chicago Press.

Wolf, E. R. 1990 [1982]. *Europe and the People without History.* Berkeley: University of California Press (2nd printing).

NOTES

1. Tony Robben, co-editor of the *Fieldwork under Fire* (Nordstrom and Robben 1995), co-directed the program focusing on cultural trauma and social suffering. Wil Pansters also occupied a core position in this research track, carrying out extensive

research on Mexican politics and violence (Pansters 2012), co-supervising a number of the doctoral dissertations. Gert Oostindie, currently Professor of Caribbean History at Leiden University and director of the Royal Netherlands Institute of Southeast Asian and Caribbean Studies (KITLV) held a part time chair in the Anthropology of the Caribbean within the program until 2006. Geert Banck, based at the University of Amsterdam's Centre for Latin American Research and Documentation (CEDLA), held a part time chair in the Anthropology of Brazil at Utrecht University until he retired in 2004. He inspired Koonings's initial work on Brazil (Banck and Koonings 1988). In 2011 Koonings was appointed his successor as part time professor of Brazilian Studies at CEDLA, University of Amsterdam.

2. See appendix 1 for a full list.

3. FLACSO research was and still is also inspired by Latin American structuralism and historical sociology. In Central America and the Caribbean FLACSO researchers studied informality, social exclusion, peace building and post war reconstruction. Francisco Rojas, Hector Rosada-Granados, the late Carlos Sojo, Abelardo Morales, Bernardo Arevalo, Lilian Bobea, and Wim Savenije were FLACSO scholars who defended their doctoral dissertation at Utrecht University.

4. At the same time, the projects also all addressed their subject in a broader social, institutional and often also historical context. This epistemological flavour was enhanced by the diverse disciplinary background of the researchers themselves: (social and cultural) anthropology, sociology, political science, international relations, history, language and cultural studies, and area studies. This made multidisciplinary work a natural quality of the program which was reflected in theoretical grounding and thematic choices.

5. However, some ethnographic methods can be experimental (see Fox 2004) and ethnographers often do resort to surveys and questionnaires (Massey 1987).

6. As Bourgois (1990: 45) highlights, "it is much more difficult—if not impossible—to satisfy the discipline-bound anthropological/methodological code of ethics if we attempt to research marginalization and oppression, than if we focus on the philosophical aesthetics of cosmology."

ONE

Researching the Politics of Aid in War-Torn Societies

The Case of Chalatenango, El Salvador

Chris van der Borgh

INTRODUCTION

This essay deals with my PhD research project in which I examined different externally funded development interventions in the period after the Salvadoran peace agreements had been signed (post 1992).[1] Foreign assistance was not new to this small Central American country. During the war years the Salvadoran government had received large sums of economic and military aid from the USA, while NGOs with links to the political-military organizations were funded by American and European INGOs. Aid was "political" and it remained a highly contested resource in the post-war years. As Boyce (1995) put it: "External assistance has played a critical role in El Salvador's peace process. . . . Aid has affected not only the balance of payments, but also the balance of power." My research dealt with the politics of these aid flows at different levels; national, departmental and village—with a focus on the latter two in the years from 1992 till 1997. The risks of this research project were minimal; the security situation in Chalatenango had improved considerably after the peace agreements and crime, and new violence did not reach the levels that it had reached elsewhere in the country. It also proved relatively easy to contact a wide range of actors and to discuss the role of aid in the post-war context. However, studying and discussing the politics of aid proved to be challenging and puzzling, as will be discussed in this essay. On one hand, I look back at the fact that the politics of aid were rapidly changing in the post-war context. On the other hand I look at some of the challenges in addressing sensitive topics like the political liaisons of aid organizations and the contestations about the use of aid. Although this research took place some two decades ago, I believe that the puzzles and challenges that I encountered during my fieldwork are still relevant for researchers of reconstruction, and development or humanitarian aid in war-torn, unstable, and "high-aid" contexts.

RESEARCH PROJECT AND CONTEXT

On 16 January 1992 the government of El Salvador and the rebel movement Frente Farabundo Marti para la Liberación Nacional (FMLN) signed a peace agreement that put an end to the civil war in that country. A few weeks later the implementation of the agreement started, a process that was verified by ONUSAL, one of the first post- cold war UN peace operations. The Salvadoran peace process has widely been considered a success story. There was no relapse into war, a new civil police was built, the guerrilla movement demobilized and transformed into a political party (FMLN), the military withdrew from political life and national elections were organized in 1994. The flow of international aid into the country increased with a view to help "reconstruct" the country and to "build peace." A wide range of development organizations—both existing and new ones—were responsible for the distribution of aid.

Although the peace agreements stipulated that the Salvadoran government and the FMLN should reach consensus on a National Reconstruction Plan (NRP), this proved extremely difficult (Murray 1994; Sollis 1993). On paper the FMLN endorsed the NRP, but during the post-settlement years the reconstruction process was highly contested between the right-wing government and the FMLN. With the elections scheduled for March 1994, it was very likely that in the first two years after the peace agreement aid served as a kind of political credit for the two political parties. For instance, the Salvadoran government had transformed the former counter-insurgency organization Comisión Nacional para la Restauración de Areas (CONARA) into a new Secretary for National Reconstruction (SRN) and a newly created Social Investment Fund (FIS) channeled large amounts of money to local communities for infrastructural works. Both programs seemed to strengthen the position of the ruling ARENA party.[2] This was what many FMLN members believed. I remember a meeting in 1992 in Europe in which a representative of the FMLN argued that his (new) party needed funds for projects in order to compete with projects of the ones offered by FIS. But the political role of aid did not simply serve short-term party-political goals, and aid also served political "projects." This was claimed by the FMLN as well as a range of

NGOs who argued that the FIS was a form of privatization of public policy and a temporary and therefore ineffective way to alleviate poverty. Instead, the FMLN and opposition NGOs said they promoted an alternative (popular) development project. Thus, an initial assumption in my research was that there were different "practices" and processes of development, informed by different ideas about development (neoliberal versus popular) and supported by different actors (left versus right).

My main question was how these projects played out locally in a politicized and polarized context. I focused on Chalatenango—a province in the north of El Salvador, because of my existing network there and— most importantly—because the department was a divided region during the war years. Although there was no clear frontline separating the different (former) spheres of influence in the province, the northeastern part had become famous as a stronghold of the guerrilla movement where the FMLN had built a form of popular power. The south and west of the province had largely stayed under government control. Since this former conflict zone was characterized by highly contested structures of authority and legitimacy, I expected this to become a minefield for international donors aiming to support some kind of political, economic, or social rebuilding.

I focused on the largest externally funded development organizations that deployed activities in both parts of Chalatenango in the fields of infrastructure and economic reconstruction.[3] These organizations had different characteristics and pedigrees. For instance, two organizations were closely linked to the government (FIS being one of them)—but they depended almost entirely on foreign assistance; one NGO had close contacts with the guerrilla movement; two programs were implemented by UN agencies and aimed to build concerted networks between the full range of actors in the department. In my research I traced the ways in which development programs were created, how policy formulation and implementation took place, and how these programs and projects embedded in local society. I also looked at the interventions of these organizations in five villages or hamlets in the northeastern part of Chalatenango and five in the southwestern part.

An important finding of my fieldwork was that while at national, departmental, and local levels the heritage of war was still quite important, the politics of aid could not simply be reduced to the contradiction between insurgents, their supporters, and "their" projects on one hand and the government, its projects, and supporters on the other. The politics of aid was much more complex and subtle than I initially assumed— even in a highly politicized post-war context. There was a multiplicity of political influences, which could not simply be seen as representations of the interests or ideas of the parties (the two sides) to the conflict. In this regard, a key change after 1992 was the dwindling political and strategic importance of scarcely populated Chalatenango both for the government and the FMLN, while at the same time the war-torn parts of the region were considered a high priority area for foreign assistance. Thus, while the presence of the top FMLN leadership and the military in the region quickly diminished, a large number of development organizations entered. The importance of aid should not be underestimated, especially in the regions that had been controlled by the FMLN and that had been most affected by the war, where foreign funds became a very important resource (and possibly the most important one) for local governments and local organizations. This led to situations of local government agencies becoming dependent on foreign assistance, while in other cases community organizations had more resources than their local governments.[4]

The growing importance of aid flows had very important consequences on local governance that may be characteristic for "high-aid," marginalized rural areas emerging from civil war. Part of my research thus consisted of adjusting my "political lens." I remained interested in "the politics" of aid, understanding politics as the "antagonistic dimension that is inherent in human societies and which is located within the struggles of diverse social groups for power and resources" (Hicky 2009, 142).[5] But gradually I realized that the struggles about aid had drastically changed in the post-war years and that the contradictions between ideologically opposed models of development were less central in this regard. This was also related to the fact that foreign assistance is supplied and channeled by a myriad of foreign and national organizations, all using their own mechanisms and channels to reach their target groups. A multiplicity of initiatives, opportunities, local practices and "ad-hoc" conflicts and contention about the allocation of aid. Aid had become a political arena in its own right.

POLITICAL LIAISONS AND CONTESTATION IN DEVELOPMENT INTERVENTIONS

In this section I discuss two particular challenges that I encountered during my fieldwork. Firstly, this was the issue to study the connections between development organizations and political actors. Starting my fieldwork, I assumed it was still key to analyze this relationship. I describe the difficulties to explore these political liaisons and my decision to adapt the focus of my research. Secondly, I reflect on the process of studying decision making and politics in development interventions. While access to development organizations and other stakeholders proved to be surprisingly easy, I encountered serious challenges to understand the types of contention and conflict between different stakeholders in selected development interventions. It was particularly hard to separate the interpretative frames used by actors (that were in a number of cases clearly affected by the war-divides) from the issues that were "really" at stake.

Political Liaisons of Development Organizations

As already mentioned, during the war years the parties to the conflict had mobilized aid in support of their political-military strategies. Aid was part and parcel of counter-insurgency operations that not only sought to eliminate the FMLN but also to "win the hearts and minds" of people. For instance, infrastructural projects that were implemented by local mayors in war zones could serve that goal. On the other hand, the FMLN sought to establish or consolidate territorial control in the areas that it considered of strategic importance. Its strategy to return people to territories that were controlled by the FMLN, to organize them, and to provide services partly depended on its capacity to mobilize aid resources through "opposition" NGOs (that had been founded by the FMLN or that sympathized with the movement) (van der Borgh 2003; Sprenkels 2014). Two of the organizations that were included in my research had such direct political liaisons during the civil war. The first one was a government organization with a background in the counter-insurgency programs, which had converted into the national secretariat of the national (but still highly contested) reconstruction program. The capacity of this organization to play that new role was obviously questioned by many (not least by the FMLN). The other organization was an NGO that had been founded by FMLN members and that had worked during the war years in the areas that were controlled by the FMLN. During the war years these political liaisons were not recognized by the "opposition" NGOs, but in the post-settlement years this relationship became somewhat less secretive. Moreover, both organizations were in a process of transition; the control of "political" actors over development organizations diminished. This often was a painful process that was, among other things, spurred by pressures of donor agencies whose staff generally emphasized the need to break these political ties.

In my efforts to understand the changing political liaisons after the peace agreements I focused at three different groups. Firstly, I talked with NGO staff and government staff of these organizations themselves. In general it proved extremely difficult to discuss the issue of former and changing political liaisons with them. Even high-level staff of left-wing NGOs that I knew quite well were not very communicative in this regard. I had expected this, since these kinds of conversations do require a dose of trust. But trust itself was clearly not enough. The heritage of secrecy and clandestinity that had been a matter of survival during the war was still tangible in the post-settlement period.[6] And even today—twenty years later—openness about the politics of aid during the war years and its aftermath is considered a sensitive topic and not easily discussed.

Secondly, I had a large number of conversations and interviews with local recipients of aid. Here it proved easier to discuss issues like decision making and to trace development interventions. These interviews did, however, not provide me with substantive information about the "higher" politics of aid after the war, but rather with local political experiences. The information I obtained did, however, make quite clear to me how strongly development aid had been part and parcel of the politico-military struggle during the war years. On a number of occasions local leaders in FMLN-controlled areas even gave examples of how (part of) development funds of European and American NGOs had been used for politico-military purposes, and even how particular projects had been a "façade" to attract aid. This helped me to understand why the wartime political liaisons were such a sensitive topic. A third group of interviewees consisted of staff of international NGOs, bilateral donors, and UN agencies that provided me with information about the changing relations between the FMLN, the NGOs, and local popular movements on one hand and the political influence in certain government agencies on the other. This "aid community" consisted of international staff and Salvadoran staff, of which many had worked in the aid sector during the war years. I interviewed members of these organizations and I often had informal conversations afterwards—over a coffee or a beer—in which we exchanged information. The information provided me with some understanding about the changing political relations between these development organizations and political actors. However, that information was still quite limited and still did not provide me with a detailed understanding of the political linkages. Moreover, the source of information had some serious flaws. Most of the international staff (both those at the left and at the right) provided for very partial information, based on their personal experiences with their counterparts or stories they had heard from others. It was difficult to delve deeper so as to verify information and to understand how these political relations worked exactly. Also, many of them saw political linkages as something negative and told or pushed their counterparts to break or loosen those political ties, while many argued that both as a result of "the transition" and under the influence of donors these ties had indeed become less important. In this regard, there appeared to be a "dominant interpretation" in the scene(s) of expats of the success of their own interventions and the question of how "the transition" was going. Thus, staff working for development organizations constructs knowledge about "the political process" and their role in it. In this case, the dominant interpretation was that despite some setbacks, the transition was going well, and that political liaisons had diminished considerably.[7]

The most important outcome of my interviews and conversations was a basic understanding of the changing political liaisons of development organizations, and insight in the changes in Chalatenango, which forced me to revise some of my assumptions. Thus, instead of looking at the ways how in the post-war process the political struggle between the parties continued in different aid projects, I decided to broaden the scope of my research and to focus on the ways in which development organizations interacted with a range of local actors and how at different moments they coordinated or negotiated with for instance political parties, government agencies, or local organizations.

DECISION MAKING AND POLITICS IN DEVELOPMENT INTERVENTIONS

An important part of my research consisted of tracing the formulation and implementation of programs and projects, by identifying key moments of decision making and politics in which different sets of actors interacted (either contesting or cooperating).[8] It proved to be quite well possible to trace processes of intervention of different types of development organizations. In general, people were happy to cooperate and they provided me with detailed information about their experiences with or in development organizations and projects. At the time, I thought this showed that people simply liked to talk about projects (while it also confirmed the reputations of Salvadorans that they like to chat). People often believed in the success of their approaches, wanted to share this with a relative outsider, or felt a need to discuss opportunities, progress, or hurdles. While this certainly was part of the explanation of the relative ease to do this research, with hindsight I realized that two factors were fundamental for this relatively easy access. Firstly, the ongoing implementation of the peace agreements led to a general belief that there would be no relapse into war. Secondly, the availability of aid caused a kind of "aid rush" in Chalatenango with many local organizations and individuals grasping or looking for (new) opportunities. There was also a kind of "aid myth" in Chalatenango about "millions of dollars flowing into the region" and there were many rumors about villages where many (more) projects had "arrived." Thus, there was a strong belief that aid that was distributed by development organizations provided people with new opportunities. Many people were interested in these opportunities, and hoped to get their share. Although I always made clear that I was not in the aid business, I was an interesting person to talk to, because I seemed "to know" about the "world of projects," while others still believed that I also "brought projects." However, after conducting an interview I might share some of my knowledge with interviewees and advice people about where they could go with certain requests. In the absence of these conducive factors, research would have been much more difficult. I experienced this when I conducted research in Kosovo ten years later. I was interested in the (parallel) governance structures of the Serbian community in Kosovo. These structures were not supported by the international UN-administration of UNMIK, but by Belgrade and they reflected the deep distrust about the UN presence as well as the ongoing disagreement about the status of Kosovo. In Kosovo, the tensions between the different communities were still tangible, and in that context conversations about programs and projects were understandably often met with distrust.

The strategy to trace interventions (from initial ideas of donors to local implementation) enabled me to contact different persons in the same development organization, as well as staff or members of other organizations they had dealt with in the different phases of intervention (such as donors, consultants, national policy makers), and the "recipients" of these interventions. In general, talking about projects and programs was relatively easy and not considered to be something sensitive or "political." By talking to different people in different contexts it was also possible to discover similarities and differences in the accounts about decision making processes. It was particularly interesting to understand that people in villages (beneficiaries of projects) had a substantially different view of the interventions than staff of these organizations had. Also, it was quite easy to move beyond the discourse and to delve deeper into particular examples and experiences, as long as there had been no (perceived) conflicts or contradictions between different stakeholders. For instance, I interviewed a mayor who told he had allocated development funds in a particular hamlet and not in other hamlets, because he came from that place. As long as this was not contested, this was not considered sensitive at all and it was very well possible to ask for details about the intervention process. Also, I found that construction firms and even a union of construction firms had played important roles in the allocation of resources of the Social Investment Fund (van der Borgh 1997, 58). While I found this practice to be questionable, this was not the case for staff of these firms and for staff of FIS. They openly shared their thoughts about this procedure and although FIS had abrogated that "channel," it argued it had been an effort to work in a "demand driven" way.

Things were obviously quite different when I touched upon issues that were considered sensitive or contested. For instance, when a mayor *was* criticized for the allocation of funds, or when a development program *was* seen as favoring one village above another. While there are many possible reasons for tensions, debates, contestations, and open conflicts about aid, I was particularly interested in the question whether there was a link with the different ideological positions of parties and their different views about (local) development processes. I found that there were many different reasons for individuals and organizations to contest aid allocations, depending on their position and location in the aid chain. Turf wars, personal incompatibilities, difference in views about priorities and implementation, as well as a range of personal, professional and group interests were generally much more important than fundamental disagreements about the envisaged development process. In general, the political agendas of the former parties to the conflict had become relatively unimportant, and only at certain moments they popped up, or seemed to pop up.

When there were issues about the allocation of aid it was generally more difficult to talk with people about these issues and when they agreed to talk, it was hard to find out what was going on. The latter is a challenge in most conflict research, since a researcher is confronted with different interpretative frames (Fligstein and McAdam 2012, 11). I found it particularly difficult to separate the opposing ideological views on development interventions from the more ordinary everyday conflicts about the allocation of aid. With hindsight I actually doubt it whether it was necessary or even possible to separate the two. It has been argued that in civil wars the motivations of people at a local level relate in complex ways to the "master cleavage" of war and that local motivations cannot simply "be derived from identities at the top" (Kalyvas 2003, 481). In a similar vein I would argue that the "post-war" conflicts about aid related in complex ways to the (former) master cleavage. While in the early years after the peace agreements (1992-1994) there was a national-level conflict between the former warring parties about the ways reconstruction aid should be channeled, this was quite different in Chalatenango in the period of my research (1994–1997). Conflicts were mostly about allocation of resources (where and for whom) and about the implementation styles (in what way), and only in a few cases about the question about "which of the former warring parties benefitted (most)" or "which kind of development" (main stream or alternative) was supported. However, in cases where conflicts had a link to the wartime divide, these mostly seemed to be "common" conflicts about the allocation and implementation of aid, where actors used "interpretative frames" in which reference was made to war-time symbols or contradictions.

An example was the experience of the agricultural development program Prochalate, funded by IFAD and the EU. The project explicitly aimed to foster coordination between the government and opposition NGOs, and at an early stage it had organized workshops in which "opposition" NGOs and government agencies were present and had committed themselves to the program. However, the program failed to reach that objective, as was concluded by several evaluation missions of IFAD. The program worked with a combined directorship of a national and a European director. Cooperation between the national director and the main opposition NGO in Chalatenango was problematic, but finding out why exactly proved extremely difficult. There were rumors about the political ties of this director to the ARENA party, which was hard to verify. Others opinioned that the national director didn't understand the participative methodologies of the NGOs, and others again argued that the opposition

NGO was reluctant to work with an organization that was part of "the government" (the former enemy). As far as I could find out, the issues that were at stake were mostly related to working methods (e.g., using existing credit committees or creating new ones; degrees of participation) and about interest rates (competitive or subsidized). But in the conflicts about these issues, reference was made to the war period.

This can be illustrated with an example of the visit of high-level staff of the Prochalate program and staff of the opposition NGO (that until that moment did not want to participate in the credit scheme) to a cooperative of former combatants that the NGO represented. The idea was to ask whether the former combatants were interested to participate in the credit scheme of Prochalate. The staff member of the NGO introduced the program, criticizing the high interest rates and the working method of Prochalate. Moreover, he mentioned that it was a "government" program. Therefore he suggested they should not accept the Prochalate proposal. The European staff member of the program, who was also present and (after years of work in Sandinista Nicaragua) felt sympathy for the people they visited, was not happy with the tense situation and took the floor. He asked the former combatants to think about it and to come up with alternative proposals. In an effort to speak their language and get in touch with them he used the term "compañeros" (comrades), and "lucha" (struggle) to express their concerns and wishes. Afterwards, national staff of Prochalate strongly criticized him for the choice of these terms. This example shows that the divisions and identities of the war period had not disappeared and that sensitivities about the war period, claims to spheres of influence, and disagreements about the implementation of the program were hard to separate. In fact, aid had become a political arena in its own right, where political tensions played out in new ways. This was something I sensed at the time but did not fully realize, nor theorize about.

POLITICS OF AID IN RETROSPECT

Looking back at research conducted quite some time ago is both fascinating and confronting. The fascinating part of it is to look back at old data and publications and to realize that the rather massive aid flows were an important reality at the time, but a temporary phenomenon. In the 1990s remittances were already an important source of income for many Salvadorans, and with aid flows drying up they became more important since then. My research took place in the period of large aid disbursements to Chalatenango. This provided me with an opportunity to study aid flows and the ways they embedded in local society. Since aid kept many organizations and individuals busy at the time, this was the right moment to study these dynamics. The confronting part is to look at my struggle to grasp "the political" in development interventions. My own mindset and assumptions were influenced by "the politics" in the period of the civil war on one hand and by the emancipatory discourse of development organizations on the other. These two narratives had a strong influence on my work and it is fair to say that I assumed that the social and political objectives (ranging from counter-insurgency, to empowerment and participation) of donors and development organizations were of considerable importance in the use of aid. While I didn't focus on these narratives alone and argued that the processes of aid disbursement had their own context-specific logic, it proved difficult to imagine "politics" beyond these narratives.

Looking back, I did (and could not) see yet that while the (local) social and political actors in the department were important players in this arena, and the participatory and reconciliatory narratives of donors legitimized the many projects and programs, aid became a key resource in the post-war years of transition and around its allocation a (temporary) political arena came into existence. This coincided with the "delimilitarization" of the department and dwindling importance of the province both for the FMLN and the military. Although he heritage of war was still tangible, the politics of aid represented only to a limited extend the interests or ideas of the former parties (the two sides) to the conflict. Instead, there were many different reasons for individuals and organizations to contest aid allocations, depending on their position and location in the aid chain. Turf wars, personal incompatibilities, difference in views about priorities and implementation, as well as a range of personal, professional and group interests were generally much more important than fundamental ideological disagreements about the envisaged development process or the noble intentions of participation and empowerment.

REFERENCES

Arce, A. 1993. *Negotiating Agricultural Development: Entanglements of Bureaucrats and Rural Producers in Western Mexico*. Wageningen: Wageningse Sociologische Studies 34.

Autesserre, S. 2010. *The Trouble with Congo. Local Violence and the Failure of International Peacebuilding*. Cambridge: Cambridge University Press.

Borgh, C. van der. 1997. "Decision-making and participation in poverty alleviation programmes in post-war Chalatenango, El Salvador." *The European Journal of Latin American and Caribbean Studies*, 63 (December): 49–66.

Borgh, C. van der. 2003. *Cooperación externa, gobierno local y reconstrucción posguerra. La experiencia de Chalantenango, El Salvador*. Amsterdam: Thela Publishers.

Boyce, J., 1995. "External Assistance and the Peace Process in El Salvador." *World Development* 23, no. 12: 2101–2116.

Corbridge, S., G. Williams, M. Srivastava, and R. Véron. 2005. *Seeing the State: Governance and Governmentality in India*. Cambrigde: Cambridge University Press.

Fligstein, N., and D. McAdam. 2012. *A Theory of Fields*. Oxford: Oxford University Press.

Hickey, S. 2008. "The Return of Politics in Development Studies (I): Getting Lost within the Poverty Agenda?" *Progress in Development Studies* 8, no. 4: 349–358.

Hickey, S. 2009. "The Return of Politics in Development Studies (II): Capturing the Political?" *Progress in Development Studies* 9, no. 2: 141–152.

Kalyvas, S. 2003 "The ontology of 'Political Violence': Action and identity in civil wars." *Perspectives on Politics* 1, no. 3: 475–494.

Long, N., and D. van der Ploeg, 1994. "Heterogeneity, Actor and Structure: Towards a Reconstitution of the Concept of Structure." In *Rethinking Social Development: Theory, Research and Practice,* edited by D. Booth, 62–89. Harlow: Longman.

Murray, K., ed. 1994. *Rescuing Reconstruction. The Debate on the Post-War Economic Recovery in El Salvador.* Cambridge: Hemisphere Initiatives.

Sollis, P. 1993. *Reluctant Reforms, the Christiani Government and the International Community in the Process of Salvadoran Post-War Reconstruction,* Washington: Washington Office on Latin America (WOLA).

Sprenkels, R. 2014. "Revolution and Accommodation. Post-Insurgency in El Salvador." PhD diss., Utrecht University.

NOTES

1. Parts of this essay were published with SAGE Research Methods Cases—Politics & International Relations (2019).

2. While there is a history of (party) political use of development aid and public funds, this is something that the founders of FIS, that promoted a technocratic view of service delivery, claimed to avoid. However , due to the visibility of these mostly infrastructural projects that were announced by huge billboards placed along the road and referring to the "the government of El Salvador" it is very likely that the "governing party" benefitted from this.

3. I used the term development organizations for those organizations that shared a number of characteristics. They provided public services such as infrastructure, credit schemes, or capacity-building programs, they worked on the basis of foreign assistance, they had a substantial national "paid" staff.

4. Foreign assistance replaces in a number of cases central government funding, due to the fact that international donors are more inclined to work in the relatively marginalized departments of the country, thus relieving the central government to attend these regions.

5. This definition is based on the work of Mouffe, while Hickey took the quote from Corbridge et al. (2005, 257).

6. See Sprenkels (2014) on the importance of clandestine relations in the revolutionary movements.

7. See also the work of Severine Autesserre who writes about the life world of international staff that works in the field of peacebuilding in DRC that this scene has "its own rituals, its own customs, its own rules, its own taboos, its own meeting places—in brief, its own culture" (Autesserre 2010,1).

8. By including different areas of decision-making I tried to look beyond the practical decisions related to the implementation of programs and was able to look at underlying ideas and political decisions about service provisioning (see van der Borgh 1997).

TWO

Dealing with Distrust

A Diplomat-Anthropologist Negotiating Obstacles in Politically Sensitive Urban Fieldwork

Ingeborg Denissen

INTRODUCTION

> "Fortunately I do not work in Mayo. Why? Because it is an area filled with rebels."

The quote here above expresses the stigma that rests on Mayo, a popular neighborhood in the Sudanese capital city Khartoum. It was made by a young female doctor who I met at a picnic of a voluntary association, when I asked her where exactly in Khartoum she was working. Her view was shared not only by many residents of Khartoum, but is also upheld by the Sudanese government. Because of the alleged presence of rebels and political opposition in Mayo, the government considers the area potentially threatening to national security. It maintains its authority in the area through a strong presence of its National Intelligence and Security Service (NISS). In this setting, I carried out fieldwork on claim-making practices of the urban poor, while I was also working for the Dutch government in Sudan as a diplomat.[1] Although both my roles were actually separate,[2] I wore two hats at a time when relations between the Sudanese and Western governments in general and the Dutch government in particular became tense due to the indictment of the President by the International Criminal Court in The Hague.

This contribution is about the challenges I encountered as a Dutch diplomat-anthropologist in Mayo between 2008 and 2011. In general, au-

33

thoritarian settings evoke challenges for ethnographers because they are ruled by informality, violence, and distrust. This is even truer when authoritarianism coincides with armed conflict and when it is maintained through the presence of a secret security service, like was the case in Mayo. In armed conflict situations, people are forced to pledge loyalty and to take sides: maintaining a "neutral" position is difficult. But when moreover a secret service is involved to control the population, identities are hybrid, loyalties are kept implicit and conspiracy theories flourish. How can a (foreign) researcher get access to information when everything is subject to distrust? How can the researcher be sure that the information that can be accessed is "real"? How to behave in such a way that neither the research objectives, nor the respondents are being compromised or put at risk? Doing research in such a setting is already a careful balancing act. But what impact does it have when the researcher him or herself also has a hybrid status? In Sudan at the time when I conducted my research, a Dutch diplomat doing interviews on governance issues in a politically sensitive neighborhood of the capital city could have been easily considered a spy.

In the coming sections I will describe the main obstacles I encountered when negotiating my presence in Mayo. They basically unfolded at two levels: the first level hurdle consisted of getting access to informants, and the second level hurdle was about getting access to reliable information. I will conclude this chapter with a reflection on the impact my status as a diplomat-anthropologist had, but before turning to the specificities of my fieldwork I will first provide some background information on Mayo.

AUTHORITARIANISM IN SUDAN AND IN MAYO

Since independence, the political history of Sudan has been characterised by the domination of one-party rule. The current regime is generally characterised as authoritarian (Ahmed and Al Nagar 2003, 97; Tilly and Tarrow 2007, 55). It came to power in 1989 through a military coup, with the aim to install Islamist rule. Soon after the 1989 coup, all political parties, trade unions, and independent media were banned and a tight security regime was established. The national security act of 1990 introduced a new intelligence apparatus, whose autonomy was expanded with arbitrary powers in 1991 and 1992.[3] The ruling party soon dominated the military, the executive, and the judiciary. Under the banner of a "civilisation project," the politics of Islamisation and Arabization lead to the army's increased involvement in the entire country (Collins 2008, 187-192). In 1989, the Popular Defence Forces (PFD) were created to discipline the tribal militia formerly used in the Southern conflict to secure the regime and expand the faith. Although the conflict with the South dates back much further than the installation of the current regime and it has its main origins in disagreements on wealth and power sharing, the regime's harsh stance on Arabization and Islamization has intensified the conflict with the South, and it also entered into conflict with rebel movements in the centre, the east and the west of the country.

Following a split within the ruling party in the early 2000s, the rule of President Bashir has become characterised as more pragmatic and more economically rather than religiously oriented. Under international pressure Bashir has also introduced some political openings (Ahmed and El Naggar 2003) and in 2005 he signed the Comprehensive Peace Agreement with the SPLA, stipulating a referendum which eventually led to the separation of South Sudan in 2011. Notwithstanding, the regime is still intolerant of potential political opponents and it uses ethnic identifications to divide and rule in order to control the ethnically-oriented rebel movements (Al Zain 2008). The various conflicts have further empowered NISS, which plays a central role in controlling political and armed opposition, particularly in the capital.

Khartoum is the centre from which the regime holds a tight grip on the country. At the same time, the capital is surrounded by internally displaced persons (IDPs) from the various conflict areas: an estimated two million IDPs resides in and around Khartoum. Many of those live in Mayo, within and outside the official IDP camp.[4] There is not much criminal violence in the area in comparison to similar areas in other large African cities, but it is defined as a priority area in terms of national security. The relation between the state and the citizens is to a large extent mediated by the security service, having a strong hold on the neighbourhoods through so-called "liaan shaabia" or "popular committees." "Popular committees" are the most important bodies of citizen representation and participation. The local governance act stipulates the establishment of popular committees per "block" of around 8,000-9,000 inhabitants[5] ; Mayo is divided into forty-two of such popular committees.[6] According to people I interviewed popular committees often have NISS agents on board:

> It is just like to organise people from A to Z. In the popular committees there are security members! . . . Just they can one day, you can get a [visit] to your house, and you can be taken with the security! . . . Because he on forehand knows, that guy is from communist party and that guy is from the other party . . . . Sometimes, people are having a meeting, . . . negotiating about their party. . . . Then, the government says oh, they are trying to do things. . . . They can beat him up. Especially the leaders from the other parties.

NISS is linked to the Presidency via systems of trust and loyalty that are mainly ethnically based (Collins 2008):

> Here in Khartoum, like the government is going to use one of the tribes against the other. Like let's say . . . the government in Khartoum is

going to use the Arabs who came from Darfur against the people who
are here. Like, . . . in the popular committees, we are dealing with the
Arabs. Ok? They, the Arabs don't like that tribe which is from the Fur
tribe. They can just whisper to the ear of the government that they are
supporting the rebels. And I can be taken somewhere . . . .[7]

This system has an effect on the relations between different groups of
citizens in Mayo and on relations between citizens and the state. Although researchers from outside do not have an ethnically ascribed status, they still risk to be drawn into the polarization of the various conflicts
through their attachment to a certain country or a specific organization.

A DIPLOMAT-ANTHROPOLOGIST NEGOTIATING ACCESS IN MAYO

The Sudanese government roughly categorizes foreigners as "helpers" or
"adversaries." For example, whereas diplomats from Arab states could
easily move around the entire country without travel permits, as Dutch
embassy staff we always had to apply for permits when leaving the capital and also when travelling to the IDP camps within the capital. After the
ICC indictment of the president the constraints put on us travelling
around got worse. At least ten foreign NGOs were expelled from Darfur
and several foreign staff members were declared persona non grata (they
were "PNG-ed" as it was called in the expat community) in the months
that followed. Several of us diplomats were interrogated by NISS on
occasion: I once spent two hours in the security office at an airport in
Darfur explaining the timing of my visit, despite already having a travel
permit. This was something that I and my colleague became rather indifferent to because we got accustomed to it, but this also implied that these
were things we more or less always expected to happen.

Traditionally, researchers had been less a focus of NISS than NGO
workers and official representatives of the international community, but
in the run-up to the Southern Sudanese referendum in 2011 it became
increasingly difficult even for them to obtain research permits, particularly for the IDP camps in the capital. So how could I as a researcher-
diplomat go find my way through these kinds of obstacles, in order to do
ethnographic field research? How could I gain access to relevant respondents and to reliable information in this context of distrust?

The First-Level Hurdle — Accessing Informants

Because of the fear that the position of the Dutch embassy, or my
respondents, or the people who helped me would fall under risk, I was
very careful in all the steps that I undertook during my fieldwork from
the beginning. With the help of my ambassador I started discussing my

research intentions with high-ranking officials of the ruling party, such as the director of the Institute for Strategic Studies, as well as the governor of Khartoum State. Although they reacted positively to my research topic (the governor even invited me to "go knock on every person's door"), this did not mean that I could actually start my field work. The main bottleneck lied in obtaining an official permit: this was usually a prerequisite for any researcher but it was unclear whether I actually needed it and how I could obtain one.

My ambassador had consulted our contact person in the Sudanese Ministry of Foreign Affairs, who suggested that I establish linkages with Sudanese research institutes. Through a befriended Sudanese researcher, I came into contact with the Anthropology Department of Khartoum University. The department head stood sympathetic towards the objective of linking academic research to policy and the dean of the Faculty of Social Sciences soon accepted me as a visiting researcher to his institute. At first the department head did not deem it necessary that I applied for a research permit, because as a diplomat I already had a residence permit. He put me in touch with his best students, who could assist me with my fieldwork. When I started looking for respondents however, I found that they would not willingly help me without a research permit, out of fear for the security service to which they would have to account for talking to me.

When I explained this to the Department Head he agreed that having a permit was a requisite, although the question at what administrative level I would have to apply for one left him puzzled. Fortunately however, an acquaintance of his worked as the head of the locality office in one of the areas where I wanted to do my research. When he explained the question and my position to her, I was welcomed to the office to receive my permit. Furthermore, she put me in touch with her administrative counterpart in Mayo. Both heads of administration held master's degrees and stood favourably towards academic research. Moreover, they were also genuinely interested in the content of my research proposal, particularly because it involved the challenges of urbanization.

I finally managed to obtain a research permit for the squatter areas and the planned areas in Mayo after having lived in Sudan for two and a half years. Although after all that time I was obviously rejoiced to have obtained both permits, this was not yet the end of the story. With the permits of the localities in hand, I still had to visit the policy offices and the security offices in the neighbourhoods to inform them of my presence and to also gain their permission.

In Mayo, I first had to pass by the head of the local NISS office to get his permission as well. Although his reception was friendly—he too stood favourably towards academic research, he said—he presented me with yet another dilemma: he generously offered the assistance of his employee who could arrange interviews and accompany me and my research assistant during our field visits. This was an offer I could not possibly refuse because the security service was present at every street corner and in each popular committee, but of course I was concerned for the effects this would have on the quality of my interviews. Fortunately however, after the security officer had accompanied us several times and had seen the content of my work, he let us move around independently. He only kept calling my research assistant to see how we were doing.

Notwithstanding, in the field I was asked for my research permit on an almost daily basis, not only by people I intended to interview but also by people in the streets who later emerged to be security officials in the local popular committees. This also happened indirectly. Once, an imam had offered to arrange interviews for me with female visitors of his mosque. One of the ladies had told her husband, a member of the popular committee, who then accused the imam of wanting to bring a spy to the community. It was only after I had handed copies of my permits to the imam that he could solve the conflict with the popular committee.

Another issue occurred when the coordinator of the state ministry of health had invited me to visit an NGO-run health centre in Mayo. Not knowing that the centre was situated in the Mandela IDP-camp (the border between the camp and the rest of Mayo is invisible to an outsider) and having been invited by a government official, I thought my research permit would grant me access. However, when I arrived, the security officer of the NGO running the camp insisted that we needed a permit from the Humanitarian Aid Commission (HAC). While he did give us a quick tour around the compound, he did not allow us to speak to the residents or the staff. Our contact at the state ministry was furious when he heard about the incident, but he could not arrange another visit for us. HAC can overrule any other government body active in the camps, because it is to a large extent controlled by NISS.

When, at the end of my research period, a renewed conflict in the Nuba Mountains pushed another wave of IDPs into the capital, my access to Mayo became practically blocked. When my research assistant, as usual, wanted to get into my car in front of the police station where we always met (for transparency reasons), she was suddenly summoned by a young officer to report to an office inside the building. When I followed her inside, I realized that all the people we had met and interviewed before in the police station were gone. HAC officers had occupied an office at the second floor of the building and four officials had already started interrogating my research assistant, asking her from which tribe she was (which she refused to respond) and what she was doing there with me. They also asked her rhetorically whether she though that the Dutch police would allow her to do research in the Netherlands. During the entire cross-examination I was not allowed to enter the room. After an hour we were both dismissed with them message that we could no longer enter Mayo to do interviews. When we talked to our contact in NISS he managed to arrange for us that we could still speak to local government officials, but access to all other persons was forbidden from then on.[8]

The Second-Level Hurdle — Accessing Reliable Information

Besides the formal permission I needed to get access to any kind of information, another challenge for me was to be able to gather *reliable* information. Any statistical information on Mayo proved hard to gather, most of the available data on population and their living situation was based on rough estimates and made available by the UN and NGOs. I was told by the local government that maps from the area existed, but that these were not allowed to be shared.

At the same time, I have been allowed by the local government to attend several official gatherings and functions. I was for example invited to the opening of the Judia (a traditional court) within the compound of the policy station, and to the popular committee elections in April 2011. The election was a government initiative in order to avoid the spill-over of the upheavals in neighbouring countries during the Arab spring. First Vice President Taha had announced renewed elections of the popular committees in order to include more of the youth. When I asked a representative of the ruling party and organiser of the popular committee elections in Mayo whether the re-elections had accomplished this objective, he responded: "Yes, we now have all the youth. This is *our* change; we are not like Syria, Libya and Egypt."[9] This was one of the most insightful events that I witnessed in order to understand how Sudanese politics actually worked.

One challenge was to gain the trust of the local government, but another one was to gain trust of the inhabitants in the context described above. Because I was posted as a diplomat, I could not go and live in Mayo as I did when I carried out my fieldwork in Mexico City for this same research project. Together with my two research assistants, I moved around by bus, in rickshaws, and occasionally also by car. I neither hid nor promoted that I worked for the Dutch government, because ultimately I visited Mayo as a researcher, but in the end I did not feel that it mattered very much. People in Mayo — as in Mexico, by the way — did not really distinguish between Western NGO-workers, researchers, or diplomats. I tried to compensate for not living in Mayo by spending as much time as I could in the area, to go back to the same respondents on different occasions and to assist in events.

The fact that I did not live in the area and that I did not speak the language made me more dependent on others in Khartoum than in Mexico City. My two research assistants greatly helped me in interpreting the things I heard. They did not accompany me on every occasion because I did conduct some interviews in English on my own (particularly with Nuba IDPs), but they were of great help in my interviews with government representatives, Islamic NGOs, and members of Northern tribes. It happened a few times that they translated issues to me that community members explicitly asked them not to translate, because it "might give [me] a bad image of the community" or because it "might sound racist." Without my assistants I would not have been given this information at all. Moreover, it was generally enriching to discuss the interpretation of what I had heard with my assistants, compared to doing the research alone in Mexico where I was not able to compare notes.

On the other hand, there was something particular about language in Mayo. Usually, knowing the local language is a first requisite for anthropologists when they go out to do field work. Therefore I did make an effort to learn Sudanese Arabic, but was far from proficient when I started interviewing. In the Sudanese context however, this was not an absolute disadvantage. Language, together with ethnicity, marks important dividing lines in Mayo. The fact that I did not speak Arabic very well may have helped me not to be perceived as a significant threat to ethnic minorities, and a better knowledge of the language might have raised suspicion of NISS as well.[10] My Arabic was good enough to earn some goodwill, but bad enough to not be suspected. Moreover, better knowledge of Arabic would have made me less dependent on translators with some respondents but it would not have helped me with all. Many of the IDPs in Mayo do not speak Arabic but Nuba, Dinka and Darfuri dialects. Particularly with the Nuba and Dinka leaders I could best converse in English, a language that also has a more positive connotation for them than Arabic. Finally, I felt that my two research assistants and myself being women helped to build trust with the communities and the government alike. It was simply less likely for people that women were part of the security services, so we were less mistrusted.

ADVANTAGES AND DISADVANTAGES OF BEING A RESEARCHER-DIPLOMAT

Doing research in Mayo was difficult particularly because of the lack of reliable data and because of the presence of an unpredictable secret service. Because I constantly had to engage with NISS in multiple ways and many people I was interviewing feared the security service, I have always been very precautious. My work as a diplomat had also primed me towards a certain fear of NISS, in the sense that I constantly felt that I was considered as an "adversary." This might have even made me too precautious at times, considering the readiness of the local government officials to help me; the truth was that I was quite intimidated by the "formally ill-defined limits" of authoritarianism. The unpredictability of NISS operations provoked me to spend a lot of time and energy on bureaucratic processes. As my fieldwork advanced I did get more confident because I got to know people in the local police and security offices and I felt more at ease in the area. But at critical times these people were then again replaced by others.

My consciousness of the presence of NISS also influenced the way in which I posed my questions to people — often in a rather indirect way, letting them choose how open they wanted to be. Sometimes I felt that people did not feel free to talk (often when they were not alone), but in most cases people where actually quite open, critical even. Interestingly enough I also found that sometimes I was more careful than my Sudanese research assistants. For example, when my one assistant was interrogated by NISS, I was genuinely concerned that she might be arrested. When I asked her afterwards however she said that she was "not afraid at all, just angry!" During the presentation of my research results three years later some Sudanese participants were so much more outspokenly critical than I dared to be, that I started wondering whether I had not exaggerated somehow. Had I maybe been too mistrustful? Or had I simply not really understood the context in which I was working? At the same time, this experience also made me realize that exactly this makes arbitrary rule so pervasive: one simply does not know where the boundaries lie. When it already had a paralysing effect on me, a diplomat who did not run any real risks except from being PNG'ed, I asked myself, what must then be the impact of arbitrary rule for people permanently living under it?

I carried out the exact same research in Mexico and in Sudan. In Mexico doing field research was easier than in Sudan in the sense that there was no secret service present (at least not in the same pervasive way) and I did not have to be careful to talk politics with people. The other difference was that in Mexico I was not working as a diplomat for the Dutch government and in Sudan I was. In Mexico I could therefore go and live in the community under study for six months, which, together with the fact that I spoke the language, helped me to feel more confident. In Sudan however, none of the foreign researchers I knew were living in Mayo or other areas of Khartoum they studied and the question is whether they would have been allowed to by NISS. The fact that I was a diplomat did make me feel vulnerable at times but it also gave me many advantages. Many fellow researchers envied me for the time I was allowed to stay in the country for example and the insights I got in the higher levels of politics and in the conflicts in the areas where many of the inhabitants of Mayo came from through my embassy work. This also greatly helped to understand the context in which I was working as a researcher. In fact, being a diplomat may have even made me a better researcher in Mayo.

My research on its turn granted me the possibility to engage on equal footing with Sudanese academics. I also saw more than what diplomats usually got to see (the popular committee elections, for example, or proceedings and punishment in the City Court). Moreover, it allowed me to personally engage with the Sudanese state and to experience how it actually *worked* at the individual level. A large part of the work of a diplomat, besides representing his or her home country, consists of understanding the country where he or she is posted and developing sound judgement of local developments. In that sense, being an anthropologist also made me a better diplomat.

REFERENCES

Abdalla, M.A. 2008. "Poverty and Inequality in Urban Sudan. Policies, Institutions and Governance." PhD diss., Leiden University.

Ahmed, A.G., and S. El Nagar. 2003. "When Political Parties Fail: Sudan's Democratic Conundrum." In *African Political Parties*, edited by M. Salih, 94-115. London: Pluto Press.

Al Zain, M. 2008. "The Political Potential of Displacement to Urban Areas: How has the "Ethnic Discourse" Transformed the Culturally Polarized Milieu in the Sudan?" *Peace and Conflict Review* 1, no. 1 (July): 1-16. http://www.review.upeace.org/article.cfm

Cavatorta, F. 2013. *Civil Society Activism under Authoritarian Rule. A Comparative Perspective*. London: Routledge.

Collins, R.O. 2008. *A History of Modern Sudan*. Cambridge: Cambridge University Press.

Denissen, I. 2014. "Negotiating Urban Citizenship: The State, Brokers and the Poor in Mexico City and Khartoum." PhD diss., Utrecht University.

Koonings, K. and D. Kruijt, eds. 1999. *Societies of Fear. The Legacy of Civil War, Violence, And Terror in Latin America*. London: Zed Books.

Luyendijk, J. 2009. *People Like Us*. New York: Soft Skull Press.

Migdal, J. 2002. *The State in Society*. Cambridge: Cambridge University Press.

Nordstrom, C., and A.C.G.M. Robben, eds. 1995. *Fieldwork under Fire: Contemporary Studies of Violence and Survival*. Berkeley: University of California Press.

Pansters, W.G., 2012b. "Zones of State Making: Violence, Coercion and Hegemony in Twentieth Century Mexico." In *Violence, Coercion, and State-Making in Twentieth-Century Mexico. The Other Half of the Centaur*, edited by W.G. Pansters, 3-39. Stanford: Stanford University Press.

Pantuliano, S., M. Assal, M, B. A. ElNaiem, H. McElhinney, and M. Schwab. 2011. *City Limits: Urbanization and Vulnerability in Sudan. Khartoum Case Study*. London: Overseas Development Institute.

Rotker, S, with K. Goldman and J. Balán, eds. 2002. *Citizens of Fear: Urban Violence in Latin America*. New Brunswick: Rutgers University Press.

Tilly, C. 2004. "Trust and Rule." *Theory and Society* 33: 1-30.

Tilly, C. and S. Tarrow. 2007. *Contentious Politics*. Boulder: Paradigm Publishers.

NOTES

1. Parts of this article are drawn from my PhD thesis "Negotiating Urban Citizenship: The Urban Poor, Brokers, and the State in Mexico City and Khartoum," January 2014. This thesis was written under the umbrella of a cooperation agreement between Utrecht University and the Dutch Ministry of Foreign Affairs, the "IS-academy," promoting the linkages between research and policy. I conducted six months of fieldwork in Iztapalapa, Mexico City, and fieldwork spread over a period of three years in Mayo, Khartoum, from 2008-2011.

2. There was no direct link between my embassy tasks (which concentrated on supporting the implementation of the peace agreement in the border areas) and my academic research (which focused on urban poverty and claim-making in Khartoum).

3. It is currently known as the National Intelligence and Security Service (NISS), in English. The NISS falls directly under the Presidential Guard.

4. There are four official IDP camps in Khartoum, one of which, Mandela, is situated in Mayo.

5. The origins of the popular committees lie in the Popular Defence Act of 1989, but they have been revised in the Popular Committee Act 1994, the Local Governance Acts 1998 and 2003 (Abdalla 2008, 106).

6. Interviews 62, March 2011, and 82, April 2011. This figure fits with an estimated population of roughly 350,000 people.

7. Interview 34, March 2010.

8. Fortunately this only happened at the end of my research period when I had already gathered most of my data.

9. Fieldnotes, popular committee elections in Mayo, May 2011.

10. Westerners who spoke fluent Arabic and had close contacts with local populations were quickly identified by NISS, as I have experienced with a friend who got the choice between either starting to work for NISS as a double spy or being "PNG'ed."

THREE

Researching Security in Africa as the "Sierra Foxtrot Golf"

Tessa Diphoorn

INTRODUCTION

During an academic discussion in early 2014, three of my female colleagues and I each presented the main findings of our ethnographic fieldwork on violence and security that we each conducted in various parts of
the world. At the end of our presentations, two separate audience members asked us how we, as women, were able to do such research. This was
not an unusual experience for me; such questions have been posed to me
at numerous academic settings. And although I understand the curiosity
and interest behind such questions, it points towards an inherent assumption that we, as women, need to further explain how we are capable
of researching violence and security. There seems to be an inherent pos-
tulation that there are inescapable methodological or practical problems
that will naturally arise. I often wonder: are these questions also posed in
a similar fashion to men?

In this chapter, I will reflect on this inherent gendered element of
researching violence and security by drawing on my ethnographic fieldwork on security in two African countries, namely South Africa and Kenya. This chapter will elaborate on what it means to be the "Sierra Foxtrot
Golf" — a nickname one company in South Africa gave me for radio communication purposes, which stands for "Special Female Guest" — and the
various roles we as female researchers are ascribed, and in turn, appro-
priate when researching violence. In the first section, I will briefly discuss
the topic of my research, namely the private security industry in South

Africa and Kenya. In the second section, I will present three ethnographic vignettes that show the three main roles that were ascribed to me, and which I enacted, during my fieldwork over the years: the "safe" one, the one in need of protection, and the emotional one. In describing these three roles, I argue that gender is a prominent "self" that must be explored in any process of reflexivity in order to analyse gendered understandings of the research setting. I contend that reflection of the "self" is not only a methodological exercise that provides insight into ourselves as researchers, but that it is also a crucial part of our analysis, and if excluded, we overlook essential insights into the lives of our research participants. I end this chapter with some concluding remarks.

PRIVATE SECURITY IN AFRICA

I base this chapter on my ethnographic fieldwork on private security companies in Durban (South Africa) and Nairobi (Kenya).[1] Durban was the site of my PhD research between 2007–2011, and Nairobi was the site of my post doctorate research location.[2] Worldwide the private security industry has an estimated global value of over \$139 billion, and with prospective annual growth rates of eight percent, the industry will be worth an estimated \$230 billion in 2015 (Abrahamsen and Williams 2011, 19). North America and Europe currently account for the largest share of the global market (70 percent), yet with higher growth rates in developing countries, one would expect these parts of the world to constitute a larger portion of the market in the near future (Abrahamsen and Williams 2011, 40).

South Africa and Kenya are both ideal contexts in which to study the relationships between policing, security, and violence: both have high rates of criminal violence, a prominence and ubiquity of non-state policing, and a leading and growing private security industry. South Africa is globally regarded as the "absolute 'champion' in the security industry" (De Waard 1999, 169); it currently has the largest private-security sector in the world, valued at approximately 2 percent of the country's total GDP (Abrahamsen and Williams 2011). In 2017, there were 8,916 registered private security providers (PSIRA 2017-2018).[3] The industry originated in the mining sector, entered the urban centres in the 1970s, exploded during the height of the political resistance of the late 1980s and into the political transition circa 1994, and has experienced continuous growth rates since. Besides its vast size, the industry is also highly diverse, being categorised into twenty different types of security services by the Private Security Industry Regulatory Authority (PSIRA), the quasi-state body that regulates the industry.

My PhD research in South Africa specifically focused on armed response officers, which refers to private security officers working for companies that provide armed reaction services, of which there were 3,451 in 2017 (PSIRA 2017–2018). Armed response officers comprise a substantial portion of the 522,542 active registered private security officers in South Africa (PSIRA 2017–2018). They are armed private security officers who patrol communities in vehicles and react and/or respond to triggers such as alarms and panic buttons that are installed on clients' premises. My ethnographic fieldwork analysed their everyday security practices in re- lation to others, which I label as "twilight policing" practices (Diphoorn 2016). Drawing from the anthropological framework of (de facto) sove- reignty, twilight policing refers to punitive, disciplinary, and exclusion- ary policing practices that emerge through the interconnections between state and non-state policing. I argue that armed response officers perform security practices in a twilight zone between state and non-state policing.

In Kenya, the industry has operated since the 1960s and has experi- enced an exponential boom in the last two decades. It is estimated that over 2000 private security companies operate in Kenya, of which only 900 are registered and it is estimated to have an annual turnover of KSh32.2.billion—US$43 million (Wairagu et al. 2004). The industry ac- counts for over 300,000 employees, compared to 40,000 police officers (Mkutu and Sabala 2007, 411). Although a range of security services are provided, such as cash-in-transit, electronic monitoring, private investi- gations, and body guarding, guarding services constitute the majority with 47 percent of the industry (Wairagu et al. 2004, 29). Unlike South Africa, there is no formal state regulation of the industry. Private security providers fall under the Ministry of Trade and Industry and wage issues are monitored under the Ministry of Labor. Although a bill was drafted in 2004 and completed in 2005 to establish a regulation system based on South African and UK legislation, no real action has been taken since (Mkutu and Sabala 2007, 406). The result is that the industry must rely on self-regulation measures implemented by two rivaling employers associ- ations: the Kenya Security Industry Association (KSIA) and the Protective Security Industry Association (PSIA).[4]

In Kenya, as a part of a larger comparative project, I analyzed the role of the private security industry within the larger "public-private security assemblage" in order to understand how the industry operates at the level of the state. In addition to analyzing the composition and regulation of the assemblage, I was particularly interested in how individuals, forms of expertise, and objects move between different security providers and shape the provision and enactment of security.

DOING RESEARCH AS A WOMAN

The concept of gender is not one that I specifically delve into in my research. Although I discuss the prevalence of a "macho culture" and explore masculinities, the predominance of males in my research population eliminates the need for a discussion about gender differences, that is, analysing the differences between male and female security officers. However, gender emerged in my fieldwork when I analysed the role and impact of my various "selves" (Coffey 1999; Denzin 1997) that shaped my role as a researcher and my impact in the field. In South Africa, I was repeatedly reminded that I was a wit stekkie—slang for white woman—further affirmed by the ascribed name "Sierra Foxtrot Golf"—the Special Female Guest—for radio communication by one of the companies.

As a white, upper-middle-class woman from the Netherlands who conducts research with and about predominantly men, my gender continuously differentiates me from my informants. Although gender plays a role in any ethnographic research, it weighs heavier for a female studying police institutions due to the inherent masculinity of such an environment. As women, we are ascribed particular roles that are based on existing gender classifications and stereotypes within the research setting, an issue also explored by other female researchers (such as Huggins and Glebbeek 2009; Hunt 1984; Marks 2004). When I "crewed" with armed response officers in South Africa, it was always assumed by others, such as clients and police officers, that I was a counsellor, psychologist, or marketing manager.

Additionally, my informants also assign a range of roles onto me, ranging from potential sexual partner, to a type of stepdaughter, to an understanding listener they can consult their problems with, to a knowledgeable academic that can assist them in their careers. In the field, I find myself manoeuvring between different stereotypes. When interviewing company owners and high ranking police officers, for example, I am generally purposely naive and subordinate. When I attended sessions at the shooting range in Durban, meanwhile, I felt compelled to act tougher and like "one of the guys." Occasionally I am purposely flirtatious, and at other times, I am deliberately non-sexual. As a researcher, I thus tactically engage in various stages of "identity negotiation" (Huggins and Glebbeek 2009, 9), while at other times my positioning is reactive, spontaneous, and identifiable only in retrospect. In the following sections, I will discuss three empirical vignettes to show the three main roles that were, and are, assigned to me: the safe one, the one that needs protection, and the emotional one.

The Safe One

In June 2014, I was in Nairobi to conduct the first phase of my fieldwork on the private security industry and how it relates to state institutions. As I lacked my own vehicle, I arranged with Jim,[5] a taxi driver, to take me around during the first few days. He was a rather quiet and reserved man who showed very little interest in the content of my research, but after dropping me off at the company offices of several private security companies, his curiosity spiked. On our way to a shopping centre for another interview, he finally asked me what I was doing in Nairobi and why I was talking to people from private security companies. I told him about my research topic, and he was in a bit of disbelief, he looked confused. He then said, "So, you came here, all the way from Holland, to talk to these guys?" of which I responded with a confirming nod. He was silent for a little while, staring out onto the road in front of him, and then suddenly looked at me, and said, "But you are a woman?" I starting laughing and asked, "Why is that relevant?" He seemed taken aback and then said, "But you are only talking to men. It is strange to me, a woman working with security . . . it is strange."

Before I had the opportunity to probe further, we arrived at the check point on the road before the entry to the shopping mall in question, a normal fact since the Westgate shopping centre was held hostage by Somali terrorists in September 2013. Having already experienced this security check on numerous occasions, I was surprised that the security officers had not checked our car and had not asked me to show my bag for them to search. I then asked the male security officer in question whether he wanted to check the car and he said no. I must have exuded a sense of confusion, as he then voluntarily clarified: "But, you are a woman, there is no problem." I immediately looked at Jim, who glared at me with big open eyes and started to chuckle, and said, "You see, he also thinks like me!!!!"

In this incident with Jim, we clearly see his confusion towards the fact that women conduct research on security, which is compounded by the security officer's perception that I do not need to be checked as I am not a threat; "there is a no problem" — I am "safe." My informants, who often described to me how other men never saw me as a threat, frequently voiced this perception and I experienced this as rather advantageous. In contrast to male researchers, such as Rodgers (2001) and Venkatesh (2008), I do not have to prove my own masculinity and participate in the macho culture prevalent among private security personnel. It doesn't matter that I don't know how to shoot properly or dismantle a firearm. Similarly, I don't have to impress my informants with my own "war stories" and use of force. The role of being the "safe" one is thus one that was rather advantageous and further highlights how women are regarded as harmless, powerless, less threatening, and in need of protection (Horn 1997; Lumsden 2009; Westmarland 2001).

The One Who Needs "Protection"

This is closely related to the second role, namely that as a woman, I needed protection. To ensure my own safety when studying a rather hazardous occupation, I implement particular measures, often in discus-

sion with company owners, such as wearing a bulletproof vest and accompanying supervisors that are generally not the first to attend a crime
scene. Although these arrangements would have been made for all researchers, including males, I am also convinced that these are highly
gendered.

An example of the type of protection I enjoyed occurred during November 2008, during my first few weeks on duty with armed response
officers in Durban, South Africa. The panic button of a small tavern located in an alleyway of a rather busy street close to an industrial area had
gone off. I was in the vehicle with Nicholas, an Indian armed response
officer of higher rank, and we rushed off to the area in question. Three
other armed response officers in the area also directed themselves there,
as they were all concerned that something serious was going on. When
Nicholas and I were close to the tavern, I could tell that Nicholas started
to worry, as he realised that I was in the car with him. Without discussing
the issue with me, he called upon two of his other colleagues from the
neighbouring area to attend the scene, so that two of his colleagues in the
area could secure the "guest." Shortly after, we stopped along the side of
the road and Nicholas instructed me to get out of the vehicle next to the
two armed response officers that were waiting for me and would "take
care of me." For the next thirty minutes or so, I stood against a wall with
two armed response offices right in front me, who completely closed me
off from pedestrian life. I felt rather uncomfortable and claustrophobic,
completely restricted to move by, what felt like my two personal bodyguards. Such forms of protection often irritated me, yet they provided
insight into their personal perceptions on security and gender. Furthermore, they also stopped me from being a victim and a user of violence. I
was therefore not engaged in "the praxis of violence" (Rodgers 2001, 3),
though I was unquestionably a part of its manifestation and interpretation.

However, there were also incidents where protecting me involved the
use of violence on behalf of my informants. In another piece (Diphoorn
2013), I discuss an incident where Kenny, one of my informants, punched
a man who had whispered something vulgar in my ear. I describe how I
felt guilty about causing my informant to use violence on my behalf,
albeit unwillingly and unintentionally. I describe how this incident is
laden with gendered understandings: it is clear that Kenny felt he needed
to protect me, a sentiment echoed by others, which shows particular
understandings of how women and men should interact in such cases,
and the responsibility a man has to defend a woman's "honour." It is also
leads me to argue that my presence as a woman may have exacerbated
their masculine behaviour.

The "Emotional" One

The third role specifically concerns how my presence evokes particular emotions on behalf of my informants. As I discuss elsewhere (Diphoorn 2013), I advocate a focus on our emotions in the field and I argue that being reflexive involves exploring "the emotional practice of doing research" (Pickering 2001, 491). This is particularly important when researching emotionally charged topics, such as violence, where our emotions are more salient and weigh heavier on our analysis (Campbell 2002). I have coined this the "emotionality of participation" (Diphoorn 2013), which refers to the dialectic between emotions and participation.

My focus on my emotions as a methodological tool unveiled a great deal of empirical data. At a certain point during my fieldwork in South Africa, I started to disclose my own feelings with my informants. One such incident took place during a night shift in May 2010 in Durban, when, due to a range of circumstances, I had given mouth-to-mouth to the family member of an informant, who, unfortunately, did not survive (Diphoorn 2013). After the incident, I resumed the night shift, but I could not shake off what had happened and continued to retch uncontrollably. I became angry with the company owner and the other security officers on the scene for not being able to perform mouth-to-mouth themselves, and I started demanding (rather rudely) that such training be provided for all of his employees. Similar to incidents described by Campbell (2002) and Punch (1986), when I got home early in the morning after the shift, I went straight to sleep but woke up a few hours later, drenched in sweat, to vomit. For weeks I had recurring nightmares of the woman's face floating out of a bathtub and coming towards me, on the verge of vomiting over my body (Diphoorn 2013).

While on a night shift a few days after this incident with Brian, who works for another company, I told him about the incident, how I vomited afterwards, and my recurring nightmares. He initially expressed awkwardness about my openness; he avoided eye contact, was continuously shifting in his seat, and changed the topic at the first opportunity. But a few hours later, while we were parked up by a gas station, he took the initiative and shared what he called "the heaviest shit" he had seen. Similar incidents happened with other informants: by disclosing my own feelings, I was able to create space for discussion between my informants and myself.

Many private security personnel present themselves as tough men; they aren't "sissies" or "faggots," and can handle the dangers of the job. Often, when I first start to discuss some of my emotions, several of them act cold and distant, treating certain dangerous incidents as mundane. Eventually, however, almost all of them start to share stories about traumatic incidents, nightmares, and domestic problems stemming from "taking the work home." As my informants regarded grief and distress as normal feminine emotions, I often purposely adopted this nurturing role, delving into my emotions in order to encourage my informants to share theirs. I am not implying that a man could not have uncovered this data. Rather, I am simply highlighting how being a woman allowed me to be "emotional," which thereby shaped my means of acquiring such information.

CONCLUDING REMARKS

In this chapter, I have analysed gender as a prominent "self" that continues to emerge throughout my research on violence and security in Africa. I have shown how gender distinguishes me from my research participants, but also how it sheds light onto particular gendered hierarchies, structures, and perceptions. The three different roles—the safe one, the one in need of protection, and the emotional one—essentially concern three different gendered perceptions of violence researchers. As women we are generally not regarded as a (security) threat, are in need of looking after, and are allowed, or even expected, to be emotional and explore our feelings. This has particular repercussions for our research, methodologically and analytically, and influences the type of data we collect and how we analyse it.

Yet these three roles also say something about the nature of my relationships with my informants and how they view me. But perhaps more importantly, they provide insight into the way they see women and thus how gender is related to issues of security and violence. In South Africa, I experienced being a woman as advantageous. Yet, in Kenya, this is not so clear-cut. When requesting permission to accompany security personnel in their vehicles in 2015, one company owner immediately denied the request on the basis that "you're a girl." Yet a few weeks later, two other company owners showed no such hesitation. This thus points to the diversity in gendered perceptions of violence and security that are worth looking further into. Furthermore, gender is but one part of the "self" and in my research on security and violence, there are unquestionably many more roles that are given to me and that I embody that are also very well worth exploring.

REFERENCES

Abrahamsen R. and M. Williams. 2011. *Security beyond the State. Private Security in International Politics.* Cambridge: Cambridge University Press.

Campbell, R. 2002. *Emotionally Involved. The Impact of Researching Rape.* London: Routledge.

Coffey, A. 1999. *The Ethnographic Self. Fieldwork and the Representation of Identity* London: Sage Publications.

De Waard, J. 1999. "The Private Security Industry in International Perspective." *European Journal on Criminal Policy and Research* 7: 143–174.

Denzin, N. K. 1997. *Interpretive Ethnography. Ethnographic Practices for the 21st Century.* Thousand Oaks: Sage Publications.

Diphoorn, T. 2013. "The Emotionality of Participation: Various Modes of Participation in Ethnographic Fieldwork on Private Policing in Durban, South Africa." *Journal of Contemporary Ethnography* 42, no. 2: 201–225.

Diphoorn, T. 2016. *Twilight Policing. Private Security and Violence in Urban South Africa.* Berkeley: University of California Press.

Horn, R. 1997. "Not 'One of the Boys': Women Researching the Police." *Journal of Gender Studies* 6, no. 3: 297–308.

Huggins, M. K., and M. L. Glebbeek. 2009b. "Introduction. Similarities among Differences." In *Women Fielding Danger. Negotiating Ethnographic Identities in Field Research,* edited by M. K. Huggins and M. Glebbeek, 1–27. Lanham: Rowman & Littlefield Publishers.

Hunt, J. 1984. "The Development of Rapport through the Negotiation of Gender in Fieldwork among Police." *Human Organization* 43, no. 4: 283–296.

Lumsden, K. 2009. "'Don't Ask a Woman to Do Another Woman's Job': Gendered Interactions and the Emotional Ethnographer." *Sociology* 43, no. 3: 497–513.

Marks, M. 2004. "Researching Police Transformation. The Ethnographic Imperative." *British Journal of Criminology* 44, no. 6: 866–888.

Mkutu, K. and K. Sabala. 2007. "Private Security Companies in Kenya and Dilemmas for Security." *Journal of Contemporary African Studies* 25, no. 3: 391–416.

Pickering, S. 2001. "Undermining the Sanitized Account. Violence and Emotionality in the Field in Northern Ireland." *British Journal of Criminology* 41, no. 3: 485–501.

Punch, M. 1986. *The Politics and Ethics of Fieldwork.* Beverly Hills. Sage Publications.

Rodgers, D. 2001. "Making Danger a Calling: Anthropology, Violence and the Dilemmas of Participant Observation." London: LSE (Crisis States Research Centre - Working Papers Series 1.6).

Venkatesh, S. 2008. *Gang Leader for a Day. A Rogue Sociologist Takes to the Streets.* London: Penguin Books.

Wairagu, F., J. Kamenju, and M. Singo. 2004. *Private Security in Kenya.* Nairobi: Security, Research and Information Centre (SRIC).

Westmarand, L. 2001. "Blowing the Whistle on Police Violence: Gender, Ethnography and Ethics." *British Journal of Criminology* 41 (3): 523–535.

NOTES

1. Within the field of private security, a common distinction is made between private military companies and private security companies. This chapter focuses on private security companies, which are primarily concerned with internal security and focus on police-like activities (e.g., guarding, access control, surveillance) as opposed to military activities.

2. In my former position as post-doctoral researcher within a research project funded by the European Research Council (ERC) Starting Grant titled "Public-Private Security Assemblages," I conductd a comparative analysis of security assemblages in Kingston, Nairobi, and Jerusalem. Due to the limited scope and regional focus of this chapter, I will not elaborate on my experiences in Jamaica and Israel in this chapter.

3. I retrieved PSIRA's annual reports from the website www.psira.co.za.

4. In 2016, the Private Security Regulation Act was finally passed in Parliament, yet it is too soon to analyze what the impact of this has been on the industry.

5. Jim, similar to all of the other names in this chapter, is a pseudonym.

FOUR

A Wolf in Sheep's Clothing

Negotiating Identity in Fieldwork Among the National Civil Police in Guatemala

Marie-Louise Glebbeek

INTRODUCTION

"I told you a hundred times. How could you be so stupid? Haven't you got any brains? What should I do with you? Go out of my sight!" I heard the colonel of the Guardia Civil shout while I was waiting in the corridor. An embarrassed Guardia Civil Officer left the room. "And what do you want?" the colonel, continuing in his bullying manner, said to me. "Well, uh, I would like to study the PNC," I answered, a bit intimidated. "You want what?" "Well, I was sent to you by the people of the European Union and I would like to study the reform process of the PNC, its overall implementation and results, and its institutional and political context, by focusing on police functioning and practices on the operational level." "You want what?" he said. "I did not understand a word you said. Maybe it's your Spanish. Just forget about the scientific bollocks and tell me precisely what you want," he said, annoyed. "Uh, well I would like to spend some time at the police academy and at a PNC precinct," I told him. "Well, let us see if that is possible, you said you were sent by the European Union Office?"

From 1998 till 2001, I conducted research among the newly established Guatemalan Civilian Police Force (PNC), agreed upon in the peace accord signed by the government and the armed opposition in December 1996.[1] The anthropological research aimed to study the objectives, implementation, consequences, and influencing factors of the Guatemalan police reform. The primary focus of the research was an analysis of how the functioning and practices of the police force at the operational level was influenced by the reform and their news tasks in a democratic society. The research was based on participant observation and interviews, primarily with police personnel but also with local NGOs, government authorities, and international observers.

Among the Latin American countries that went through successive cycles of authoritarianism, conflict, violence, and (re)democratization, Guatemala stands out for the long duration of its low-intensity civil war (surpassed only by the Colombian conflict), the number of civilian victims of repression, and the degree of tutelary powers preserved by the military throughout the protracted period of democratization and peace negotiations (Kruijt 1999; Plant 1999; Schirmer 1998). At the same time, however, the Guatemalan peace process has mobilized a variety of domestic civil actors who contributed to the formulation and acceptance of a wide-ranging set of agreements on fundamental social and institutional reforms. Alongside issues related to changing the long-standing status of exclusion and repression suffered by Guatemala's indigenous people, the reform of the so-called security forces can be seen as key to the consolidation of democratic governance and the ending of violence as an arbitrary instrument for state repression, political contestation, or criminal activities.

During the armed conflict between the army and the insurgents, over 200,000 people were killed or disappeared as a result of political violence (Kruijt 1999, 45). According to the Commission of Historical Clarification (CEH) set up under the Peace Accords, 93 percent of human rights violations were committed by government forces and related paramilitary groups. During the conflict, the military institutions directed their institutional strength against all organized segments of society, thereby creating a hybrid civil-military political regime of violence and repression. Over the years a system of repression developed towards civil society in which the use of terror and the dominance of fear became "normal." The Guatemalan National Police (Policía Nacional, PN) played a significant role in these violations. Although various powerful actors had previously manipulated the police forces, they had always succeeded in retaining a certain level of autonomy. During the armed conflict this partial autonomy was lost when the army took over the control of the police forces. The police were used to carry out counter-insurgency operations, in which virtually everything was allowed: illegal detentions, threats, intimidation, torture, extra-judicial killing, and disappearances. Under military command the police forces formed death squads responsible for many killings and disappearances during the armed conflict. The objective of these death squads was to eliminate alleged members, allies, or collaborators of "subversive" movements, using the help of civilians and lists prepared by military intelligence. Public security and military defense were in practice fused. The police forces were feared or despised, often both.

With the signing of the peace accords between the Guatemalan government and the former guerrilla group Unidad Revolucionaria Nacional Guatemalteca (URNG) in December 1996, a thirty-six year civil conflict was not only ended, but a foundation for extensive reforms was laid as well. One of the reforms agreed upon in the Agreement on Strengthening of Civilian Power and on the Role of the Army in a Democratic Society, was the creation, in 1996, of a single National Civilian Police (Policía Nacional Civil, PNC). This new police force would be based on civilian and democratic concepts of security and would be free of ties to the old institution, the PN.

According to Bayley (1999, 5) a solid indicator of the "democraticness" of a police force is whether they are open to monitoring by outsiders, and whether foreigners are permitted to study police operations, because this suggests openness to outside examination. As far as I was informed, before starting my research among the Guatemalan police force, the PNC was not known for its openness; on the contrary, it seemed to be a closed institution, secretive and seclusive to outsiders and with their notorious past probably not an institution that would welcome a researcher with open arms. Consequently, my main concern was how to get access to this closed institution.

This chapter will first elaborate on how researchers, especially in intergender research in male-dominated institutions, have to negotiate their research identity and one's positionality within the hierarchy of power. Ethnographic positionalities can be ascribed (given), selective (chosen and worked out), and enforced; they are dynamic and multiple rather than static opposites; and are shaped by gender, nationality, age, race/ethnicity and other parts of one's identity. As will be shown, the objective of anthropological research to produce non-hierarchical and non-manipulative research relationships between the researcher and the researched and to overcome hierarchical differences, is hard to create in intergender research in male-dominated institutions such as police institutions, when sexually charged remarks can easily result in sexual abuse of the female researcher and where research information can be secret and potentially dangerous knowledge for the researched.

This negotiation of ethnographic positionality and research identity will then be illustrated by four paragraphs that elaborate on my entry to the field, the actual fieldwork, the research identity that was negotiated upon, and how in spite of the anthropological imperative to create non-manipulative relationships the research among the PNC in Guatemala was a kind of Machiavellian endeavor by playing with my research identity and role in order to get as much as possible out of the fieldwork.

INTERGENDER RESEARCH IN MALE-DOMINATED AND CLOSED INSTITUTIONS

The identity of the researcher facilitates and/or inhibits the research process, researchers' and research populations' safety, and researchers' ethical choices and outcomes. Within the field, fraught with difficult choices at every turn, each researcher has to discover and imply strategies for negotiating within, around, and through the research challenges associated with gender, danger, identity interactions, and ethics.

Most challenging in this research was the perception of the policemen but also women of me "being a woman," which they associated with stereotyped roles of women: "the good wife," mother, sister, or daughter—or into a "sex object," but not as a "research scientist." Being a woman profoundly shapes the researchers' interactions with interviewees and associated actors. While such identities, like gender, ethnicity, nationality, or age are fixed, perceptions and associations can be influenced and therefore "identity negotiation" and "negotiation positionality" are important methods for researchers, even more for female researchers studying males.

Identity negotiations as a process begins with Franks's (2002) three static "ethnographic positionalities"—ascribed (given), selective (chosen and worked out), and enforced. Sehgal (2009, 331) defines positionality as "a researcher's location within existing hierarchies of power and the ways in which the researcher's identity and affiliations are positioned among and by others." An identity assertion or positionality is presented by the researcher and then either fully accepted or rejected by the interviewee, if so then the two actors need to renegotiate and reshape their relative positionalities. Subramaniam (2009, 221) argues that identities are "dynamic and multiple" rather than "role-set static opposites."

Identity negotiations often proceed by trial and error as they are renegotiated within each changing field setting (Subramaniam 2009, 205). One outcome of such negotiations is what Huggins and Glebbeek (2009) has been labeled as "identity approximation": the coming together—at least temporarily within each trial-and-error, give-and-take identity negotiation—of researcher and interviewee positionalities. Each actor in an interaction goes as far as she can and will go in creating and accepting her own and the others' selective positionality. Sometimes researchers even accept certain aspects of a culturally defined ascribed gender positionality in order to craft a status that would produce a safer space for researcher and researched, enhance research outcomes (i.e., data collection), and protect research ethics. The negotiation in which a researcher's sexuality or ethnic-religious positionality can for example being backstaged, or the status of "honored guest" front-staged relative to other positionalities, shape a researcher's "field persona"—"an amalgamation of who, by local cultural norms, [the researcher] *should be* and who [she *is*], according to [her] own and [her] discipline's expectations" (Huggins and Glebbeek 2009, 10).

In this research gender-related factors interacted with such associated status characteristics as age, professional status, nationality, and class and had various consequences about which I will write in the next paragraph. While gender complicated my research in many ways, it also opened doors.

ENTRY IN THE FIELD

In October 1998, I made my first exploratory visit to Guatemala, which lasted three weeks. Based in Hotel Spring in Zone 1 of Guatemala City, I visited most NGOs involved in monitoring the PNC. I spoke with people from MINUGUA and to representatives from the Dutch Embassy, who observe the police through their Consultative Committee meetings. In those three weeks I not only became familiar with the civil and non-governmental organizations surrounding the PNC, I also became an expert on the complex Guatemalan bus system and knew the city map by heart. However, this short fieldwork period was poorly timed, since simultaneously with my visit Hurricane Mitch raged through Guatemala, throwing the country into chaos. As a consequence I spent my time running from interview appointments to my economy hotel room in an effort to keep my belongings from being destroyed by the rainwater streaming through the hotel's leaking roof. Nevertheless, this exploratory visit and all the networking I had done proved to be very fruitful during my second fieldwork period.

When I returned to Guatemala in spring 1999, I was soon invited by the NGOs to join their weekly meetings at which they discussed the functioning of the PNC. I spent one and a half months interviewing human rights organizations, people from local NGOs, research institutions and so on. However, after two months in Guatemala studying the police force, I had not spoken to one single policeman. I doubted that the PNC would allow me to study their institution. From meetings with the NGOs it became clear that they had problems themselves getting information about and entrance into the closed police organization. Official permission would be hard to get. I could have decided to study the police force in a semi-illegal way by visiting local police stations in the hope of being able to interview its personnel. However, in order to be able to walk freely through the police institution and to interview whomever I wanted, I realized that my best bet would probably be to get introduced by an organization that was well respected by the PNC. This could certainly not be one of the NGOs or MINUGUA, which were known for their critical opinion about the PNC. Finally, the Dutch Embassy, for which I had carried out a temporary assignment, became the starting point of my long journey to the main gate of the PNC.

The Dutch Embassy introduced me to the right people in the European Union (EU), the main donor to the Guatemalan police reform. The executive of the EU was enthusiastic about my study and was willing to help me get entrance into the PNC. They introduced me to the Guardia Civil Española (GCE), the Spanish police who provided the actual technical assistance to the PNC in the EU project. It was clear from the beginning that the GCE, which was more or less forced by the EU to help me get my entrance, was less enthusiastic about my research and considered me a nuisance they were unable to avoid. As a consequence contact with the GCE and especially the Colonel in charge was anything but easy. The Colonel, who was feared by most NGOs for his blunt behavior, did not forget to remind me during each meeting that my Spanish was terrible, that my research would be an absolute disaster, and that I was naive and ignorant:

> "Don't you get it by now? I explained it to you over and over again. Where are your brains? Well then, I will start at the beginning again. You know what, let's stop talking. Let us drink our coffee peacefully. You know, your Spanish is getting worse every day?" the Guardia Civil colonel exclaimed when I asked a critical question about the PNC.

Despite his often blunt behaviour, he did make time to listen impatiently to my wishes and it was he who got me into the PNC. In the years that followed I could walk in and out of his office without appointments, and he always made time in his grumpy way.

During our first meeting I told the GCE colonel I wanted to spend some time at the police academy to observe practices there and to get to know the future police agents. I wanted to start my PNC "career" where every police officer started his or her career, at the academy. Consequently, the colonel introduced me to the GCE staff at the police academy, who introduced me in their turn to the director of the academy.

THE FIELDWORK

As said, I first travelled to Guatemala for a preliminary exploratory visit of one month in November 1998. My second fieldwork period lasted from April 1999 to December 1999, followed by two further fieldwork periods, from August to November 2000 and from January to April 2001.

In July 1999 I was introduced by the GCE to the director of the police academy. I told the director of my wish to spend some time at the academy grounds, to participate in and observe classes, to interview students and personnel. I was very surprised when he agreed to all my requests without any restrictions. He allowed me to stay at the academy for two weeks every day from 6 a.m. to 10 p.m. I could walk around the academy grounds freely and interview whomever I wanted. That day he personally gave me a tour around the academy grounds, during which he offered me, very attentively, several moments of time and privacy (he took a few steps backward) to talk to some students. It all felt too easy, and I felt sorry about not having asked for more, such as more weeks and permission to sleep at the academy as the students did, and so on. After our talk and tour he ordered the head of study to make the logistic arrangements for my stay. However, on my first day of fieldwork, I was stopped at the gate of the academy and not allowed to enter. After some minutes of talking and explaining an agent was ordered to escort me to an official of the study department, who finally cleared up the misunderstanding. He provided me with a letter, signed by the director that "authorized my entrance to the academy from 5.00 a.m. to 21.30, to be able to undertake a study of the police institution." In the years that followed this letter proved to be extremely handy each time I visited the academy.

In July 1999, I became a student of the fifth promotion of new recruits at the academy. This promotion consisted of 1,500 young people, between 18 and 30 years old, who followed a course of six months. During the course they stayed at the academy and were allowed to leave the barracks only during the weekends. The students were subjected to an iron military discipline. Much time was spent on marching and physical exercises, in which I participated fanatically, though it must have been a funny sight, with my clumsy efforts to keep in time with the others, bumping into the person in front of me once in a while. I followed the theoretical, practical, and self-defense classes. The high walls, closed gates, strict discipline, and lack of any free time or privacy were bearable to me because it was only for a few weeks and I could leave whenever I desired. Yet for the students it was a reality they had to face every day for six months; and even after the course personnel could not escape the characteristics of the closed police institution: isolated and closed barracks, strict discipline, no privacy, and hardly any spare time. One day during classes I had an appointment with the director; when I arrived at his office, he was not there yet. I waited at the entrance leaning against the doorpost (very inappropriate behavior at the academy). An officer who entered the office asked in an authoritarian tone: "Attention! What are you doing here? Do you have permission to leave your class?" I was surprised because normally people would not bother to enforce the academy rules in my case, since it was obvious I was odd. I never found out if the officer was joking or if he seriously thought I was one of the students. However, I made a mental note not to wear exclusively blue clothes, which resembled the academy dungarees.

The *siesta* between the morning and afternoon classes I spent hanging around the female barracks, chit-chatting with the students. It was during these conversations that I got to know all about them, their motivations for joining the PNC, their family life, their love life, and their concerns. It amazed me how easy it was to talk to them and how quickly they accepted me as a comrade. While it was relatively easy to build a rapport with the female students, with the male students, instructors, and officers it was more difficult. Male students from my class (10 female and 48 male) remained silent and on their guard for the first day, but during the break of the second day a crowd of curious males and females surrounded me. Male and female students were allowed to talk to each other only during classes or during breaks; it was forbidden to talk to the opposite sex without permission after class. Since I did not want to break the rules or to be an exception, I talked to the male students only when this was officially allowed. That is why I hardly talked to instructors and officers during these weeks at the academy. Most of the instructors and officers and some of the male students of the fifth promotion I got to know after my stay at the academy, when I visited the academy or the precinct where they were working.

After my stay at the academy, I continued to visit the students of the fifth promotion every week at the Wednesday afternoon visiting hour until they graduated. During the graduation ceremony I was given a seat in the area for dignitaries, only a few seats away from the ministers, the director, and ambassadors. I took photographs of them during their graduation ceremony and distributed them among the students. After their graduation and their deployment, I continued to visit several students on a regular basis throughout the country. They were the richest source of information about the life in the PNC.

After my "training" at the police station I returned to the Guardia Civil, this time with the wish to spend some time at a local precinct. With the help of MINUGUA I gained some general information on each capital's precinct, after which I selected one I wished to observe more closely. Besides practical criteria such as being not too far away from where I lived and easily reachable, other criteria were that it had to be an average precinct in size, in personnel, in criminality, and in the socio-economic characteristics of inhabitants of the area.

Together with a captain of the GCE I visited some precincts, or comisarías, in the capital and in other cities such as Antigua and Chimaltenango. In each comisaría he was received with respect; all personnel jumped into position and saluted. The captain remained authoritarian during each lunch we had together. Each time he ordered me a complete lunch or dinner without asking me what I wanted. When I objected during the third time he ordered for me, he was sincerely surprised, telling me that in Spain a man always decided for a woman what she was to eat.

One day he took me to the precinct I had chosen to stay at for six weeks and gave me a tour through the comisaría. Although I asked many questions, my introduction was kept vague. The captain murmured, when asked about me, something about me being a member of the GCE, studying the PNC. After this tour he said: "well, now you know the comisaría, so I leave you here." I never got to know if the PNC actually gave me permission to study the comisaría and I thought it would be wise to let sleeping dogs lie.

THE IDENTITY OF THE RESEARCHER

Before my first visit to Guatemala I worried and doubted if the PNC would allow me to study their institutions. My university had established some contacts in Guatemala which could help me with my entrance in the PNC, but these contacts proved to be of little help after arriving in Guatemala because they had no entrance or contact whatsoever with the PNC. It was all up to me to establish the right contacts to be able to perform my research.

Philosophizing about the time I spent within the PNC, it is my conviction that my entrance and acceptance into the PNC was facilitated by the fact that I was a young and foreign woman. I was not considered a threat and as such I did not encounter much hostility. Since I was young and foreign, my ignorance was accepted and this enabled me to ask many questions that otherwise would probably not have been answered. Men were honored by my interest, and I quickly gained the trust of the female students and police personnel. The director of the police academy told me afterwards he had given me permission to join the students only because I had much in common with them, in age and physical shape. It was true that I did not encounter serious problems getting along with the students. It was relatively easy to establish a good rapport with them.

However, being a woman, young, and foreign did not always facilitate the research, but sometimes complicated it. Most of my interviews were held, for privacy reasons, outside the precincts, which meant that I had to make appointments with policemen when they were off-duty. Quite often these appointments were misunderstood as dates, as if I was interested in them in a non-professional way. Over and over again I had to explain that I was not available and that I was interested in them solely as employees of the PNC. I lied that I was married, and although I was not lying about having a long-standing relationship, I did wear a fake wedding ring. Serious interviews, especially with middle-ranking officers, were often interrupted by remarks about the color of my eyes, or questions such as what I was doing later that day, if I liked to dance, if I was a natural blonde. While I got used to the macho, Latino culture of whistling and remarks on the street, and even the sometimes denigrating pinch on the bottom, I was not prepared to find the same behavior in the PNC. But it was sometimes funny to see how a group of policemen that I had passed on the street and who had made the usual remarks were shocked when they arrived at the precinct and found me talking to their superiors.

Those advances made me very careful in giving my address or phone number to officers. Only the ones I trusted had my phone number, but even from them I received phone calls in which they asked for a meeting since they had interesting information. However, those appointments appeared to be, when we finally met, nothing more than another effort to get a date with me. These experiences made me somewhat suspicious and made me avoid any risk of being alone with them. I always made appointments in public, busy restaurants and at decent hours. Whenever I felt nervous about a meeting, I left a note in my room, with the name of the person I was meeting, the time, and the destination. This was bound to be found if I disappeared. Most of the time I told the policemen beforehand and quite bluntly that I only wanted to talk about their profession. However, my study dealt also with the person behind the police uniform and therefore I had to ask personal questions as well. Consequently, I was always walking on a fine line between strictly professional and personal interest, which was likely to be misunderstood by some policemen. Never before had I been so clearly aware of my actions, behavior and attitude towards men.

While I could navigate relatively freely through the police institution, since I was not considered a threat, this also meant that I was not always taken very seriously. It was, for instance extremely difficult to get the police director to give me an interview. It took me weeks, and with some government officials even months, to get an appointment, which was, when I finally succeeded, easily cancelled or nobody showed up. However, this lack of esteem enabled me to raid their offices and take them by surprise, using a little charm, which a distinguished person would of course never have done.

The main focus of study was on the new police force (PNC), established after the Peace Accord. However, I was also eager to know about the performance of the former police force (PN). Because I had introduced my study as being about the new police force, people got suspicious whenever I started asking questions about the old force or about related topics such as corruption and human rights violations. Therefore, I tried to avoid asking sensitive questions and concentrated, at least at the beginning, on asking questions about the more technical aspects of the work. I did ask some questions about corruption or violations, but I was very careful not to coax statements they would later regret or which would put me in a difficult position, because I knew something I was not supposed to know. I kept my eyes and ears open and made mental notes of some illegal things I got to know about or witnessed by accident, which I later wrote down in my notebook (in Dutch), but I never asked an official about it. I tried not to attract suspicion and hoped to gain more trust in this way, after which I could ask more sensitive questions. This strategy worked rather well. It amazed me how freely some policemen spoke to me, probably no longer realizing that, after fifty cups of coffee together, I was still this researcher who was writing a book about them.

A WOLF IN SHEEP'S CLOTHING: THE SWITCHING ROLES OF THE RESEARCHER

While I tried to be as honest as possible about my study, my research sometimes felt as if it were guided by a cold-blooded Machiavellian, manipulative strategy. To gain people's trust and to establish a rapport, I constantly adapted my role as researcher. As explained above about my time at the academy, one moment I pretended to be tough or macho and the next moment I talked about girlish things. It took me a few minutes in each interview to establish the role that was expected from me or which would suit me the best. When I noticed that someone liked to display his knowledge in a teaching style, I switched into the role of the eager-to-learn pupil. In some interviews I played ignorant, yet in others I gained trust by showing them I knew a lot about the police institution. When someone was authoritarian I automatically became subordinate. When I discovered that someone was susceptible to my female charm, I used it. When someone asked for a lot of attention, I gave it.

The formal or informal nature of the interview depended on the situation. It happened a few times that I had prepared a formal interview with certain questions, but that during the first minutes of the interview it became clear that I had more chance of getting my questions answered with an informal interview, with a few jokes and chit-chat. In this way most of the people I interviewed felt at ease and opened up, which contributed to the interview in a positive way.

This switching of roles required flexibility and was not always easy to do. On many occasions it felt unethical and dishonest. Despite my changing attitudes, I did try to be the impartial observer and remain neutral in my interviews with police personnel, government officials, NGOs, or citizens, but this neutrality could be easily misunderstood as sympathy with them. I hardly ever publicly disapproved of what people told me, I simply asked more questions. By showing interest and not stating my opinion about things, I probably gave them the impression that I was on their side when I actually disapproved of many of the things I heard. I constantly had the feeling I had to choose between the critical NGOs and the police force, between donors with different opinions, between the police and the population. While I got more and more access into the police, the NGOs invited me less to their weekly meetings. In the meetings I did attend, I mostly listened to what others had to say, I hardly spoke myself. I found it difficult to share my opinions with them; it almost felt that, if I did, I would betray my informants. At the same time I had to be careful while talking to people from MINUGUA or local NGOs in the presence of my police informants, because it would make them suspicious. On the other hand, I could also not ignore the MINUGUA and NGO people totally, that would arouse suspicion too and would moreover damage my relationship with them.

The schizophrenic situations my research got me into were confusing. One moment I talked with someone from MINUGUA about the importance of a democratic police system that respects and guarantees civil and human rights. The next moment I talked with someone of the GCE, who stated that democratic Spain today was worse off than Spain during the Franco dictatorship because criminality was repressed with a firm hand during Franco's regime, which he considered a good thing. One day a top police official gave me important permission necessary for the continuation of my research, which made him in my eyes the most sympathetic police official of the PNC. However, the next day the newspaper told me that this high official used to be in charge of a death squad that was formed in the 1980s. How could I have sympathies for such a man? Sometimes I shook hands of which it was known that they were not clean; and the same day I interviewed someone whose family members had been killed by the hands of one of these men. On my way to an important police conference, the road was blocked by protesting villagers, and on the roadside was lying the dead body of a man who had been shot by an impatient and angry passer-by. Later, I heard that this impatient and angry passer-by was a policeman on his way to the same conference.

Conflicting situations and feelings sometimes made it difficult to remain impartial or to sympathize or not sympathize with "sides." I became aware of my sympathy for the PNC when I read a thesis by an American student about the ill-treatment of arrested persons by PNC personnel. Her conclusions were that about 90 percent of all arrested persons were severely harassed by PNC personnel. My reaction to this research was not to believe her; I doubted her analyses and even more her research methods. I believed it could not be as bad as she stated. After returning to Holland and having a bit more distance, I became more critical and impartial about the PNC again, but it still feels unethical and dishonest to write critically or negatively about the PNC, although I can also not refrain from it. This will make it hard to write a balanced account on the Guatemalan police reform, because when solely focusing on certain aspects of the reform I could make it a success story, while by focusing on others I could make it a total failure.

In conclusion, I would say that the fact that I am a foreign, young woman was of more benefit than disadvantage in my research on the Guatemalan police force. I was not always taken seriously because of my age, being young and female: "What damage can she do?" My Spanish, which is still far from perfect, also contributed to this. However, this enabled me to walk freely through the police institution, observing and interviewing the people I wanted to. It appeared to be more problematic to remain the impartial, objective researcher. I now recognize that switching roles during interviews did not cause failures of neutrality—even though this might have given the persons interviewed the impression that I sympathized with them—but in fact forced me to constantly think during interviews about my own positions regarding an interviewee's testimony.

REFERENCES

Bayley, D. 1997. "The Contemporary Practices of Policing: A Comparative View." In *Civilian Police and Multinational Peacekeeping. A Workshop Series. A role for Democratic Policing,* edited by J. Burack, W. Lewis, and E. Marks, 3-7. Washington: U.S. Department of Justice.

CEH. 1999. *Guatemala. Memoria del silencio. Tomo II: Las violaciones de los derechos humanos y los hechos de violencia.* Guatemala: Comisión para el Esclarecimiento Histórico.

Franks, M. 2002. "Feminisms and Cross-Ideological Feminist Social Research: Standpoint, Situatedness and Positionality—Developing Cross-Ideological Feminist Research." *Journal of International Women's Studies* 3, no. 2: 38-50.

Glebbeek, M. 2001. "Police Reform and the Peace Process in Guatemala: the Fifth Promotion of the National Civilian Police." *Bulletin of Latin American Research* 20, no.4: 431-453.

Glebbeek, M. 2003. *In the Crossfire of Democracy. Police Reform and Police Practice in Post-Civil War Guatemala.* Amsterdam: Rozenberg Publishers.

Huggins, M. K., and M. L. Glebbeek. 2009a. "Introduction. Similarities among Differences." In *Women Fielding Danger. Negotiating Ethnographic Identities in Field Research,* edited by M. K. Huggins and M. Glebbeek, 1-27. Lanham: Rowman & Littlefield Publishers.

Huggins, M. K., and M. L. Glebbeek. 2009b. "Studying Violent Male Institutions: Cross-Gender Dynamics in Police Research—Secrecy and Danger in Brazil and Guatemala." In *Women Fielding Danger. Negotiating Ethnographic Identities in Field Research,* edited by M. K. Huggins and M. Glebbeek, 353-377. Lanham: Rowman & Littlefield Publishers.

Kruijt, D. 1999. "Exercises in State Terrorism: the Counter-Insurgency Campaigns in Guatemala and Peru." In *Societies of Fear: The Legacy of Civil War, Violence and Terror in Latin America,* edited by K. Koonings and D. Kruijt, 36-62. London: Zed Books.

Plant, R. 1999. "Indigenous Identity and Rights in the Guatemalan Peace Process." In *Comparative Peace Processes in Latin America,* edited by C. J. Arnson, 319-338. Washington and Stanford: Woodrow Wilson Center Press and Stanford University Press.

Schirmer, J. 1998. *A Violence Called Democracy: The Guatemalan Military Project.* Philadelphia: University of Pennsylvania Press.

Sehgal M. 2009. "The Veiled Feminist Ethnographer: Fieldwork among Women of India's Hindu Right." In: *Women Fielding Danger: Negotiating Ethnographic Identities in Field Research,* edited by M. K. Huggins and M. L. Glebbeek, 325–352. Lanham: Rowman & Littlefield Publishers.

Subramaniam, M. 2009. "Negotiating the Field in Rural India: Location, Organization, and Identity Salience." In: *Women Fielding Danger. Negotiating Ethnographic Identities in Field Research,* edited by M.K. Huggins and M. Glebbeek, 201-226. Lanham: Rowman & Littlefield Publishers.

NOTE

1. Parts of this chapter draw on Glebbeek (2003) and Huggins and Glebbeek (2009).

FIVE

"*Doctor*, How Can We Improve Our Image in Europe?"

Researching War and Peace in Colombia as an Ethnographer-Consultant

Kees Koonings

CONSULTANCY: APPLIED OR ENGAGED ANTHROPOLOGY?

Early in the morning of a grey Thursday in July 2012 I was waiting in our Villavicencio hotel for the heavy rain to stop.[1] The weather was delaying my transfer to one of the small towns in the La Macarena area. My schedule called for a lunch meeting with the (female) mayor of the town and the (female*) personera* (local ombudsperson). After that, a meeting with a (female) president of a producer Association was planned. Fortunately the rain subsided, and the one-hour flight in a small single-engine plane proceeded under sunny conditions. The La Macarena area covers a range of hills and low mountains surrounded by tropical plains: ideal country for a range of activities in one way or another related to the violent history of the area: coca cultivation, agribusiness, environmental degradation, strategic hinterland for the insurgency. When the small aircraft descended in its approach of the airfield two military Hercules transport planes parked alongside the runway came in sight. Once on the tarmac the heavy military presence in the town was obvious. La Macarena had in the past been one of the redoubts of the FARC, but now the place looked like an army garrison. The area had come under military control, and since 2006 it had been one of the priority zones of the Colombian government's Plan Consolidación, aimed at strengthening state presence in areas recap-tured from the guerrilla or the paramilitary. The Dutch government had been actively involved as a *cooperante* (external donor) supporting different parts of peacebuilding and reconstruction strategies of the Colombian government, NGOs, and multilateral organizations. My assignment was to gather data and insights into the relevance of Dutch support for the strengthening of peace, democracy and human rights in Colombia. Dutch involvement in La Macarena was highly controversial, as are many donor-supported efforts in peacebuilding in Colombia. The meeting was in fact fruitful, or so I told myself; the three courageous women apparently spoke frankly about their predicament, the challenges they faced, and their commitment to helping bring peace to these troubled lands. With this comforting thought I (and my companion—counterpart-cum-fixer—from the Colombian NGO) boarded our little plane late in the afternoon back to the provincial capital to catch our immediate connection to Bogotá. We made it back before nightfall.[2]

This singular experience embodies much of the challenges that social scientific researchers, in particular anthropologists, encounter when acting as advisors or consultants for policy-makers, be they governments, politicians, bureaucrats, NGO staff, or program and project officials. Often, reflection on the fit or misfit between ethnographic research and the world of policy and intervention focuses, as I see it, on two questions: can the ethnographer seriously perform such a role? Should the ethnographer earnestly accept such a role? However, my actual aim in this chapter is different. I want to explore the possibilities and limitations that being an occasional "ethnographer-consultant" implies for gathering and using ethnographic data as part of an autonomous research project, designed within the usual boundaries of academia. And even if, as I will argue, this is indeed possible, can such a researcher role and the research carried out really be seen as "ethnographic"? This question not only relates to the overall design of the research but also to the nature, quality and validity of the data obtained and the positionality of the researcher.[3]

In my case what is at stake is a longitudinal research project that started in 2003 and as far as fieldwork goes lasted until 2012. In my research I focus on the two-pronged strategy of the Uribe administration (2001-2010) to wage war on the FARC guerrilla and to seek peace through "disarmament, demobilization, and re-integration" (DDR) and transitional justice with the right-wing paramilitary. What in fact are, in such a risky and charged environment, the possibilities, limitations, pitfalls, and risks of undertaking ethnographic research in combination with a role as hired consultant to international cooperation agencies? I will reflect on how my consultancy work was connected to a broader research agenda, facilitating a longitudinal "multi-scalar ethnography" (Xiang 2013).

Advisory and consultancy work in support of governance and policy interventions is a specific variety of applied social science (including anthropology). During the twentieth-century heydays of late colonialism and imperialism this type of involvement acquired a dubious reputation as it positioned social scientist as supporter of colonial governance and counterinsurgency (Bourgois 1990, 44). In recent years this debate flared up again in the wake of the U.S.-led "war on terror" waged by a number of NATO member states, including The Netherlands, in Afghanistan, Pakistan, the Middle East, Somalia, and Libya. The debate linked especially anthropology to dubious practises such as the U.S., military "Human Terrain System" (HTS) in Afghanistan (Gardner and Lewis 2015, 69) and to what has been dubbed "armed humanitarianism" (Omidian 2009; Forte 2010; Price 2014).

It seems to me that applied (qualitative) social science work provokes important questions as to whether ethnographers "can seriously" and "should earnestly" be engaging in consultancy-type applied research. Are ethnographers sufficiently in tune with institutional, policy, and "technical" issues? Can ethnography yield the kind of data and recommendations that policy-makers and practitioners need or like? Can typical consultancy conditions (pre-framed "terms of reference," time constraints, stakeholder pressure) leave enough room for the ethnographic method (that as a rule requires time, deep understanding, rapport, and critical positionality)? Will anthropologists be able to maintain ethnographic integrity given the biased and pressured environment of contracted, policy-related research? Should ethnographers have a professional and ethical duty to be "public," "engaged" or even "militant," generally in favour of the "subaltern"? Authors like Mosse (2004) seek to steer clear from either an instrumental or critical stance. His perspective suggests an ethnography of development interventions that in such a charged field shows "not whether but how development projects work; not whether a project succeeds but how 'success' is produced" (Mosse 2004, 646).

Being an ethnographer-consultant made me more aware of this. Mosse and Lewis (2006) argue that ethnographers (in particular, anthropologist) can have a valid role in understanding and contributing to development by mobilising the potential of the anthropologist to unpack development practises as complex fields of interests, power, and meaning. The ethnographer-consultant is a "cultural politician" precisely because she or he mobilises the particular epistemological capabilities of the field to address questions and interests posted by development's stakeholders. This underlies my idea that conducting applied ethnographic research, which explicitly includes the writing up of conclusions and recommendations, is in essence a political activity. Stakeholders know this and anticipate this through various forms of engagement with the consultant.

THE CONTEXT: BECOMING AN ETHNOGRAPHER-CONSULTANT
IN THE COLOMBIAN CONFLICT

My longitudinal work as an ethnographer-consultant within the armed conflict and peacebuilding in Colombia spanned the time frame between 2003 and 2012. The peace processes under the aegis of the governments of Alvaro Uribe (2002-2010) and Juan Manuel Santos (2010-2018) constituted the direct context for my endeavours as an ethnographer-consultant and also framed the object of my autonomous research on war and peace in Colombia under Uribe leveraged by the consultancy assignments.

Since the 1980s the armed conflict had proliferated into a complex web of interlocking political and criminal armed actors including the state *fuerza publica* (military and police), a variety of guerrilla organizations, a growing network of paramilitary groups, drug cartels, and a wide variety of local gangs and militias, most notoriously in the city of Medellín (Pizarro Leongómez 2004; Restrepo and Aponte 2009). President Alvaro Uribe (2003-2010) embarked on a quite different course, under the name of "democratic security policy." He pledged to be uncompromising with respect to the FARC, stepping up military efforts to push them back. At the same time he started to test the waters for a round of negotiations with the paramilitary of the AUC that should lead to a DDR agreement. Under pressure from the Colombian civil society, the Constitutional Court, and Congress the Uribe administration enacted legislation to embed the negotiations in a broader frame of transitional justice (the Justice and Peace law of 2005; cf. García-Godos and Lid 2010). It served as a foundation for posterior transitional justice legislation by Uribe's successor Juan Manuel Santos (2010-2018) such as the "land restitution law" and the "victims law" and indeed the peace negotiations with the FARC that led to a final accord in 2016.

The Colombian peace efforts in the 2000s and 2010s generated substantial involvement of transnational policy-making and development assistance institutions seeking to support local and national level efforts at DDR, transitional justice, and reconstruction. Hence a large number of Colombian and foreign consultants were employed to offer analytical knowledge and grounded advice. In my case, this included first and foremost an assignment to assess, together with my Swedish colleague Kjell-Åke Nordquist (then at the University of Uppsala), the operational and political merits of Dutch and Swedish support to the Misión de Apoyo al Proceso de Paz (Mapp) of the Organization of American States (OAS). I carried out this assignment in 2005, making three trips to Colombia; the first two (in April and June) to gather data, and the final one, in October, to report preliminary findings and recommendations to various groups of stakeholders (see Koonings and Nordquist 2005).

The "Mapp/OEA assignment" not only turned out to be the first of a series of consultancy assignments related to various aspects of the conflict, peace, and development in Colombia but also inspired me to include the Colombian conflict and peace process into my "autonomous" academic research and teaching agendas. [4] In a sense this inverted the usual route where ethnographers are drawn into consultancy because of the expertise built up in their academic work. My academic research on Colombia has been focused on the dynamics of the Colombian armed conflict and the peace and transitional justice agenda during the Uribe and (early) Santos governments. I look at this as two interrelated processes that are at the same time contradictory and mutually constitutive: while Uribe combined a stepped-up military offensive against the FARC with an agreement with the paramilitary commanders of AUC to demobilize and subject themselves and their troops to transitional justice, Santos struck a comprehensive peace accord with FARC while largely ignoring the re-mobilization of paramilitary groups and drug trafficking networks at that time euphemistically labelled BACRIM (*bandas criminals emergentes*).

IS THIS ETHNOGRAPHY THAT I'M DOING?

Ethnographic research seeks engagement with "natural" social conditions through prolonged and sustained presence in the field. The "rapid appraisal" work of the ethnographer-consultant usually violates this foundational principle of the trade. When doing our October 2010 evaluation of Pax Cristi's regional peace building program in Cauca, we stayed for a little less than week in the department of Cauca (in and around the town of Santander de Quilichao). As is usually the case, our counterpart, the local program coordinator, acted at once as gatekeeper, key informant and fixer. We went through an intensive program of site visits, meetings, and individual and group conversations. The peace building program focused strongly on working with so-called affected populations. Given the social and ethnic diversity of this northern part of the department of Cauca, this meant both indigenous and Afro-Colombian local communities.

> One day was used to visit one of the tightly organized communities (*cabildos*) of the Nasa (or Paez) indigenous people. During the day, their spokespersons received us in the association's headquarters and provided us with an assertive narrative about the association's work for peace. Their activities included community DDR for indigenous youngsters that had been recruited by the FARC and unarmed community patrols. Another day was used to meet with 'board members' of an Afro-Colombian grass roots organisation. This group worked with Afro-Colombian families that were victims of recent paramilitary violence. The meeting took the form of an afternoon of "shallow" (rather than "deep"; cf. Clifford 1997) hanging out with our interlocutors. We could clearly grasp the difficulties this group experienced in keeping

their organization together and in their work with the families, many of whom continued to live in fear of paramilitary coercion. In both cases we had to rely on the contextualization provided by our counterpart to make complete sense of our observations.

The obstacles and restrictions I encountered in this particular evaluation study forced me to mobilize various ethnographic skills: in situ observation (although hardly participant), establishing "rapport" (although with participants that were keen on obtaining some benefit from the encounter), and interpreting a diversity of narratives. In other words, the consultant relies on the ethnographic toolbox (or "methodological sensorium") to build rapport, to develop a sense of connection, and to embed the findings in a holistic perspective by contextualizing the case under study.

As my work as ethnographer-consultant developed over time, my engagement with the Mapp/OEA came much closer to a sustained ethnographic effort. The initial assignment (in 2005) occupied the better part of a year. It was the spin-offs during subsequent years that actually deepened the ethnographic quality of my work. Between 2005 and 2012 I had the opportunity to observe and experience the work of two consecutive heads of mission with whom I developed a classical form of positive rapport. They and the various staff members in the Bogotá office were generous with their time, experiential narratives, and access to documents and other data accumulated by the mission. I had the good fortune to be able to visit and observe up close a number of regional teams fielded as part of the verification and support work of Mapp/OEA.

Not only did this provide me with a gradual deepening of understanding of the way the mission worked and evolved but it also contributed to my decision to define the "War and Peace in Colombia under Uribe" project as one of my academic research lines. Part of this emerging synergy was the willingness of Mapp/OEA to regard me as a sympathetic researcher (*"amigo de la casa"* — "friend of the house") who could count on their cooperation after my consultancy work with them had been concluded.[5] This cooperation not only became part of my independent academic research (and graduate students and trainee placement and supervision) from 2006 onward but also extended to Mapp/OEA turning into a "resource organization" for subsequent assignments. Mapp/OEA offered me periodic updating on their appreciation of the dynamics of war and peace and allowed me to grasp the practical and political complexities of the efforts made by this multilateral "third party" in the process. This doubtlessly produced synergy but also created a pro-Mapp/OEA bias in my interpretation of their role in the peace process.

PITFALLS AND RISKS

I explore four pitfalls and risks for ethnographic research and the researcher that stem directly from the consultancy role, namely the risk of lack of depth in data (and related data validity and reliability problems), the pitfall of ethnographic seduction, the risk of political interference, and the pitfalls surrounding the researcher's positionality and integrity (including the near-impossibility of replication studies).

Shallow Data?

Conventional ethnographers often dismiss rapid field appraisals because of this first risk (for classical anthropologists perhaps the "mother of all risks"). The alleged methodological and epistemological uniqueness of the discipline is founded on long and deep involvement with the research population in their "natural" social and cultural environment. Compared to this, the quick-and-dirty quality of consultancy work is not seen as up to standard: no rapport, no trust, no grounded understanding of peoples' positions, interactions, and subjectivities. Let us look a bit closer at the "quick" part of this criticism.

The first example comes from our April 2005 visit to the Urabá region in northwest Colombia where the paramilitary Bloque Bananero had demobilized.

> We were visiting the Urabá region for a couple of days in April 2005. Urabá is the strategically important lowland extension of the department of Antioquia. It has been a zone where for generations guerrilla and paramilitary armed actors carved out their spaces of domination. The Bloque Bananero was active in the region since 1994 and demobilized in November 2004. An encounter with its former commander "alias HH" and a visit to his "demobilization facility" was included in our program. On the designated morning we were picked up close to our hotel in the town of Apartadó by "HH" himself and his retinue. "HH" occupied the middle of the three 4x4 vehicles while his visibly armed bodyguards travelled in the other cars. After visiting various micro-enterprises, we were levied off to the *finca* (rural estate) occupied by the group. During our conversation it was noticeable that our interlocutor was constantly on his guard. Looking around we could see armed guards at the perimeter of the property. The reason was a plain and simple fear for his life. The various units (*bloques*) within the AUC and their principal commanders were notorious for their internecine feuds and fights, fuelled by issues of power and territorial control, interests in the drugs trade and other illicit economic activities, and personal animosities. "HH" didn't trust his comrades; the Colombian state facilitated, so we were led to believe, his transfer to Urabá with an army helicopter.

The second example comes from our June 2005 visit to the demobilization site of the paramilitary Bloque Heroes de Tolová near Valencia, a quiet village in the department of Cordoba, two hours south of the capital Montería.

> To get to the DDR site we travelled in an official Mapp/OEA vehicle from Montería where the mission had one of its not-so-many regional representations. The site appeared to be a *hacienda* commissioned for this purpose. DDR sites are places where the paramilitary units that agreed to demobilization gathered at a specified date to enter the formal DDR process. On the day of our visit the troops (mostly men, very few women) had just settled after coming out of the bush and the procedures were in full swing. Striking up casual conversations here and there, we learned that, in the perceptions of the young rank-and-file paramilitary, their "work" had been necessary to contain the "terrorists" of the FARC (". . . they are still around, very close. . ."). Some of the wounded were in bad shape, laying with blood-soaked bandages and amputated limbs on the bare concrete floor of one of the semi-open buildings. At some point, we were invited to sit down with the commander of the group and his legal counsel for a conversation. The legal advisor cut to the chase, looking directly at me (the "Spanish speaking" of the two consultants): "Doctor, the commander would like to know, how can we improve our image in Europe?" The first thing that occurred to me was answering in equally plain terms: *"paran de matar!"* (stop killing). My response condensed my understanding, maturing at the time, that the principal argument to support the "peace process" of the Uribe government and the involvement of the Mapp/OEA was the prospect to end the often massive violence against the civilian population unleashed by the paramilitary.

What do these vignettes show? On the one hand, they convey the opportunity the ethnographer-consultant has to experience the density and complexity of the subject that I had only started to study. These ethnographic encounters gave me the opportunity to get in touch quickly and directly with the world of the paramilitary and their controversial DDR scheme. On the other hand, the examples demonstrate the limits of learning and understanding. Encounters are indeed brief and by necessity fleeting. Every and each of the observations included in the example could, or maybe even should, be followed by in depth exploring their details, implications, and the personal stories that lay behind them. As a matter of fact, some of this was done subsequently by graduate students and doctoral candidates under my (co-)supervision. Still, these stories and many of the complexities that I came to understand along the way were not immediately known by me at the time. They only emerged later through additional research and progressive insight. Over time, these "quick" ethnographic encounters have been acquiring new meaning as part of my longitudinal and multi-scalar approach.

Not everything the ethnographer-consultant does is "ethnographic." A large part of this work is usually dedicated to studying documents and conducting formal open and in many cases lengthy and in-depth interviews. Here the issue of the quality of data is less of a problem. Open interviews are most of the time comprehensive and frank but very often also selective or biased given the specific aims (called "terms of reference") of evaluation or advisory research and the issues that are at stake. If the ethnographer-consultant lacks the embedded knowledge to follow up on answers given to interview questions the risk of superficiality is real. In my case this improved to the extent that I became more knowledgeable about the many dimensions and stages of the Colombian conflict and peace process. Being able to spent time in Colombia often and in many different places also gave a certain "macro-ethnographic" understanding of war and peace as a nationally and locally "lived experience" (Lubkemann 2008).

Ethnographic Seduction?

In April 2005 I was interviewing a high-profile (former) paramilitary commander that had accepted demobilization within the process set in motion by the Colombian government one year before. Until shortly before that encounter this particular commander was a prominent power broker in Montería and one of the frontmen in the efforts of the paramilitary leadership to consolidate the AUC and to include this fragile confederation into the "legitimate" politics of war and peace. While his fellow travellers were still weighing their options while residing in nearby Santa Fé de Ralito where the "negotiation table" with the government was set up, this commander had decided to give himself up, at least for now. As the interview progressed the man showed increasing unease, constantly looking around in the hotel dining room where we were talking and seemingly not focusing on the interview. At a certain moment he turned directly to the coordinator of the local Mapp/OEA office who was sitting in as a listener to the conversation. I knew already that the two had been in contact over the previous months, and apparently he trusted her when he asked her whether the Mapp/OEA mission could facilitate a safe place abroad to stay for his wife and children, preferably a Spanish-speaking country such as Costa Rica, Argentina, or Spain itself. If I recall well (my notes do not specify this, unfortunately), this direct request came at the moment in the interview when we were discussing issues like rivalry and distrust within the cabal of paramount paramilitary chiefs. Among them, rivalry may well be lethal.

Although strictly speaking this is not an example of ethnographic seduction because it was not an effort to ". . . influence the understanding and research results of [the] interviewer" (Robben 1996, 72), I use this to highlight the fact that in any ethnographic research, but perhaps in particular in consultancy work with reasonably high stakes set in a charged environment (as was obviously the case), informants or participants try to steer the ethnographic encounter in a direction that may be favourable to them without making overly explicit demands.[6] Seen in this way, a much more intriguing example of ethnographic seduction occurred before I even had properly started my first field visit for the Mapp/OEA assessment, and its seductive significance within an ethnographic encounter as such only occurred to me much later.

> The Ministry of Foreign Affairs of one of the patron countries of the assessment arranged my travel to Bogotá in April 2005 insisting that I should fly business class. This was justified, it was argued, because I had to arrive well rested given the importance of the assignment and the intensity of the work schedule that I was about to face. Arriving at Eldorado Airport I was instructed not to follow the ordinary exit route for passengers leading to the long immigration queue. Instead I was gently guided to a VIP space where my passport was promptly stamped and one of the Embassy diplomates was waiting for me. She led me directly to her CD-plated car and drove me to my hotel, making sure everything was fine and that I was ready for the following day's briefing with the ambassador and Mapp/OEA leadership.

I reconstruct this seemingly minor logistic detail as an example of implicit "ethnographic seduction" because of my subsequent experiences within the Mapp/OEA assignment. After the conclusion of our work in October 2005 there was no doubt that the patrons and all other stakeholders had been anxious to steer the results of the research.

Political Pressure

In fact, in consultancy work in which research is directed at the evaluation of outcome, impact, and relevance of the intervention, the pitfall of ethnographic seduction is often trumped by the far more explicit risks stemming from political pressure. Political pressure of any sort is always part of consultancy work and that is why I argue that this type of research is in itself also (but not only) a political activity. The risk of political influencing is, as I see it, not so much that it affects the quality of research findings due to a certain (biased) interpretation by the ethnographer, but rather that it may affect the explicit framing of the analysis and in particular the formulation of conclusions and policy recommendations. Political pressure seeks to achieve precisely that. Obviously, political pressure is part and parcel of consultancy work. Hence, navigating this is a common challenge for consultants.

In the case of the ethnographer-consultant, the "politics" of assignments even create additional and often unexpected ethnographic spaces and encounters. For instance, during the formal debriefings following the presentation of our final report on the Dutch and Swedish support to the

Mapp/OEA, in October 2005, the two embassies had organized *conversatorios*, round table meetings with stakeholders. A small meeting, rather intimate and informal in its setup, took place in the offices of the Swedish Embassy in Bogotá. During this meeting, the director of a prestigious Colombian NGO and former ELN *guerrillero*, asked me how it could be possible that The Netherlands and Sweden supported a peace scheme designed by the Uribe government. Was it not common knowledge that this DDR program was only meant to protect and legitimize the paramilitary who were responsible for extra-legal violence and atrocities? It is interesting to note that his organization had been and continued to be a prominent recipient of Dutch and Swedish aid money. The larger, more formal stakeholders' meeting took place in the residence of one of the ambassadors. The cleverly framed purpose of the meeting was not only to communicate the outcomes of our assessment but also to generate consensus behind the decision to support the Mapp/OEA and to propagate the notion that more donors should step in to increase the budget, making Mapp/OEA a more effective and legitimate mission. As it turned out these objectives were met despite the sometimes intense nature of the debate. The only notable challenge was put up by the local branch of an international human rights advocacy organization. They argued that the peace process with the paramilitary was illegitimate and that support to Mapp/OEA should not be endorsed. The organization had even written a formal letter to the Dutch and Swedish governments to demand an end to their support.

There were other instances, however, in which political pressure was brought to the fore while gathering data or drafting the report. Again, the Mapp/OEA assessment provides a few tell-tale examples. When visiting the Zona de Ubicación in Santa Fé de Ralito, Cordoba, in April 2005 we were given the opportunity to interview three prominent paramilitary commanders on a single day. All of them were notorious in their own particular way. I will offer a descriptive vignette of this visit in the next section. Here I only recount an element within the second of the three lengthy interviews. When the conversation, held over lunch offered by the commander, came close to its conclusion, our interlocutor rose from the table and invited us to join him to an adjacent room. There he proudly presented his "project": a scale model of a condominium-style apartment building that, so he claimed, would house his "boys" (*muchachos*) as they worked on cash crop farms that were also part of the project. The commander argued that this was his contribution to the "R" of DDR: reintegration into society. He added the question if this would not be an excellent opportunity for the Dutch and Swedish governments to support the peace process with their aid money. I replied evasively that these kinds of "commercial" projects were not within the spending remit of our development co-operation and that he maybe should try the Inter-American Development Bank. I thought it wise not to speak my mind: that our governments would surely find the idea preposterous of supporting agents that were suspected of massive violence and sought ways to legalize their land grabbing and launder illicit money.

The second example is about another commander, residing in Urabá, who had been transforming himself into a "social entrepreneur" and civil society leader. We spoke to him and a few of his *muchachos* in the premises of the government-run CRO (Centro de Referencia y Oportunidad) in small town Turbo. CROs were set up to assist the reintegration of demobilized paramilitary. They presented themselves as representatives of the "Association of Demobilized of the South," supposedly a civil society organization representing the interests of the demobilized. Again, one of the issues was the precarious situation of the former soldiers; support by donor governments would be important to alleviate their plight, so the commander insisted. Later it became clear to me that, at that stage of the process, paramilitary commanders had an interest in keeping their soldiers at hand, possibly to preserve the command structure, the unity of the bloque, and the financial and social dependency of the demobilized on the so-called *estructuras paramilitares*. These kind of political plea-making by *paracos* for obvious reasons did not inspire me to include them into our recommendations.

Political pressure is stronger than ethnographic seduction but also more explicit and hence easier to detect. It is more likely to affect the immediate product of the ethnographer-consultant, that is to say, the contracted report, but it does not necessarily harm the validity of the underlying data—after due reinterpretation and elimination of bias. The potentially biased report itself can be justified by the researcher as a necessary element of a politically charged assignment that required this kind of product. Yet this kind of justification can never be absolute. I strongly hold the view that applied researchers should at all times monitor their own professional and moral bottom lines. There is no excuse for forfeiting professional and personal integrity.

Researcher's Integrity

This brings me to the final pitfall I want to briefly discuss here: the positionality and in particular the integrity of the ethnographic-consultant as researcher. Ethnographic seduction and politics do put, as we already saw, the researcher's positionality to the test since they present in a way *external* temptations or pressure. The dimension of integrity that I want to discuss here is about dilemmas that are *internal* to the ethnographer-consultant's pondering and choices. I am talking about considerations that have to do with the integer handling of the protection of informants (due anonymity, confidentiality, and safety) and the proper use (or abstention to use) data gathered as part of the consultancy work. As a rule, conversations are granted and access to often internal and confidential documentation is given under the (often unstated) assumption that they will be used for the purpose of the assignment only. This poses an obvious complication when the researcher wants to put such material to scholarly use. Were the interlocutors made aware of this purpose that often emerges *ex post facto*? Can there have been informed consent? Will posterior re-use of findings pose any harm to informants or the agencies they represented at the time? Let me briefly illustrate these important dilemmas with two experiences.

The first one happened in October 2009 during a brief visit to Colombia in my "autonomous" capacity. I had decided to go for a couple of days to the department of Nariño to visit one of our doctoral candidates. As part of her fieldwork she had arranged an internship with the Pasto office of the Mapp/OEA (this in itself a product of the rapport I had by then established with the mission). As it turned out, during the days of my visit she was staffing the office "alone" (as an "intern-observer"). This proved to be no obstacle to her plan to carry out a verification in a remote highland Andean community where a peace march would be held. Nariño still had at the time many areas controlled either by the FARC or the BACRIM. The small town we went to visit was situated in BACRIM territory. We drove there in an official Mapp/OEA vehicle, the driver being careful to comply with the security routines dictated from the head office in Bogota. The two passengers, a doctoral candidate and her supervisor, constituted the (in)formal delegation of the day. In the community the first business the doctoral candidate-slash-international observer had to take care of was talking to the local police chief about intimidating behaviour by men on motorcycles that had been watching the march, taking pictures. Other activities of the day included participating in mural painting celebrating peace and reconciliation, and meetings with local peasants that complained in unison about the damaging effects of aerial spraying of coca fields. Addressing me, assuming the "old guy" was in charge, they insisted that the Mapp/OEA should try to end this practice (and come up with other resources to support local development). I respectfully told the meeting that the "young lady" was the responsible person in the delegation and that I was merely a guest; she would duly convey their views so that they could be included in the trimestral reporting. In addition to the dilemmas I already mentioned, this experience also points at the blurring of field roles. To what extent is it acceptable to transgress boundaries between researcher and operative?

The second example comes from an informal meeting, in April 2005, with the ambassador to Colombia of a leading power. This meeting—set up by the ambassador of one of the European countries that supported the Mapp/OEA mission at the time—was not so much about fact finding but about political feasibility: hearing directly "from the horse's mouth" that the process between the Colombian government and the paramilitary would, if not openly supported, then at least be tolerated or endorsed by the government of this country. The evening progressed under the enjoyment of a good glass of whisky, contributing significantly to the frankness of the conversation. I had to make a good effort to stay focused while staying in sync with the "old hands" vibe of the evening. This was a fascinating experience; even now, more than thirteen years later, I still hesitate to write about it. There can be no doubt that the meeting and everything that transpired while we had it had to be seen as confidential and off the record, for strictly political reasons. As is probably clear from the above, I make an effort to be as "anonymous" as possible narrating this event. Still I fear that this effort has its limitations: a horse is a horse is a horse, of course.

In a general sense I feel that the answer to the question of if, when, and how the research material obtained in this way can be used—a question my interlocutors will not be able to answer—depends entirely upon choices I have to make. Apart from guaranteeing "doing no harm" and confidentiality, such choices have to be informed by my assessment of the relevance of the material and its re-interpretation within my longitudinal approach and the degree of integrity. I agree with Kovats-Bernat (2002) and Verhallen (2016) that a form of "situated research ethics" is preferable. The researcher decides to (re-)use the research findings while making sure that participants are protected and that no confidentiality rules are violated. This practise also puts clear limits on the sharing of data packages derived from this type of work.

OPPORTUNITIES

My discussion of pitfalls and risks may suggest that consultancy work and ethnographic research are uneasy bedfellows. Indeed, many hardcore ethnographers will argue precisely this. I am prepared to go along with this position, to a certain extent; after all, ethnography's strength is, as noted before, strongly based on long-lasting involvement in the sociability of the research participants. Still, this does not exhaust its methodological potential. There are at least three ethnographical benefits to be derived from (qualitative appraisal) consultancy roles: access, quality of findings and interpretation, and researcher's positionality and reputation. I'll provide examples of each but it goes without saying that these opportunities do not materialize automatically. As I will illustrate below, they require what I call "ethnographic awareness," an intangible quality that combines training, experience, and (iteratively expanding) knowledgeability of a particular field. Ethnographic awareness then means that one tries to grasp the "real-life" qualities of the encounters and events the researcher engages with as a consultant.

Access: "Close Encounters of the Third Kind"

When I talk about access I'm referring to access to informants, places, events, and documentation. Short-term consultants as a rule need and acquire access to key informants, documents, and events to gather the inputs for their analysis and recommendations. The "counterpart," that is to say the agency or program under scrutiny, is obliged to organize or facilitate this. Although this by definition generates bias and brings the consultant into a political force field (already noted in the previous section) it also enables the consultant to have extraordinary access to research material and informants in a short period of time, something that would be much harder, time consuming, or even impossible under standard ethnographic conditions. In my experience as a consultant in Colombia it was quite common to be able to talk to a wide variety of people as part of any single field visit. These encounters often included rural community members, demobilized paramilitary rank-and-file, paramilitary commanders, municipal authorities, representatives of the Roman Catholic Church, trade unionists, indigenous leaders, mid- and high-ranking government officials, cabinet ministers, high-level members of the judiciary, senior diplomats, officials of multilateral agencies and missions, and so on.

Although in my general experience in Latin America many of such interlocutors would make themselves generously available also without the clout and sense of urgency produced by the consultancy context, the latter unmistakably serves as leverage. This is especially the case when it comes to having access to persons that would otherwise be most likely beyond the reach of the researcher. My encounter with a few (former) paramilitary commanders in April 2005 offers a particularly vivid illustration.

> After my interview with one of the former commanders in a Montería hotel the previous evening, we (the Mapp/OEA's local team leader and me) headed for the so-called Zona de Ubicación near the village of Santa Fé de Ralito in the department of Cordoba. This zone was not far away from Montería but to enter it we first had to pass an army checkpoint and then checkpoints put up by the various paramilitary *bloques* of the AUC. The Mapp/OEA's local team leader who accompanied me assured me that those we selected for a conversation that day were willing, and even motivated, to present their views on the peace process and the role of the multilateral mission. Although I was prepared, or so I told myself, for the paramilitary political framing that would undoubtedly be forthcoming (which indeed it did) I was also surprised by the range of issues brought forward by the commanders and, even more, by their conduct and the spatial and material arrangements of their outfit. I came to think later these displayed in an ethnographic sense the different personalities and roles they represented within the paramilitary leadership. Without, for my present purpose, going into

the content of the interviews as such, I label the three settings and encounters of that day as, respectively, the "guerrilla encampment," the *"paisa hacienda,"* and the "conference centre." The first of these encounters brought me and my company to a couple of barracks where one of the notorious *bloque* leaders received us in battle dress wearing rubber boots similar to those generally used by the guerrillas of the FARC. *Couleur locale* was added by two jaguars kept in cages outside the main barrack. After this first interview it was almost lunch time and our second interlocutor, carrying an even stronger notoriety than his colleague, had invited us to lunch to his residence that was styled after a country estate of wealthy *Antioqueña* landowners. The rustic interior decoration relied heavily on leather, wood and horse paraphernalia and was filled with household staff and uniformed armed guards. After having been placed in the antechamber for almost an hour (there can of course be only one *patrón* after all) we were invited into the main dining room for a typical *paisa* lunch of beans, rice, *chicharrón*, meat, eggs, and fried *plátanos*. The third encounter brought us to the compound of a commander that had been assuming a role as political strategist and intellectual within the AUC. The premises he occupied included a (small) lecture facility and conference hall; during the conversation our interlocutor mentioned, *inter alia*, the academic support he had been organizing to bolster the political project of the *autodefensas*. Needless to say, all three confirmed their belief in the peace negotiations and the valuable role played by the Mapp/OEA support mission. As it turned out a number of the paramilitary commanders gathered here in Ralito were a few years later arrested and extradited to the U.S. on the orders of president Uribe on the charge of drug trafficking.

The question is, of course, if such extraordinary access can compensate for the limited ethnographic depth of such a singular visit. I argue that the value of such encounters often only comes out later in the longitudinal work as they are absorbed in the growing body of findings and the increasing levels of understanding that this brings.

Quantity and Quality of Data

The same holds true for a second opportunity brought on by consultancy work, namely the possibility to quickly raise a sizable body of good-quality data. Apart from quick and high-intensity access to persons, locations, and events, this also refers to (internal) documentation and (non-public) statistics. Consultancy assignments are regularly fed with this kind of material by the counterpart and third parties. Although this might be done selectively, experienced consultants usually know what relevant material should be available and insist on having access to it. In my experience the scope and reach of information obtainable from consultancy assignments is often remarkable, offering possibilities for triangulation. Of course, much of this material is also confidential and cannot be directly cited as such.

There is also another aspect of consulting which relates to the quality of data that I want to mention briefly. I call this the "pressure cooker effect" of being immersed in the field in the capacity of a consultant. As a rule, the short time available during field trips is intensively used for interviews, meetings, and site visits. At first this may be overwhelming but it also creates an ecology that, in my experience, facilitates constant triangulation and re-interpretation in reflexive encounters with a diverse array of interlocutors and, sometimes, fellow-evaluators. This broadening and deepening of insight occurs not just within the scope of the particular consultancy assignment but also incrementally within the longitudinal frame I adopted over a number of years. I argue that this builds up to a holistic vision that may be different from but not necessarily less valuable than the conventional format of sustained ethnographic fieldwork.

Building an "Autonomous" Reputation

The final opportunity I want to briefly bring up is that a longitudinal approach in which one can manage to incorporate a number of specific, though thematically related, consultancy assignments works as a kind of springboard. Reflecting on my own work in Colombia since the mid-2000s, I was fortunate to have accumulated not only research data and insights but also a growing network of policy operators, advocacy workers, and researchers that, by being open-minded and generous, continued to facilitate my (field) research and participation in technical and academic events after and beyond the requirements of my consultancy stints. In the course of my research often a blending of contracted and autonomous work appeared. I could mobilize contacts acquired during consultancy at a later moment for autonomous follow-up or update interviews. Similarly, consultancy liaisons often facilitated new encounters during independent visits and, inversely, networks built in my autonomous capacity were conveniently available for subsequent advisory work. Importantly, this beneficial effect was not limited to my personal academic activities but extended into the opening up of intern and research opportunities for graduate students under my supervision.

CONCLUSION

In this chapter I have reflected upon my own work as consultant within the field of conflict resolution and peace-building in Colombia between 2005 and 2012. My initial assignment to assess donor support to the Mapp/OEA verification and support mission for the demobilization of the paramilitary inspired me to embark on autonomous research into the dynamics of war and peace in Colombia. This resulted in an eight-year period in which successive consultancy assignments, independent field-work, and the supervision of graduate students blended into a program that, I argue, qualifies as "longitudinal multi-scalar ethnography."

As I have tried to show, the work of an ethnographer-consultant deviates in a number of ways from conventional ethnographic designs. It affects key features of ethnographic research such as access to the field and to key informants, rapport, and trust. Engagement with "the field" is often limited in time, fragmented, politically charged, and addressing specific questions ("terms of reference"). As a result, classical ethnographic report and sustained exposure to sociability with and subjectivity of research participants is, in principle, limited. In addition, important questions regarding research integrity and ethics can be raised such as safe-keeping, confidentiality, and informed consent. Yet, consultancy work also offers a number of opportunities to facilitate a broader research agenda. The design that I choose (admittedly framed as such mostly in hindsight as my work unfolded) arguably fits the nature of the research problem: making sense of the dynamics of conflict resolution and peace-building in a complex and protracted conflict in which many stakeholders are engaged at different levels. I suggest that my approach can be seen as (partially) ethnographic not in a classical sense but in a new sense, responsive to my role and limitations and fitting for the problem under investigation.

At the same time, if qualitative consultancy research, as a type of fieldwork, can be considered ethnographic, it also risks lacking depth, autonomous rapport, and certain ethical safeguards. It also shapes researchers' positionality, research ethics, and, most importantly, the imperative of preserving relative autonomy in a "risky" environment that steers the ethnographer-consultant towards performing like a political knowledge broker. On the other hand, however, it also makes good on this, in part, through enhancing the scope, reach, and intensity of research. Being an ethnographer-consultant can be used to leverage autonomous research but care is required in (re-)interpreting the findings as well as in accounting for the overall integrity of the research as the researcher moves from "political translator" (back?) to critical scholar.

REFERENCES

Bourgois, P. 1990. "Confronting Anthropological Ethics: Ethnographic Lessons from Central America." *Journal of Peace Research* 27, no. 1: 43-54.

Clifford, J. 1997. *Routes: Travel and Translation in the Late Twentieth Century*. Cambridge, MA: Harvard University Press.

Forte, M.C., ed. 2010. *The New Imperialism, vol. 1: Militarism, Humanitarianism, and Occupation*. Montreal: Alert Press.

García-Godos, J., and K.A. Lid 2010. "Transitional Justice and Victims' Rights before the End of a Conflict: The Unusual Case of Colombia." *Journal of Latin American Studies* 42, no 3: 487-516.

Gardner, K., and D. Lewis. 2015. *Anthropology and Development Challenges for the Twenty-First Century*. London: Pluto Press.

Koonings, K., D. Kruijt, and P. Valenzuela. 2013. "Evaluación de la política de los Países Bajos en apoyo a la paz y los derechos humanos en Colombia." Amsterdam: CEDLA (Informe de la investigación *Derechos Humanos y Construcción de Paz*. IOB—Evaluación de la política exterior de los Países Bajos con respecto a América Latina).

Koonings, K., and K.-A. Nordquist. 2005. "Proceso de paz, cese al fuego, desarme, desmovilización y reintegración—cddr—paramilitar y (apoyo internacional a la)Misión de Apoyo al Proceso de Paz de la OEA—Mapp/OEA—en Colombia." Uppsala/Utrecht: Valoración conjunta comisionada por las embajadas de Holanda y Suecia. Informe final.

Kovats-Bernat, J. C. 2002. "Negotiating Dangerous Fields: Pragmatic Strategies for Fieldwork amid Violence and Terror." *American Anthropologist* 104(1): 208-222.

Lubkemann, S. 2008. *Culture in Chaos. An Anthropology of the Social Conditions in War*. Chicago: The University of Chicago Press.

Mosse, D. 2004. "Is Good Policy Unimplementable? Reflections on the Ethnography of Aid Policy and Practise." *Development and Change* 35, no. 4: 639-671.

Mosse, D., and D. Lewis. 2006. "Theoretical Approaches to Brokerage and Translation in Development." In *Development Brokers and Translators: The Ethnography of Aid Agencies*, edited by D. Lewis and D. Mosse, 1-26. Bloomfield, CT: Kumarian Press.

Omidian, P.A. 2009. "Living and Working in a War Zone: An Applied Anthropologist in Afghanistan." *Practising Anthropology* 31, no. 2: 4-11.

Pizarro Leongómez, E. 2004. *Una democracia asediada: balance y perspectivas del conflicto armado en Colombia*. Bogota: Norma.

Price, D. 2014. "Counterinsurgency by Other Names: Complicating Humanitarian Applied Anthropology in Current, Former, and Future War Zones." *Human Organization* 73, no. 2: 95-105.

Restrepo, J.A., and D. Aponte, eds. 2009. *Guerra y violencias en Colombia: herramientas e interpretaciones*. Bogota: Editorial Pontificia Universidad Javeriana.

Robben, A.C.G.M. 1996. "Ethnographic Seduction, Transference, and Resistance in Dialogues about Terror and Violence in Argentina." *Ethos* 24, no. 1: 71-106.

Verhallen, T. 2016. "Tuning to the Dance of Ethnography: Ethics during Situated Fieldwork in Single-Mother Child Protection Families." *Current Anthropology* 57(4): 452-473.

Xiang, B. 2013. "Multi-Scalar Ethnography: An Approach for Critical Engagement with Migration and Social Change." *Ethnography* 14(3): 282–299.

NOTES

1. These and all following vignettes, quotes from mostly informal ethnographic conversations, and experiences in the field are documented in a large number of field note books and diaries that I kept between 2005 and 2012.

2. This particular field visit was part of the Colombia case study for the comprehensive IOB (2013) evaluation of Dutch foreign policy for Latin America. See Koonings, Kruijt, and Valenzuela (2013) for the published country study.

3. I am grateful for the incisive comments from Dirk Kruijt, Dennis Rodgers, and Andrea Damacena Martins on an earlier draft of this chapter.

4. The consultancy assignments in Colombia comprised work for: the Clingendael Institute (The Hague) and the Dutch ministry of Foreign Affairs in April 2007; the Dutch Christian Labour Confederation (CNV) and their Colombian counterpart CGT in April 2010; the Dutch NGO IKV Pax Christi in Cauca in October 2010; the general evaluation of Dutch foreign policy towards Latin America carried out by IOB in July 2012. I undertook independent research visits in November 2006, March/April and October 2009, July 2011, March 2012. Integrating teaching and research included placement and supervision of a total of 13 graduate students from the Utrecht University

master programme of Latin American and Caribbean Studies, one from the Utrecht University research master program CASTOR, and two researchers from the PhD programme of the Department of Anthropology of Utrecht University.

5. For the sake of clarity, I re-state that Mapp/OEA did not act as principal in the 2005 assessment, but as counterpart (and research subject). The Netherlands and Sweden (through their Ministries of Foreign Affairs and Embassies in Bogotá) were the principals for the assignment.

6. I embrace this understanding of ethnographic seduction rather than Robben's (1996) psychoanalytical approach.

SIX

Interviewing Revolutionary Generations in Latin America

A Personal Memoir

Dirk Kruijt

INTRODUCTION

In the forty years or so that I worked at Utrecht University or was seconded to the Dutch Ministry of Foreign Affairs, I was involved in several major research projects. Most of these were collective endeavours. I for example wrote about labour relations, entrepreneurial elites, the informal economy, and economic development issues with (the late) Menno Vellinga (the Peruvian mining proletariat and regional bourgeoisies in Peru and Colombia and Mexico) and Carlos Alba (the regional bourgeoisie and the informal economy and society in Mexico). I also published a series of edited volumes and articles on the relation between urbanisation, violence, and exclusion, as well as the role of the military in politics, with Kees Koonings (informality, exclusion, and violence in Latin America). On one topic, however, I have tended to work alone, and this is in relation to the oral histories of revolutionary generations in Latin America, about which I have published three single-authored monographs. The first was about the generation of progressive, nationalistic colonels and generals that carried out the "Plan Inca" of the "Revolutionary Government of the Armed Forces" in Peru (1968–1975). The second focused on the guerrilla generations of the Central American civil wars between the 1960s and the 1990s. Finally, the third considered the Cuban generation of the insurgents against dictator Batista and the subsequent generation engaged in the "international solidarity," the liaison and support to all Latin American and Caribbean rebel movements between the 1960s and the 2000s.[1]

Revolutions are often generational affairs, associated with the emergence of a particular cohort of individuals who engage in collective political action and are motivated by common ideological sentiments.[2] The latter are frequently presented as combining a legacy of the past and dreams of the future, be these in the form of shared frustration, an ethos of sacrifice, a new moral commitment, or a "historical calling," while the former aim at achieving profound transformations of the economy and society, rebuilding a new (and better) class structure, accompanied by favourable political reforms, encouraged by a new (and nobler) power elite. A new ideology will be dominant, new cultural expressions, and lifestyles emerge. Cultural role models will be different. It will generate new family and gender relations. Sometimes even different moral and religious expressions and concerns will surface.

A revolution also implies destruction, however. The radical restructuring of the old economic, social, and political order, resistance and migration of the old elite and adherents to the former regime, or reorganization of the key institutions of security and defence, order and justice, are all "classic" features of post-revolutionary societies. The old leadership will disappear in favour of new forms of governance (or new leadership). Representatives of the new classes and new social strata establish new boundaries of equality, inequality, and opportunity in society. Career paths will be completely different. Maybe a dream of a classless society will become reality. New political parties and social movements substitute the movements and institutions supporting the old regime. Utopias about a "new world" populated by "new men and women" will be accomplished.

Understanding the balance between hope and fear, pragmatism and aspiration, creation and destruction that revolutions entail is never easy, but always comes down to individuals' perceptions and understandings. The leaders and adherents of the Cuban, the Peruvian, and the Central American Revolution had in common a fervent patriotism, strong anti-imperialist and anti-American feelings, pro-poor sympathies, and conviction of urgency of social justice and social reform. They all venerated revolutionary heroes of the past. Roots and triggers of the rebellions were: being confronted with situations of extreme social injustice; the visible presence of extreme poverty; the shared despise of a negligent economic elite; the national, political, and economic dependence of the United States; and the sycophant behaviour of the ruling class with respect of representatives of the "Colossus of the North." In the case of Central America and Cuba, the presence of a brutalizing dictatorship, supported by the United States, generated the idea of a legitimate armed confrontation against a hated regime. The Peruvian military had fought against—and crushed—three independent guerrilla forces. But the counterinsurgency campaign had convinced them that they were fighting against the wrong adversaries. Even during their military campaigns they had formed clandestine reading and discussion groups, discussing the texts of the Mariateguí, a Peruvian Marxist who admired the Inca regime as a protective, Spartan empire of the past and the cradle of pro-poor and pro-indigenous governance. It was their source of inspiration when they drafted the Plan Inca, the reform programme of the military revolutionary government.

This chapter explores various dimensions of my research into revolutionary generations in Peru, Central America, and Cuba. It begins with a description of my methodological approach, and more specifically the way that my research was very much embedded in my own personal and professional life, before then considering different specificities of the different research projects. In doing so, I highlight both some of the benefits, but also the "riskiness" inherent in such oral history research.

ORAL HISTORY RESEARCH AS PERSONALLY EMBEDDED RESEARCH

At one level, my methodology for my research in Peru, Central America, and Cuba was very "classic" and followed roughly the same pattern in each contexts. The most important source of primary data were in-depth interviews, complemented with multiple secondary sources: academic and journalistic publications, testimonial editions, information offered by diplomatic observers, government reports, reports published by truth and reconciliation commissions, sometimes supplemented by radio and TV documentaries, or published and unpublished diaries or memory notes by the interviewees. The primary interviews took in general a couple of hours. In some cases they were extended over several days and in exceptional situations over a period of months.

The first thing I learned was the importance of an introduction by trustworthy intermediaries, persons of prestige in the social environment of the interviewed ones who stood for my reliability. Without that kind of introduction I could never have initiated my interview series in Peru, Central America and Cuba. After the initial interviews, contacting new persons was easier. Once properly introduced, others were more confident to tell me their life histories and let my share their memories. I also apprehended that new interviewees consulted the previously interviewed about who I was, who had authorised or initiated the interview series, and if they could speak without fear of being lured into half-truths. The fact that I offered the transcriptions for review or corrections was also helpful.

I generally use a qualitative interview style, a conversation between two or more persons at ease. All interviews were achieved on the base of shared confidence. In the Peruvian case I transcribed the complete text of the interviews and let the interviewees correct the first draft. In some case I received in return new manuscripts of many pages, some of them a résumé of their own diaries. Also in Cuba I had the full text transcribed. Every interviewee could read the text and comment on it. Only one interviewed officer decided to retire his text. All others skipped, added, or corrected their interviews and agreed on their use in subsequent publications. In Central America, I also taped the interviews but did not return them to those I interviewed. But I always asked them for permission for publication. Everyone had the opportunity to stop the recorder and some made use of it.[3]

At the same time, my research was also embedded in my personal and professional life in an extremely intimate manner. My Peruvian research was a direct consequence of the fact that in 1970, I (temporarily) gave up the stability of a position at Utrecht University in order to work at both the (upper-middle-class) Catholic University and the (proletarian) San Marcos University in Lima. I arrived in Peru in the early years of the Revolutionary Government of the Armed Forces in Peru, led by General Velasco Alvarado (1968—1975), a year after the announcement of the Land Reform. It was the first time in my life that I was able to directly experience a revolutionary fervour during the years of continuous economic, social, and political reforms. A decade later, in the mid-1980s, I started my oral history study, that led me to dialogue with nearly all of Velasco's military ministers and civilian advisers. I discussed with the core members of his military team their life histories and experiences during the military government. Interviewing them took me several months in 1985, 1986, and 1989, and it was not until the early 1990s that I published the first results.

Similarly, between 1988 and 1992, I was seconded from Utrecht University to the Dutch Ministry of Foreign Affairs, and worked in the Dutch regional embassy in Central America. I spent most of my time travelling between El Salvador, Guatemala, and Nicaragua. Edelberto Torres-Rivas, then the secretary general of the FLACSO system (Facultad Latinoamericano de Ciencias Sociales), invited me to become a research member on civil-military relations. In both capacities I became acquainted with Central American intellectuals in exile, and with some of the peace negotiators at the end of the civil wars in these three countries. In 1999, I participated in a TV documentary about the peace process in Guatemala. With the TV crew I interviewed two actors who had greatly influenced the outcomes of the peace negotiations: Rodrigo Asturias and Julio Balconi. The first was the commander-in-chief of one of the three guerrilla movements; the second, first as colonel and the as general, had been a member of the negotiating team and, in the crucial peace year 1996, the minister of defence. In 2004, I started a comparative study, based on interviews with key players during the war and the peace negotiations—former presidents and cabinet members, retired generals and intelligence officers, the leading guerrilla comandantes and their field comandantes, the official and unofficial peace negotiators, and academic scholars who had already published on the civil wars.

The Central American study was my introduction to the Cuban Revolution. In 2009, I presented the book at the University of Havana. After a discussion with the staff members of the Cuban FLACSO institute, we agreed on a joint research project about the former urban underground and the rural guerrilla during the insurgency period against dictator Batista. This interview round took the most of 2010 and 2011. During these interviews I became acquainted with other Cuban researchers. With one of them I agreed on a second interview series, this time with the (retired) officials of the Departamento América, Cuba's liaison with all revolutionary and political movements in the region. We interviewed around forty of their members between 2011 and 2013. The next section explores in more detail how the personalised embedding of my research fundamentally shaped it, both methodologically and epistemologically.

PERSONALISED EMBEDDING AT WORK

In Peru, I was particularly helped by a good friend and colleague, Maria del Pilar Tello, a well-known journalist and author of a collection of interviews with the military ministers that she had recently published. Her father had been an associate of Mariateguí and was the co-founder of the Socialist Party. She initiated my access to the first interviews. During these first couple of interviews, I was more or less tested. The fact that I had two children born in Peru certainly facilitated the initial conversations. In the course of my interviews I was sort of "adopted" by three key members of Velasco's generals—Jorge Fernandez Maldonado, Miguel Ángel de la Flor, and Ramón Miranda. These three officers were widely regarded as honest, loyal and outspoken, also among their fellow generals. I could balance their opinions with officers from other factions within the military and with Velasco's civilian advisers. The three generals guided me through the difficult process of "do-and-do-not" during other interviews, telephoned colleagues and prepared me for delicate themes: about the counter-coup against Velasco in 1975, about excessive self-esteem of some of their colleagues ("Probably he could not have done it; he was drunk at that moment"), about Velasco's adversaries within the Marine. But in order to balance my information, they also contacted me with retired admirals with whom they were on speaking terms, with the explicit message that they might get me in touch with relevant colleagues. After the initial interviews, contacting new persons was easier.

To my good luck I met and befriended the former secretary of the council of ministers, Arturo Valdés Palacio, a lawyer with the military rank of brigadier, also Velasco's personal legal adviser. To my surprise — and delight—he kept at home a complete photocopied archive of the cabinet sessions between 1968 and 1975.[4] We carried out many interviews together, each of which invariably started with the question where we had left off last time: "Was it July 1971?," Arturo would say, and on receiving confirmation, he would then open the dossier for "August 1971," I would start the tape recorder, and he would read paragraphs from the papers in the dossier, commenting them with his entertaining, ironic interpretation of the situation.

These interviews were my basic referential points. I could always refer to the cabinet discussions and the decisions afterwards. When I interviewed the next generals and admirals, they were always impressed by my detailed "knowledge" of the lingering course of the revolution. In the mid-1980s, when I conducted my interviews, it still was habitual that the generals went to one special bank office to receive their monthly pension check. Several times they asked one another: "What did he ask you?" My detailed questions were commented on. I never mentioned the source of information during the interviews, but it certainly facilitated the atmosphere during my conversations.

When I published my book with a biographical chapter about Velasco, Generals De la Flor and Miranda wrote a foreword. It resulted to be a sort of golden credit card during my other two other research projects in Central America and Cuba. Velasco had all the military virtues of leadership, generalship, courage, discipline, loyalty, and dedication to his institution, patriotism, honesty, sympathy for the poor and underprivileged, and incorruptibility. In the case of the Salvadoran generals (they had recently introduced the rank of general in the Armed Forces) and of the Guatemalan generals (there were twelve of them in active service, two division generals and ten brigadiers), some of them gratefully compared themselves with general Velasco, saviour of the nation. In Guatemala, the then Minister of Defence gave me permission to interview several generals in active service.

In Central America, working at the Netherlands regional embassy as an adviser between 1988 and 1992 enormously facilitated access to military and political key persons. Basically, I circulated during four years between El Salvador, Guatemala, and Nicaragua. Unavoidably, I became acquainted with the personalities and institutions directly involved in the peace negotiations and the post-war reintegration process. In these three countries, civil wars were fought by the military, paramilitary forces and guerrilla organisations, unified under umbrella structures (the Sandinista FSLN [Frente Sandinista de Liberación Nacional] in Nicaragua, the Salvadoran FMLN [Frente Farabundo Martí de Liberación Nacional], and the

Guatemalan URNG [Unión Revolucionaria Nacional Guatemalteca]), headed by a generation of intellectuals, former lieutenants, former members of the Communist Youth, and students leaders. After the war I maintained good working relations with the local FLACSO establishments in Guatemala City and San Salvador; in Managua I became incorporated in the IHNCA institute (Instituto de Historia de Nicaragua y Centro América).

After the already-mentioned TV documentary about guerrilla leader Rodrigo Asturias and army general Julio Balconi, I started interviewing in Guatemala. Balconi and Asturias had maintained confidential communications aside from the official negotiating rounds. After presidential permission they had extended their off-the-record conversations to formal Army-UNRG consultations. In March 1996 the army and the guerrilla organised a decisive meeting in Cuba, with the assistance of the Cuban liaison officer for Central America, Ramiro Abreu. During this meeting, and with the good offices of Fidel and Raúl Castro, the higher echelons of the armed forces and the leadership of the guerrilla achieved an agreement on all pending affairs, even on a cease-fire and a disarming scheme. In December 1996, the official peace agreements were signed.

Afterwards, when Balconi's published his memoirs, I assisted him as a kind of ghost writer. I noticed that Balconi had developed a relation of trust with the leading Guatemalan guerrilla comandantes. Interesting enough, the first interviews were obtained after an introduction by Balconi. The URNG, then, was divided and already had been split up in two smaller parties. The larger one was headed by Rodrigo Asturias who also provided me with access to part of his personal archive. They, and Héctor Rosada-Granados, peace negotiator 1993 and 1996, gave me a helping hand in scheduling appointments. I already had worked with them during my years at the embassy and I had been the supervisor of Rosada-Granados's PhD thesis at Utrecht University. Sometimes one has good luck by pure coincidence. While interviewing political key persons I met someone who had been the lover of a guerrilla comandante. She invited me for a breakfast in one of Guatemala's elegant hotels and there she told me, discreetly, about schisms, splits and personal antagonisms within the Guatemalan guerrilla leadership.[5]

In El Salvador, Héctor Dada and Ruben Zamora were extremely helpful. Dada had been a member of the progressive civil-military junta whose dissolution initiated the civil war in 1979. In the 1990s he was a leading peace negotiator on behalf of the FMLN and as an independent member of parliament he still was highly respected by political friends and foes. He also had been the director of the local FLACSO centre in San Salvador and was so kind to introduce me to many of his FMLN colleagues in the parliament. Zamora, the first FMLN presidential candidate after the Peace Agreements in 1992 and himself author of standard works on the FMLN, generously offered me free access to his private and his research archives. Once having visited several MP members at their parliamentary offices, their network of secretarial support made my appointments with other colleagues. During my embassy period I had assisted the Secretary of National Reconstruction of President Cristiani's post-war government; it facilitated an interview with him. And the interview with Cristiani, in turn, smoothed the process of interviewing his military and political advisers.

In Nicaragua, the start of the interviews was surprising. I remembered that the former secretary and chauffeur of the Netherlands embassy office in Managua had been related to the Ministry of the Interior and I asked them their assistance. To my astonishment I got the next day, still jet lagged, a call that comandante Thomas Borge, the former minister, expected me at 9:00 a.m. at his office. I took a taxi, completely unprepared. The interview started as an interrogatory but after half an hour, after knowing that we both had been married to a Peruvian, he suddenly softened and became helpful. He told me that I still had another 30 minutes and that he would give me his honest opinion about all delicate matters I would present him. Effectively, it was one of the best interviews I got in Nicaragua. I returned to my hotel with a collection of his most recent poetry and a copy of his memoirs.

I was greatly aided by Margareta Vannini, director of the Instituto de Historia de Nicaragua y de Centroamérica (INHCA), the former Instituto de Estudios Sandinistas, who personally made appointments with leading comandantes. When the interview round was underway, some comandantes—Humberto Ortega was one of them—called me to invite me for an interview. One of his bodyguards picked me up to drive me to his walled townhouse. The FSLN was then split up in several factions, and most comandantes had joined the "new Sandinista" opposition or left the Frente. It made it easier to ask about ideological preferences then and now. Most comandantes were modest and reflexive, some were pompous and self-indulging. Several wanted to settle an old account with Daniel Ortega; without being asked about it, they volunteered with gossip and unflattering anecdotes about his political and private life and that of his wife, Rosario Murillo. It resulted impossible to interview Ortega himself. There was never a clear "no"; but I had always to call to the assistant of his wife "compañera Rosario" who diligently assured me that tomorrow he would be able to give me the place and hour of an interview. After weeks, it became a matter of honour to continue. After three months I gave up.

In Cuba, I researched and interviewed as a member of a team. My first round of interviews was facilitated by a three FLACSO professors. The FLACSO director, somewhat uneasy about a foreigner interviewing veterans, had decided that I always should be accompanied by one of my three colleagues. They were both colleagues and minders. It is only fair to mention that, without their presence, I would not have had access to the veteran insurgents who were most willing to converse about their memories and experiences. My colleagues provided me with "orientations" about what to do and not to do. The general research theme was the "history of the revolutionary generation, 1953–1961." I was not used to the Cuban style of interviewing: questions and answers. The first couple of interviews were half-interrogations, but afterwards we agreed on easy conversations that could be taped.

I also was astonished when my Cuban colleagues were inclined to end the interview when we had reached the year 1961 in our conversations. It became clear that they took the permission to research the period between 1953 and 1961 quite literally. But happily enough, most interviewees wanted to continue: their life history had not ended in 1961. We reached a compromise: after the first interview I was permitted to return for a second or third interview some days thereafter. And I have to admit that nearly all interviewees were open, hospitable, speaking quite frankly, providing detailed information, and offering their help with identifying others, friends and former colleagues. Sometimes they let us copy some of their private memoirs, unpublished manuscripts or historical documents they kept at home. Those who had published books or articles let us copy gave a copy or made us available their own personal copy for reproduction.

By gentlemen's agreement it was established that every researcher could use the interviews after the explicit approval of the respondents and the publication, in a somewhat reduced form, of the interviews in Cuba. Cuban professionals earn very little in cash: between 30 and 40 euro per month. I paid them "incentives" in cash for their assistance, advise, transcription of the interviews, and mini-seminars to discuss with the interviewees their consent to publish the final draft of the interviews. It produced an unintended consequence of several efforts to convince the respondents to agree on the publication, complicated negotiations with editorial houses, re-budgeting publication costs, delays in printing, and sometimes even the import of toner, packets of A4 paper, travel allowances, and additional tasks to be fulfilled. Once, when I had to import new packets of A4 paper when there was a shortage of printing paper or toner in Cuba, it happened that a customs functionary patiently opened a package and reviewed page after page in order to verify that I was not entering the country with forbidden publications. Email contact was another source of frustration. Sometimes the server of the FLACSO institute did not function. It is very difficult to transmit annexes per mail. It complicated the correspondence and sometimes we had to spend an entire day in order to buy toner or to photocopy transcriptions.

When we started, with a new team, with a second round of interviews among the (retired) members of the Departamento América, Cuba's foreign intelligence and liaison with the Latin American guerrilla movements, things changed. Later I got to know that I was vetted and that also Cuba has a "Vatican" where decisions are made about yes or no. In my case, I was "oriented" to move to another apartment, the property of former colleagues and the party secretary of a municipality of Greater Havana, a trusted ambience. There, many of the retired members of the Departamento were interviewed; sometimes we travelled across Havana to visit the older ones at home. Without exception, the interviewees were very frank, outspoken, without evasion or explicit political correctness. Of course, they had been "the eyes and ears of Fidel," an elite group within an elite organisation, hand-picked by their chief, Manuel Piñeiro, who had direct access to Fidel Castro and one of the very few who had the right to say "no" to the Comandante-en-Jefe. I remember the conversations as fascinating. Sometimes there were three, four, or five members present, fervently discussing and forgetting that they were taped. But with the exception of one functionary, all interviewees agreed afterwards the publication of their interviews. They only complained when we reduced the initial texts of, say, 30,000 words, to 5,000 or 6,000 words.

The only negative aspect of this style of working is that it requires a lot of patience. Organising interviews is not as complicated as it seems, once a relation of trust is established or permission is given to speak without reserve. But the procedures of transcription, re-phrasing, correcting, re-transcribing, re-correcting, and especially the negotiations with the editorial houses are time-consuming and irritating. Especially in the case of Cuba it required time, much time again. In retrospect, though the interviews took several periods of months, the transcriptions and small corrections were the cause of delays. The procedure of publishing the two interview books inevitably led to postponements. In the case of the publication by the University of Havana, we had to get permission of the vice-rector to co-finance the publication with the editorial house; the process of the financial transference took half a year. No one was opposed; the proper procedures are slowly progressing. Afterwards (but only afterwards), I was quite happy with the experience: At already I had some work experience in the Peruvian and in the Central American public sector and I thought that I knew the knacks to get things done. Cuba was a new experience and all previous bureaucratic reflexes proved to be unsuccessful. It only took me quite much time to learn how Cuban informal structures are functioning.

CONCLUSION

In all three of the studies that I have mentioned in this chapter I did research on revolutionary generations and soldiers in arms, of regular armies, or of guerrilla movements. I interviewed politicians, senior officers, guerrilla leaders, and civilian advisers, both active and retired, and I worked with the explicit—or at the very least unambiguous implicit—permission of the institutions involved. In the sense of personal risk, the situation was never dangerous, but it clearly required significant navigation of political sensibilities and an acute awareness of how different individuals and groups interrelated with each other. In particular, in the case of Cuba I had to acquire a sensitivity of the "otherness" of its society and political structure, the etiquette and the implicit ranking of veteran guerrila participants and subsequent generations, their loyalty to the system they had built, and their latent and sometimes candid irritation about the fusion between the "real fighters" and the cadres of the old Communist Party that had not participated in the insurgency but enjoyed the confidence of the Soviet advisers who were present until the late eighties.

I became very aware of the similarities—rather than the differences—between the various revolutionary generations: a fervent nationalism, patriotism, a sense of "calling," personal courage (both military courage and civil courage), loyalty to their institutions (or, in the case of the guerrila movements, their factions), the expressed need for considered to be decent and proven to be capable of sacrifices, and their pride to have contributed, of course modestly, to the course of history. At least partially, these feelings were the reason that individuals were willing to be interviewed.

At the same time, historians have traditionally felt uneasy about oral history. What is not explicitly mentioned in primary sources of archives and secondary sources of books, diaries, memoirs, or letters is "risky" for reasons of "subjectivity." Of course, working with written documents and archives is not a certification of objectivity. Additionally, what do you do in the absence or closure of archives? Then your only primary sources are interviews, supported by secondary scholarly sources, and the "grey" literature of books, pamphlets, underground journals and unpublished diaries. The advantage of oral history, however, is that you can discuss and ask for the specifics. Then there is always the possibility of balancing information by interviewing key persons or obtaining written information of rivalling factions (I do not know any guerrilla movement, armed institution, or political movement that does not have competing and rivalling factions!). Then there is the risk of memory failures due to age or over-loyalty with respect to the dirty laundry of their former institutions. But again, adversaries will disclose with gusto what really happened. Eventually, the greatest risk of oral history is a kind of self-censorship: you interviewed someone about sensitive issues, you did so in an agreeable context, you sympathized with the interviewee, you socialized with them—and to criticize them afterwards is difficult, unfair, potentially jeopardizing of your relationship with them and others . . . I certainly became aware of this danger in all three cases of oral history research, and have had to navigation difficult dilemmas in this respect, but ultimately, it is a risk that you have to take in order to carry out good oral history, which like ethnography, depends very much on the establishment of a sense of rapport and frank exchange. Seen from this perspective, it can be argued that the risk is an inevitable one.

REFERENCES

Balconi, J., and D. Kruijt. 2004. *Hacia la reconciliación. Guatemala, 1960–1996*. Guatemala: Editorial Piedra Santa.

Bell Lara, J., T. Caram León, D. Kruijt, and D. Luisa López García. 2013. *Cuba: La generación revolucionaria, 1952–1961*. La Habana: Editorial Félix Varela (second edition).

Bell Lara, J., T. Caram León, D. Kruijt, and D. Luisa López García. 2014. *Combatientes*. La Habana: Editorial de Ciencias Sociales.

Kruijt, D. 1994. *Revolution by Decree. Peru 1968–1975*. Amsterdam: Thela Publishers.

Kruijt, D. 2008. *Guerrillas. War and Peace in Central America*. London: Zed Books.

Kruijt, D. 2013. "Research on Latin America's Soldiers: Generals, Sergeants, and Guerrilla *comandantes*." In *Qualitative Methods in Military Studies. Research Experiences and Challenges*, edited by H. Carreiras and C. Castro, 158–177. London: Routledge (Cass Military Studies).

Kruijt, D. 2017. *Cuba and Revolutionary Latin America*. London: Zed Books.

Suárez Salazar, Luis, and Dirk Kruijt. 2015. *La Revolución Cubana en Nuestra América: El internacionalismo anónimo*. La Habana: Ruth Casa Editorial, 2015 (e-book).

NOTES

1. Oral history research is by its very nature a collective endeavour, of course, and it should be noted that I did co-publish a number of the auxiliary studies to my monographs, in order to make the primary (interview) sources available in book form. In the case of Balconi and Kruijt (2004) this referred to the war memories and a detailed account of the peace negotiations by one of the key Guatemalan actors. In the case of Kruijt and Van Meurs (2000), Bell, Caram, Kruijt and López (2014) and Suárez Salazar (2015) we published the (partial) transcripts of the interviews with key actors in Guatemala and Cuba. The publications on Peru (Kruijt 1994) and Central America (Kruijt 2008) were also edited in Spanish. My own account about Cuba's influence on the Latin American revolutions was published as Kruijt (2017).

2. Here I paraphrase Kruijt (2008, 39).

3. This paragraph quotes and rephrases some parts of Kruijt (2013).

4. Eventually, his son donated the entire archive to the Catholic University in Lima. From 2015 on, parts of this archive are gradually being digitized and published.

5. She also was helpful to obtain the permission of the Guatemalan Minister of Defence to interview the generals in active service.

SEVEN

"You Are Not Like the Ladinos at All"

Reflections on Fieldwork, Cataloguing the Researcher, and Knowledge Production

Elisabet Dueholm Rasch

INTRODUCTION

The *fiesta* has ended. There are still some people around, scattered over the streets; some too drunk to stay on their own feet, others already unconscious. In some cantinas the music is still playing, people still dancing. As Judith and I stroll through the streets, we find a little girl. She is looking for her parents. We ask her if she knows where to go; she doesn't. We take her into doña Martha's small shop at the corner of the street and ask whether she knows who she is and where she comes from; she doesn't. "And," she says, pointing at me, "you'd better be careful. She's from the rural area, that's for sure, and if they see you (pointing at me, the white, female anthropologist) with her, they might just lynch you, because that's the way they are" (fieldnotes November 2003).

Although I knew that some tourists had been lynched recently because people had thought they would abduct their children, I was shocked. I had already become to consider myself as an insider of the community where I was doing my PhD fieldwork and the idea that I could be a possible victim of such a thing—a thing that would happen to outsiders hostile to the community—stood diametrically opposed to this. Apparently, I was considered an outsider to the community; a *gringa* that could possibly abduct Guatemalan children. It was only after several reflexive sessions that I could see that *doña* Martha's comment was in a way interesting and valuable for my research: the identity she attributed to me and to the inhabitants of the rural area disclosed some of the workings of identity at my fieldwork location. The identity she attributed to me, in relation to the inhabitants of the rural communities, informed me about the ways she categorized the rural population. It also clearly demarcated the boundary between the inhabitants of the town and the people living in the rural communities. So, I concluded, the way people would categorize me (the researcher) along the insider/outsider as well as the indigenous/non-indigenous continuum in relation other inhabitants of the municipality was actually part of the process of knowledge production. At the same time I realized that *doña* Martha's comment, as well as the way I reacted to it, revealed a recurring dilemma during my fieldwork: balancing between intimacy and distance, being a friend and a professional, being an insider and an outsider. A dilemma that I experienced as an anthropologist and that became more manifest through the different and changing ways research participants would catalogue me.

What I will do in this methodological essay is explore how the (attributed) identity of the researcher informs the production of knowledge during fieldwork. It will become clear that insider/outsider distinction is "frequently situational, depending on the prevailing social, political, and cultural values of a given social context" (Kusow 2003, 592). The identities attributed to us define our role along the insider/outsider continuum and what research participants share with us. A number of factors inform this nature of interaction between researchers and informants and insider/outsider positions: class, nationality, gender, marital status, profession, religion (among others, see also Ergun and Erdemir 2009). For a fieldworker to be considered as an insider requires negotiations that often revolve around the strategic highlighting of commonalities and the downplaying of differences, neutrality, and political differences (Ergun and Erdemir 2009). In this process, fieldworkers go to and from distance and proximity, stepping in in order to get close, stepping out in order to be able to analyze and theorize (Madden 2010). I will show how this works on two levels, one, on the level of how fieldworkers' attributed identity inform the social interactions in the field, and, two, the ways these social interactions in themselves contribute to knowledge production in a more substantive way. Before I go on to do that, I will briefly introduce the topic of my PhD research and the methodology I applied.

GENERAL TOPIC AND METHODOLOGY

The idea for my PhD research originated in 1998 when I was doing fieldwork in a remote municipality in the department of Huehuetenango in Guatemala for my master's thesis. Before moving to this Mam municipality I had lived two months in the capital, Guatemala City, where I did an internship in a Maya organization and was struck by the different ways in which Maya identity was articulated in those two places. Whereas Mayas working in the capital's NGOs constantly referred to indigenous rights and authenticity, in Huehuetenango people applied a much more local language in their articulations of indigeneity. So, when I started out my PhD research I wanted to find out which views the Maya Movement had about both "traditional" indigenous authorities and indigenous may-ors, and about the role of the latter in the democratic reconstruction of Guatemala. I considered municipal government not as the main subject of the study but as a site wherein constructed indigenous identities are contested and practiced.

So I studied how indigenous identity takes shape and how people give meaning indigeneity within the context of the governing of a munic-ipality. In doing this, I followed three lines of inquiry: first, I looked into national and local narratives with respect to indigenous and Maya iden-tity constructions. Second, I examined the ways indigenous people par-ticipate in spaces of participation defined by the state as a way to claim citizenship. Third, I analysed ways the indigenous population gives form to their claim-making through participation in sites that have been de-fined as characteristically Maya, such as local systems of community ser-vice and boards of elders. In this essay I will focus mostly on the first line of inquiry, identity. I approached indigenous identities as "historical and contested in practice" (Holland and Lave 2001, 6). This resulted in ethno-graphic fieldwork that studied the cultural production of identity begin-ning from specific conflictive situations: the election of Rigoberto Quemé Chay as the first Maya mayor of Quetzaltenango, and the contesting of the traditional system of community service in Santa María.

During my 17-month fieldwork I unravelled the contentious local practices that evolved around the above-mentioned cases employing anthropological research methods: participant observation, open semi- and unstructured interviews, life histories, and document analysis (NGO documents, meeting minutes, newspapers articles [local and national], and policy reports). The fieldwork itself was maybe most characterized by a continuous process of role shifting between the more mundane, cosmopolitan, rights-conscious, indigenous bourgeoisie, and the much more poor and rural population, that would be considered, often, as "really" indigenous by the former. In these different "ethnographic places" I was assigned different roles on the insider/outsider continuum, depending on peoples, places and phases of my research, obviously af-fecting the type of information they would share with me. This happened in, roughly, two ways: it affected my methodology, that is, what kind of interviews I could conduct and with whom, as well as kind of knowledge would be produced during these interviews. Additionally, the way re-search participants would catalogue me (Paerregaard 2002), the research-er, and the identity they would attribute to me during this process provided me with substantive knowledge as well about the ontologies that were maintained.

QUETZALTENANGO—ON POLITICAL COMMON GROUNDS AND DIFFERENCES

My first fieldwork location was Quetzaltenango—the "Greatest Indian City in the World" (Thompson, quoted in Grandin 2002, 25). With Rigoberto Quemé Chay having been elected the first Maya mayor of Quetzaltenango in 1995, I had to go there. Of course, Quetzaltenango had more going for it than a Maya mayor to make it an interesting site for research on indigenous government. As the second largest city of Guatemala and the unofficial capital of the Mayan Western highlands, Quetzaltenango was at the very centre of Maya K'iche activism. With its population of approximately equal numbers of ladinos and Mayas, a small indigenous Maya K'iche bourgeoisie, and many, many poor *indígenas*, Quetzaltenango is also marked by profound racism. Until the election of Rigoberto Quemé Chay of the political committee Xel-jú, Quetzaltenango's indigenous population had been excluded from the economic, political and cultural arenas. Those characteristics, I presumed, would generate dynamics different from those that were to be found in a rural municipality.

In Quetzaltenango my research was centred around the political committee Xel-jú and the representatives of the rural communities that were part of the municipality. It was not very difficult to become friends with Xel-jú members, as many of them are very receptive and open-minded. Apart from that, I sympathized with their political project from the start. In due course, I was invited to the Xel-jú meetings, to the houses of Xel-jú members, and to lunches in the communities. I interviewed founders, members of its governing board, and almost all members that held office in the municipal council during the two Quemé administrations (1996–2000 and 2001–2005). I participated in meetings of the board and general meetings and, of course, also socialized in more informal settings over meals or drinks. We would talk about the origins of the organization, the necessity to found an indigenous political space, their political careers, what it means to be indigenous in Quetzaltenango, and about the politics of Xel-jú.

I approached the community representatives through workshops, organized by the municipal council and several NGOs, for community leadership. During those workshops, we had breakfast, lunch, and dinner together. We discussed, worked, played basketball, and watched movies. After a while, my participation in these workshops resulted in invitations for me to come and visit different communities. In most instances, I also made follow-up visits, which allowed me to get to know several of those communities better and to participate in meetings of the local authorities, community meetings, and inauguration ceremonies. At other times we watched soccer games, went to dance rehearsals, or just sat and chatted. The numerous interviews and informal conversations that I held on all these occasions more or less addressed the same issues as the interviews with Xel-jú members, although in a more scattered way: their work as community leaders, their thoughts about Quemé's indigenous policies, and the reality of being indigenous in the rural outskirts of Quetzaltenango.

It was not always easy to deal with the enormous differences among the people with whom I worked. One day I would be invited to a big estate near the coast to discuss possible outcomes of the elections of the governing board over a glass of wine, and the following day I would find myself enjoying black beans and tortillas near the fireplace in a small community, listening to stories about the poverty and racism that my interviewees had been experiencing. Different research participants, would assign me different roles and would highlight or emphasize different elements of my identity. This informed my social interactions in the field in several ways.

Interviewing and being with municipal politicians, meant presenting myself as a professional: well educated, knowledgeable, well informed, but also engaged with the indigenous cause. At first, I was perceived as naïve, but I think that I eventually gained the respect of those I spoke to as a critical thinker, an academic and a political analyst. I know that many Xel-jú members still consider me a friend of the committee—in both the personal and political sense—and they have often asked for my advice outside the meetings I had organized to share the findings of my research. During my visit in 2007, for example, I held extensive discussions with Jordan Rodas, candidate for mayor, as he was struggling to put together his list of candidates for the electoral slates. He asked me my opinion and, for an hour or so, we discussed different proposals. In this case, as during many other instances during my fieldwork, a shared political ideology was an important level on which my insider status was negotiated (Ergun and Erdemir 2010; Shariff 2014). As for my identity as a researcher, this made me feel accepted as an insider, at times making it difficult to distance myself from the political project. However, engaging with the rural communities and, in a later stage, doing fieldwork in Santa María, made it possible to understand Xel-jú from a more distanced perspective (and the other way around).

In the communities, where I mostly engaged with more poor representatives of the rural communities, my role and the identity assigned to me, also changed over time, as well as the way I presented myself. In the beginning they would see me as a Xel-jú municipal representative, which made them hesitate to share a critical view on municipal policies. It became crucial to present myself as engaged (which I of course also was), curious and understanding. I could only gain trust by not doing the things municipal politicians an urban residents (Mayas and ladinos alike) would do when they engaged with them: distancing myself by coming by car, demand cutlery when everybody was eating without, imposing ideas. These people started trust me, because I did the same thing they did, from playing basketball to climbing the mountain in order to get me to a community and eat loads of tortillas, and because we could engage in open talks, while we did one of all these things, about the policies of Xel-jú. The "downplaying of differences," rather than the "embracing of com-monalities"—because there weren't any—as Ergun and Erdemir (2010) call it, were crucial elements in the process of gaining trust and rapport with the representatives of the communities.

SANTA MARÍA

I came to Santa María (located in the mountains of Totonicapán and populated by 30.000 inhabitants of whom 92 percent identify as Maya K'iche) partly because of the presence of and indigenous authority called "Alguaciles and Mayores of the Corridor," which had the customary right to fulfil functions of the (national) police. I found that interesting, because this would be an example of those authorities the Maya Move-ment considered an expression of Maya identity. Claiming indigenous citizenship would entail demanding respect and the continuation of this kind of indigenous authority. Thus, Santa María was an evident place to study such articulations and expressions of indigenous identity. To my surprise—and also, to a certain extent, to my disappointment—the inhab-itants of Santa María had decided to abolish the Mayores and Alguaciles of the Corridor just a couple of months before I arrived. In the end, however, this proved to be the perfect way to explore the nature of the discussions about multicultural democracy in the municipality.

Doing research in a rural municipality is fundamentally different from doing fieldwork in a city, even a city as small as Quetzaltenango. Where-as in Quetzaltenango my mobile phone was one of my most important research tools, one that directed me from event to event, from interview to interview, in Santa María I spent most of my time in the streets, trying to find out what was going on—or what was about to happen. I was not connected to any institution, NGO, church, or school. After a while it became normal that I just appeared everywhere: right-wing as well as left-wing political meetings preceding the 2003-elections, evangelical prayer meetings and Catholic masses, commencement ceremonies at the end of the school year, the Independence Day parade, and as a player in the village basketball competition. I was everywhere, and talked to al-most everyone. In this process, neutrality as a level of negotiating insider/outsider status became important in order to ensure continuing access to conflicting groups in the municipality and building relations of trust with the informants (Ergun and Erdemir 2009).

Because of the intertwinement of religion and politics (in this locality, but also in indigenous world view), the array of research participants not only included local politicians, but went from evangelical pastors to right-wing community leaders to Maya spiritual leaders. Gaining rapport took time, also with the group of indigenous authorities that were central to my research. The first time I showed up at the "Auxiliatura del Centro" I could not have imagined how those persons would become some of the persons with whom I would develop the highest level of trust. However, this was the day that what would become my regular routine every Thursday began: chatting, observing, reading newspapers, posing questions regarding what I had seen. After a while began to feel like the office of the local authorities—with its neatly painted green walls and its benches arrayed along the walls—was becoming my home. I had my own, regular seat, close to the elders, who were in attendance almost every Thursday. They probably thought of me as a naïve girl, one of many. The whole difference was, that I was very persistent and that I adapted to rural life in as many ways as possible. As a consequence they came to see me as someone capable of collecting and understanding parts of their culture.

I started to have many homes in Santa María, where I gradually became an insider. Eating chile, *caldo rojo* and entering the typical sauna (*tuj*) all proved to be ways to downplay the differences between me and them and gain rapport. I would also help teaching English, prepare documents, fold envelopes in the middle of the night, and help prepare PowerPoint presentations. Eventually, people would start making comments as "you are not like the ladinos at all" and "you talk and make jokes with us," referring to numerous state and NGO representatives that would show up in the municipality without—apparently—connecting up to the people. This also involved distancing myself from people from the capital and Quetzaltenango and as such create some common ground. So, becoming an insider in Santa María, made me distance myself from Quetzaltenango. Again, reflecting on my changing relationships and levels of intimacy in Santa María in my fieldnotes made me see how this was also necessary in order to understand the different forms of indigeneity. Interviews were always informal or unstructured because of the precarious process of gaining rapport. I almost always began by asking for the community career of the interviewee as this proved to be the most natural way to move to generate a discussion about issues of identity and politics. Another favorite starting topic was the *vara*, the wooden staff that symbolizes authority, as those accounts often offered a starting point for many about the importance and uncertainties surrounding the system of community services.

It was easier to downplay the difference of my class and national identity, than it was to do so with my gender identity. I often felt "quite out of space" (Gelsthorpe cited in Huggins and Glebbeek 2003, 369) because I participated in many male-dominated activities, but especially because women are not supposed to go out on the street alone in municipalities such as Santa María. I am not sure how the fact that I am a woman affected the results of my research, but I am aware of the fact that a man would have been able to participate on a more equal footing. For example, it was never possible for me to go to a cantina and have a few drinks with the council members: this would have ruined my reputation—I will come back to that later. For that same reason, there were even so many social interactions that could not take place.

CATALOGUED IDENTITIES

Above I have sketched how the identities that research participants assigned to me shaped the encounters I had in the field. As I described in the introduction, it was only after a while that I realized that these processes not only shaped my social interactions in the field and the kind of knowledge people would share with me, but that analyzing the way they catalogued me in relation to others and themselves actually would be insightful to understand different meanings of indigeneity (Paerregaard 2002). My role of the knowledgeable anthropologist in Quetzaltenango, for example, also meant that I was considered knowledgeable in the field of "real" indigenous culture. This disclosed that middle-class indigenous people, identifying as Maya, in the end thought of indigeneity in quite static and essentialized ways. In Santa María, where my biggest challenge was to stay neutral, it depended heavily on the situation whether I would be categorized as insider or outsider of the municipality. In my role of the engaged, naïve, and always curious researcher it appeared that time and the downplaying of differences were the most important mechanisms to become an insider. Being part of Santa María meant not being like the ladinos, first, and second, having lived the daily life there for a long time. The way research participants in both Quetzaltenango and Santa María categorized me, the white, female, university-trained researcher, disclosed and confirmed important articulations of identification and indigeneity. These categorizations shaped insider/outsiderness and to a certain extent determined and changed my levels of intimacy and distance to my research participants. On the one hand, this at times created insecurity on my side about being accepted as a researcher. On the other hand moving between being an insider and an outsider forced me to engage in processes of reflexivity (Madden 2010)—literally moving between different fieldwork locations at times facilitated such moments of introspection. Let me exemplify how this worked out in practice by way of three vignettes that describe different situations in which different identities were attributed to me. Of course these attributions were informed by the processes described above.

After having lived in Santa María for a few months, I invited some of my Quetzaltenango friends over for lunch with my host family in Santa María. I already felt part of the village and was eager to share my experiences with them. They were high-profile Xel-jú members, people that had taught me a lot about being Maya in the city and were very politically engaged in indigenous issues. They were excited about the visit; many *Quetzaltecos* do not get to know rural municipalities from the inside. They consider these places as really indigenous; as places where true Mayaness is safeguarded. When they arrived, they parked the car, said "hi" to my host mom, who was preparing the traditional meal, *caldo rojo*, and went out to have a look around the village. They rapidly disappeared into the *cantina* around the corner. Whereas in Quetzaltenango I would drink beers and smoke cigarettes with these folks, here I could not enter the cantina with them. I lived with a Protestant family and had been able to establish and image of myself as a kind and chaste ethnographer (Fine 1993). I could get along with everybody and put a lot of energy in safeguarding this neutrality. I would certainly not drink nor smoke. For my friends, however, going in to this cantina was clearly part of an "indigenous" experience. When I showed them around the village after lunch, it became clear that they considered me as a cultural expert, someone who could inform them about the ins and outs of what they considered a real indigenous village. It occurred to me that they really considered everything in this village as more indigenous than themselves. It felt like I was showing around tourists, rather than people that would say to represent indigenous populations of the country in politics.

It felt really awkward, maybe because it made very visible some uneasy findings of my fieldwork. It confirmed the enormous differences between urban, middle-class Mayas and poor community representatives. Additionally it also confirmed what I had found while doing fieldwork in Quetzaltenango; that many "city Mayas" maintained a very essentialist, static idea of being Maya and de-coupled it from the way they would live and from daily realities. At the same time, they did not seem to acknowledge the fact that there were so many differences within the municipality itself.

This tension between different meanings of indigeneity also came to the fore in an encounter between different indigenous peoples, in Santa María. Again, the way I was identified during this encounter, helped me understand who was considered and outsider. This is what happened. On a day (one of these days of hanging around in the streets), the news was spread that "our" town would be visited by indigenous people from up North—United States, Alaska, nobody really knew from where, but it was from far away. They would arrive running and would have been running for days, weeks, and would continue running all the way to Patagonia after their visit in the context of a relay-race run that had been organized. Underway they would stop and have meetings with governors and politicians about indigenous rights and spirituality. Objective: to touch all indigenous lands and free it from colonization. We went down to welcome the runners in pickups. The girls dressed up in the traditional dress of the village that they would only wear at ceremonial activities. While we were waiting for them to arrive, we were still wondering about the whereabouts of these people. Then the first one arrived. We offered him—a longhaired and shirtless young man—a ride into the center. He didn't jump on, as the idea was to cross the continent running. Nobody understood why you would do such a thing.

In the evening there was a gathering organized by one of the municipal council members. I stood in the back of the room, but could see clearly how our visitors danced around a fire, accompanied by a monotonous drum. I felt as if I was looking at a textbook ceremony. It felt awkward not to be able to take it completely seriously what was happening on the stage. This was enhanced by the giggling behind and next to me. None of us felt part of the ceremony that was performed on stage. At that moment, I felt part of Santa María, which I considered "my town" and the way these indigenous people from up North performed authenticity seemed strange, too explicit, and out of place, almost inappropriate. I kept thinking about how this worked, and questions like "where do I belong" and whether "my" research participants connected up to the globalized indigenous identity that was performed on the stage in front of me kept me busy for the night. The next day however, my friends and research participants came to me to ask what my nationals (*paisanos*) were doing here and why. Obviously they considered me as part of exactly that which I did not feel part of. They considered our visitors as outsiders. And as I was an outsider as well, they thought as these people as my nationals.

This occurrence confirmed something I had sensed before: there was a big distance between a globalized indigenous identity and the reality of being indigenous in a small rural town in the highlands of Guatemala. The difference was that big, that they would rather categorize them the same way as they catalogued me: as an outsider. Apparently, being indigenous from the United States and performing textbook ceremonies would not bridge the distance between United States and Guatemala. Being from rural Guatemala was thus stronger than a globalized networked indigenous identity. As the next and final vignette shows, it was not the performance of rituals, the discursive identification with anything indigenous, nor was it "looking indigenous" that would transform an outsider into an insider in Santa María. It was a question of time, of "being." This came to the fore in the discussion on my participation in the basketball competition of the municipality.

In my first year of fieldwork in Santa María, I had successfully participated in the municipal basketball competition. This had more to do with my height (in comparison to indigenous women) than with my qualities as a basketball player. Our team had reached the finals—in which, due to personal circumstances, I could not participate. Having returned to the field, I was again asked to participate in the basketball competition. We formed our team and registered for the competition. However, the next day we were informed that I could not be part of that team because I was "not native from Santa María." According to the rumors, several members of another participating team did not want me in the team because of my height and our team's success of the year before. However, a discussion started in the board of the basketball competition about whether or not I was from Santa María. It turned out that they considered me part of the town for several reasons, of which the most important was time. I had been there for a long time. I had left, but I came back. This argument was embedded in a broader idea of what I was: I endured (*aguanté*) chiles, I entered the *tuj*, I consumed *caldo rojo*. I had successfully downplayed some differences.

FINAL REFLECTION

In Santa María it was not my color, my cultural expertise, wearing the traditional dress or not, speaking K'iche or not that were important elements in negotiating my position of outsider or insider. Whereas the first two snapshots showed how indigenous life in Santa María is not represented by national or international indigenous movements, the third vignette makes clear that being part of everyday life, expressed by participation in everyday practices during a long period of time facilitate processes of identification and sameness. The role as (cultural) expert that was assigned to me by my Quetzalteco friends made me understand even more how diametrically opposed this idea of "indigeneity" and "that what is ours" was to the more essentialized idea of Mayaness that was maintained by urban Mayas. In both locations these dynamic negotiations of my position as a researcher informed the production of knowledge during fieldwork; being an insider and having close contacts with research participants was an important element of knowledge production in the field. Moving between different places—not only on the insider-outsider continuum, but from literally one ethnographic field to the other—facilitated processes of anthropological reflexivity (Marcus 1998), inquiring the interrelation between my partial identities as a researcher and the ways and character of knowledge production during my research. Both being an insider and outsider, friend and professional, were crucial in this process.

REFERENCES

Ergun, A., and A. Erdegan. 2009. "Negotitating Insider and Outsider Identities in the Field: 'Insider' in a Foreign Land, 'Outsider' in One's Own Land." *Field Methods* 22, no. 1: 16–38.

Fine, G. A. 1993. "Ten Lies of Ethnography: Moral Dilemmas of Field Research." *Journal of Contemporary Ethnography* 22, no. 3: 267–294.

Holland, D., and J. Lave, eds. 2001. *History in Person: Enduring Struggles, Contentious Practice, Intimate Identities*. Santa Fe: School of American Research.

Huggins, M. K., and M. L. Glebbeek, eds. 2009. *Women Fielding Danger: Negotiating Ethnographic Identities in Field Research*. Lanham: Rowman and Littlefield Publishers.

Kusow, A. M. 2003. "Beyond Indigenous Authenticity: Reflections on the Insider/Outsider Debate in Immigration Research." *Symbolic Interaction* 26, no. 4: 591–599.

Mahony, D. 2007. "Constructing Reflexive Fieldwork Relationships: Narrating My Collaborative Storytelling Methodology." *Qualitative Inquiry* 13, no. 4: 573–594.

Marcus, G. E. 1998. *Ethnography Through Thick and Thin*. Princeton: Princeton University Press.

Paerregaard, K. 2002. "The Resonance of Fieldwork. Ethnographers, Informants and the Creation of Ethnographic Knowledge." *Social Anthropology* 10 no. 3: 319–334.

Shariff, F. 2014. "Establishing Field Relations through Shared Ideology: Insider Self-Positioning as a Precarious/Productive Foundation in Multi-Sited Studies." *Field Methods,* 26 (1): 3–20.

EIGHT

Keeping a Distance?

Dealing with Perpetrators of Violence in a Guatemalan Town

Simone Remijnse

TRIGGERING MEMORIES

When I started writing this article on fieldwork in sensitive settings, it took me back to the time that I actually carried out fieldwork for my own PhD dissertation, almost 15 years ago.[1] Since then, I have been working in conflict areas worldwide, with the Dutch peace movement, PAX.[2] I had not touched my PhD research in years, and a large part of the information I had gathered I had actually given to an American researcher, who worked in the same region as I did: a small town called Joyabaj, in Guatemala.

At the same time I started on this article, I was also looking into dilemmas and possibilities to focus my current work with PAX more on Dealing with the Past and Transitional Justice. That way I came across a review of a recently published book by Eve Zucker, an ethnography of the way in which locals in the Cambodian village of O'Thmaa try to come to term with the violent past (Newman 2013, 1–8). [3] She focussed on the role of a village leader, Ta Kam, who had collaborated with the Khmer Rouge. What struck me in the review was the following part:

> In the early stages of her fieldwork [. . .], Zucker perceived Ta Kam not as a killer, but "as a warm, grandfatherly, and revered elder" (78). She could not conceive of the possibility that the people whose husbands or fathers Ta Kam had delivered to the Khmer Rouge would "allow him

to live in their midst." Another quote: He [Ta Kam] was the embodiment of all the betrayals by his generation (80). The villagers focused
"the immorality of all the acts that occurred in that period, perpetrated
by him and others in the village, only to him" (80) (Newman 2013, 3).

FIELDWORK IN GUATEMALA: CIVIL PATROLS IN JOYABAJ

This triggered memories of my own fieldwork, especially the way I myself related to and consequently wrote about perpetrators in the village of
Joyabaj. I carried out fieldwork from 1998–2003, while Guatemala was
emerging from a prolonged civil war. The town of Joyabaj was hit hard
during this conflict, and its residents found dealing with their past
fraught with difficulties. This was even more so the case because in the
early 1980s the military had institutionalized its control over the western
highlands of Guatemala, by organizing the local population into so called
civil defense patrols (*Patrullas de Autodefensa Civil*—PAC) (Remijnse 2005,
70–71). These patrols were established by the military to "defend" the
villages against guerrilla attacks.

Participation in the patrols was obligatory for all men and many of the
patrols were involved in gross human rights violations. Civil patrol
members heavily influenced local relations in the communities at that
time, and people lived in fear under constant surveillance (Foucault 1977,
195–228; Remijnse 2003, 27–28). The legacy of the patrols extended after
the civil war had ended, in 1996. Their often violent behaviour had a
lasting impact on people's memory of the civil war. The civil patrols and
people's memories of them were the focus of my research.

After reading the review of Zucker's book, I kept thinking of the way
in which I myself had dealt with interviewing perpetrators of violence,
more than a decade ago. It especially made me think of a civil patrol
commander in Joyabaj, Leonel Ogáldez, who played a prominent role in
my dissertation. It forced me to take a critical look at my own fieldwork
and the way I had apparently avoided, rather unconsciously, establishing
any relationship with him.

TALKING ABOUT ATROCITIES

For many people it was difficult to talk about the civil war and about
their experiences during that war, but only a few people refused to talk to
me outright, although they never said so directly (Remijnse 2003, 50–51).
They maintained that I was very welcome to talk to them and that they
had a lot to tell me. However, when I showed up on their doorsteps they
sometimes backed out, ever so gracefully, saying that there was no time,
that their son had the flu, or that the rain had flooded their yard. I never
pushed people into talking to me, knowing that there would always re-

main untold stories in Joyabaj. Some people were just not interested, too afraid to tell their story because they were too traumatized, afraid of the consequences of talking to me, or thought I might use the information for other purposes, such as trials or intelligence work. One indigenous man who was also a left-wing activist told me that, when he and his group were first introduced to me, they had joked among themselves that I must be working for the CIA. They agreed to talk to me only because I was introduced by the proper person who could be absolutely trusted.

After the initial barriers came down, most people were quite willing to talk about the past, opening up more and more as the fieldwork progressed. Some of the people I interviewed told me afterwards that they felt relieved about telling their story, although their memories also made them sad. One man said after a two-hour interview, during which he described in detail how he had lost several members of his family, that "It was good and necessary to get it out of my heart, because it has been there too long. It is a relief, but it also hurts. Thank you."[4] It was difficult to listen to the sometimes very personal and horrible stories people poured out to me. In such situations one stops being the objective listener who loosely sympathizes with his or her informant. Feelings of unease and helplessness surface, although it is often enough just to listen.

The situation became even more complicated when I started interviewing people who had been active in the patrols and directly involved in the atrocities committed. I found it sometimes difficult to listen to their views on the past, in which they often portrayed their own role very differently from what I had read in human rights reports or heard from other villagers. Although I wanted to hear "their side of the story," I was continuously looking for holes in it to prove them wrong.[5] Although at that time I did not confront people with gaps in their stories during the actual interviews, since I did not feel safe enough to do so, I always checked these stories more thoroughly than I would normally have done with my interviews.

Besides, conducting a group interview in the morning with six indigenous widows who all lost family members during the civil war, then conducting an interview in the afternoon with one of the most notorious patrol commanders in the area, sometimes stretched my chameleon capabilities to their limit.

CIVIL PATROLLERS BECOME INDIVIDUALS

My first encounter with civil patrols in Guatemala was in 1995, when I was accompanying refugees going back to Guatemala. My view then was influenced by the fearful attitude of the returning refugees towards the civil patrols, of which I heard only stories of abuse and violence. At that time I could see only "agents of the state," carrying rifles and being hostile towards anyone connected to human rights organizations, which clearly included myself. When I returned for my PhD research in 1998, slowly a different picture emerged in which patrollers became individuals who had their own stories to tell, their own memories and their own reasons for participating in the patrols (Remijnse 2003, 17–18).

However, the review of Zucker's book, made me look again at my research material, and the way in which I had portrayed the civil patrollers, especially the patrol commander, Leonel Ogáldez. Going through my material after having it stored in cardboard boxes in my attic for the last 15 years, I realised that not all patrollers I had met and interviewed in Joyabaj had become individuals in my perception. I realised that during my fieldwork I had looked upon Leonel Ogáldez as the "bad guy," without being very aware of the fact that I did at that moment. As if I had projected the crimes that were committed in Joyabaj on one single person, although I knew very well that many of the men I chatted with on a daily basis had also been involved in the same atrocities. Many of them were present during some of these horrific acts, but presented themselves as an innocent "bystander," to use the words of Cohen (2001, 142–155).

Had I presented him in his other roles? As father, brother, teacher? Had I focused too much on his role as patrol commander, leaving his other roles aside? Did I make him into "the other," making it easier to attribute to him the atrocities that the civil patrollers in Joyabaj had committed? And in the meantime making it easier for myself to relate to the other patrollers, because they were not as "bad" as Leonel? Was I afraid of him, and had this fear influenced my sound judgement? Did my reading of his atrocities in human rights documents and the stories local people told me, influence my position towards him?

FIRST SIGHTING AND NOT NAMING

As a proper anthropologist you immerse yourself in written sources, before starting your fieldwork, so you are well prepared before entering the actual field. In my case, I had read a lot of material on civil patrols in Joyabaj, and encountered the name of Leonel Ogáldez many times in human rights reports, before ever setting an eye upon him. During the fieldwork I gathered more information on his apparent involvement in human rights abuses, from victims statements made to truth commissions, and information gathered by interviewing other people inside and outside of Joyabaj. Thus a picture emerged of an important local commander, who had been heavily involved in human rights violations and who was still living in Joyabaj at that time (Remijnse 2003, 159–161). The Ogáldez family had always been one of the important ladino families in the community, with several family members involved in local politics, as mayor or otherwise, and in commerce. However, when I was actually doing my fieldwork, the local influence of the Ogáldez family had somewhat diminished and Leonel Ogáldez did not appear in public very often.

In my field diary I distinctly describe the first time I laid eyes on Leonel Ogáldez on the street: "I finally saw him today, during the procession. [. . .] pointed him out to me. He looks young, dressed in beige trousers and a jeans blouse, wearing cowboy boots, a cowboy hat and big sunglasses, so I could not really see his face. He walked around somewhat grumpy, but he held his body posture in such a way as if he was saying: don't dare talk to me. He kept his distance from the crowd, and did not engage in conversation with others around him."[6] Somehow I found this encounter important enough to mention in my diary. It is interesting to read how by only looking at his body posture, I was sure enough to write down the words "don't dare talk to me." I had definitely risen the barriers for approaching him.

Until this sighting of him on the street, I had refrained from talking to him, although he had been the most important local patrol commander and someone I really should interview. Some of the villagers offered me, already in the early stages of my fieldwork, to introduce me to him. I decided to wait until I had done some more fieldwork. I was afraid that his understanding of my research in Joyabaj could close other doors for me. Other people warned me not to talk to him. One older ladino lady told me: "it is not a good idea to go and talk to him. It is not so dangerous now anymore, but they are not to be trusted."[7] Looking back now, after almost fifteen years, I realize that during my fieldwork I had never really asked myself the question if I was willing to listen to some of the people. Had I been really willing to listen to Leonel Ogáldez? Was it not just ordinary fear that kept me from knocking on his door?

While going through my original fieldwork material again, checking my notebooks and diaries, I discovered that I hardly ever wrote down his whole name. I mostly jotted down his initials, L.O. I remember that I was afraid that my fieldwork material could come into the wrong hands, and I took the precaution to store the material in different places, outside Joyabaj. Using his initials instead of his whole name was part of my precautions. However, I realize now that his name was the only one that I consciously put down in initials. The other people I interviewed were addressed by their full name. I came across his initials on several to-do lists in my notebooks and diaries . . . but really doing the interview never came of it, until April 2001, during my last fieldwork visit to Joyabaj.

THE ACTUAL INTERVIEW

It took me a long time to build up the courage to conduct the interview, and it turned out to be my only interview with him (Remijnse 2003,

219–221). It lasted for more than 3 hours. And I never had the chance to meet him informally, because, as I said before, he did not participate much in daily village life, and kept to himself.[8]

The interview itself was nothing very special. Although I knocked on the door with sweaty hands, this went away when I finally sat across of him in the patio of his mother's house. Two of his grandchildren were running around, and the laundry was hanging out in the sun. I had my questions prepared, and he quietly answered most of them. He did not directly evade questions; he just had a different opinion on some issues, as had so many other villagers. He also corrected me on several occasions, stating that I had some of my facts wrong. Facts which I had gotten from several human rights reports, truth commission reports and which were corroborated by information from police files and information I had received from other villagers. He quite openly talked about the time he was patrol commander and explained why he had been willing to take up the task of patrol commander. He talked about his mother and other brother who had been kidnapped by the guerrilla (and later on released), and the killing of his brother by the same group. But the whole time during the interview, I was very aware that I was sitting across someone who had been responsible for terrible acts of violence. The thought did not really leave my mind during the whole interview.

I did try not to depict Leonel Ogáldez as a villain in my dissertation. I quoted several villagers who had a mild view on his activities during his time as patrol commander (Remijnse 2003, 161). Especially many of the ladinos tried to explain to me why they thought Leonel had accepted the position of commander, and why he had done some of the things he was accused of in human rights reports. Many explained, just as Leonel had done himself, that he had acted out of revenge for the kidnapping of his mother and brother by the guerrilla, and the subsequent murder of his brother. As someone told me, he had "a lot of personal anger and hatred."[9] Many of them added that they would probably do the same, to protect their family.

MY OWN CONFLICTIVE MEMORIES

When I started working on this paper, I was convinced that I had written explicitly about the interview with Leonel Ogáldez in my dissertation, and how I had experienced it. But I never had. I did use a lot of information that came out of that one interview, but I did not write about the interview itself, how I had dreaded it and how I had postponed it several times. Presumably I only wrote it down in my diary; those sweaty hands, this postponing of knocking on the door of his mothers' house, the fact that I could give a very good reason why it was not a good idea to interview him that day. After a long search among my fieldwork material, I finally found the interview jotted down, not in my field diary as it should have been, but in a small notebook I normally used for taking notes during Quiché language class. I evidently had tried to "hide" the interview.

It is interesting to see that the theory on constructing memory[10] which I used in my dissertation to explain the multiple stories of individuals in Joyabaj of the same events, was now also applicable to my own work. Presumably enough time had elapsed for me to look back "because distance can give people historical perspective on matters that may have been hard to grasp at the time they happened" (Schudson cited in Schachter 1995, 87, 112). That is not to say that me doing the interview with Leonel Ogáldez was an historical occasion, but for myself it presumably was a major event during my fieldwork, something that I actually dreaded. One of the question that I had used in my dissertation to guide the research and the reader, "How do *Joyabatecos* today remember and represent their own past behaviour [. . .]" had become applicable to my own behaviour during my fieldwork, 15 years ago (Remijnse 2003, 30).

UNDERSTANDING THE INCOMPREHENSIBLE

In this article I revisited an important occasion during my fieldwork period, which is the interview with civil patrol commander Leonel Ogáldez.[11] The review of Zucker's article on the role of Ta Kam in Cambodia during the Khmer Rouge period, triggered memories of my own attitude towards Leonel Ogáldez. Distance in time gave me room to take a different look at events, and especially on the way I had conducted some of my fieldwork in relation with Leonel Ogáldez.

I can see now the fear I had at that time of him, fear to interview him, thus leaving the actual interview until my last stay in Joyabaj. But it was not only fear. It was also convenient, I realize now, to attribute the atrocities to one specific person, thereby giving myself space to enter into relations with other patrollers, who had, at least in my mind, been "less bad."

I could ask myself the question, looking back now; should I have done things differently? In this respect it is important to take a look at the work of Hannah Arendt (1965), who stressed the normality of Eichmann during the reporting she did of the Eichmann process in Israel (Achterhuis 2008, 415). Her views on the normality of Eichmann made "normal" people feel uneasy. "The demonic vision of a Nazi torturer as a psychopath was extremely reassuring for any normal human being. Evil and violence lay outside of him, so he could feel himself being good and peace-loving" (Achterhuis 2008, 416). Bearing this in mind, it would have had added value for my dissertation had I described the different roles Leonel Ogáldez in more detail, as a father, a family man, a teacher. To stress his

normality, rather than adding to his myth be only conducting one interview with him towards the end of my stay in Joyabaj, when I had filled in
most of the blanks with material from other sources. To stress the fact
that this could happen to everyone, even normal people.

But a better question would be: had I been able at that time, to do
things differently? I don't think so. Although you try to prepare yourself,
when interviewing perpetrators, it is always difficult to predict what it
does to you as a person. But it should be a topic explicitly described in a
PhD research dealing with conflict and perpetrators. Because, as in my
case, writing about "the other," and "dehumanizing the other" should
not only be done in the theoretical part of a dissertation, but also when
describing the relation between researcher and the ones who are being
researched (Remijnse 2003, 157). Apparently I had needed an "enemy,"
and placed Leonel Ogáldez outside the world (or "moral universe," to
use Cohen's words; see Cohen 2001, 90). Just like the Cambodian villagers in O'Thmaa focused on the person of Ta Kam, thereby placing "the
immorality of the acts that occurred within their village [. . .] on him,
perhaps erasing the blemish on the community as a whole" (Zucker
2013b, 1).

REFERENCES

Achterhuis, H. 2008. *Met alle geweld. Een filosofische zoektocht*. Rotterdam: Lemniscaat.
Arendt, H. 1965. *Eichmann in Jerusalem. A Report on the Banality of Evil*. New York:
    Viking Press.
Cohen, S. 2001. *States of Denial. Knowing about Atrocities and Suffering*. Cambridge:
    Polity Press.
Foucault, M. 1977. *Discipline and Punish*. London: Penguin Books.
Heitz Tokpa, K. 2013. "Trust and Distrust in Rebel-Held Côte d'Ivoire." PhD diss.,
    University of Basel.
Nelson, D.M. 2009. *Reckoning. The Ends of War in Guatemala*. Durham & London: Duke
    University Press.
Newman. K. 2014. "Book Review: Forest of Struggle and Intimate Enemies." Historical
    Dialogues, Justice, and Memory Network. A Platform for Issues Relating to Histori-
    cal Dialogues, Historical and Transitional Justice, and Public and Social Memory.
    http://historicaldialogues.org/2014/01/21/book-review-forest-of-struggle-and-
    intimate-enemies/.
Remijnse, S. 2003. *Memories of Violence. Civil Patrols and the Legacy of Conflict in Joyabaj,
    Guatemala*. Amsterdam: Rozenberg Publishers.
Remijnse, S. 2005. "Dealing with the Past: Conflicting Memories in Joyabaj, Guatema-
    la." *Politics and Ethics Review* 1, no. 1: 70–80.
Schachter, D. 1966. *Searching for Memory: The Brain, the Mind, and the Past*. New York:
    Basic Books.
Schudson, M. 1995. "Dynamics of Distortion in Collective Memory." In *Memory Distor-
    tion. How Minds, Brains and Societies Reconstruct the Past*, edited by D. Schachter,
    346–364. Cambridge: Harvard University Press.
Zucker, E. M. 2013a. *Forest of Struggle: Moralities of Remembrance in Upland Cambodia*.
    Honolulu: University of Hawai'i Press.

Zucker, E.M. 2013b. "Trauma and its Aftermath: Local Configurations of Reconciliation in Cambodia and the Khmer Rouge Tribunal." *The Journal of Asian Studies*, September: 1–8.

NOTES

1. Parts of this article draw on Remijnse (2003).
2. Formerly known as IKV / Pax Christi (www.paxforpeace.nl).
3. For an in-depth analysis of the Cambodian collective trauma see Zucker (2013a).
4. Interview 20-99 (5/7/1999).
5. This reminds me of a quote I came across in an article of Heitz Tokpa (2013: 139) when a mid-ranking rebel officer from Côte D'Ivoire whom she was interviewing said: "You listen to everybody, but you don't hear everyone."
6. Quoted from my field diary, 10/8/1998.
7. Quoted from my field diary, 10/8/1998.
8. Quoted from my field diary, 10/8/1998.
9. For an insightful discussion on civil patrollers and victimhood, "using the language of indemnization and reparation" see Nelson (2009, 301).
10. Bartlett (1932) was among the first to describe memory as an active process during which individuals reconstruct rather than remember a story (Remijnse 2003, 34; see also Schachter 1996).
11. "Understanding the unimaginable." Title translated from Achterhuis (2008, 345).

NINE

From "Broder" to "Don"

Methodological Reflections on Longitudinal Gang Research in Nicaragua

Dennis Rodgers

INTRODUCTION[1]

On 13 July 2012, I was conducting an interview with Kaiton,[2] a 23-year-old ex-gang member in *barrio* Luis Fanor Hernández, a poor neighbourhood in Managua, the capital city of Nicaragua, when he said something that shocked me profoundly. We had been talking about his recent involvement in a particularly violent mugging, and I had asked him to explain to me what had motivated him to be so brutal. He told me that his victim had resisted the mugging, pulling a knife on him and slashing him, which had "pissed [him] off" and prompted him to "really do him in," including "disarm[ing] him and then . . . [sticking] his knife in his stomach, to teach him a lesson." It was however neither the violence of the mugging, nor Kaiton's explanation for his brutality that shocked me, but rather the fact that he began his account by saying: "*Pues, usted sabe como es, Don* Dennis . . . (Well, you know how it is, *Don* Dennis. . .)." Since I had at that point in time spent over a decade and a half working with gang members in *barrio* Luis Fanor Hernández, including one year as an actual gang member (see Rodgers 2007), I *did* know "how it was," but this was not the issue. What was, rather, was that Kaiton was calling me "*Don* Dennis," and addressing me as "*usted,*" despite the fact that this was not the first time that I was interviewing him. We had previously always used the familiar "*voseo*" rather than the formal "*usted*" to address each

123

other, and also generally called each other *"broder"* (brother) or *"maje"* (mate) during our exchanges. I was perplexed by Kaiton's sudden formalism, and in fact interrupted him, exclaiming somewhat forcefully: *"oye, que la verga* (what the fuck), Kaiton, since when do you say *'Don'* and *'usted'* to me? Am I not your *broder*? What's got into you?"

Kaiton looked a bit nonplussed, shrugged, and then pressed ahead with his narrative, but he also continued to address me formally, so at the end of our interview, I persisted further on the issue. What transpired from our subsequent discussion was that Kaiton felt that I had crossed a boundary line at some point between my 2009 and 2012 visits, and that I had gone from being "one of us" to somebody who was now *"mayor"* (old), *"una persona seria"* (a serious person), and *"respetable"* (respectable). It furthermore rapidly became apparent that Kaiton was not the only gang-related individual calling me *"Don* Dennis" and treating me in a formal manner—almost all the ex-gang members of his generation, as well as current gang members, were doing so too. This contrasted starkly with previous visits, and also with the way that ex-gang members from the 1990s treated me, insofar as they continued to call me *"broder"* and treat me with great familiarity. There is no doubt that I have been getting old(er) during the course of my fieldwork, and also that my social status has changed over the course of the past 18 years, for example from graduate student to professor. However, my personal development is only a partial explanation for the evolution of my relationship with Kaiton and other gang-associated individuals in *barrio* Luis Fanor Hernández. Much more important is the particular nature of the research that I have been conducting in Nicaragua, and more specifically, its longitudinality.

Although longitudinal ethnographic research is by no means uncommon, especially within anthropology, its methodological ramifications are rarely explicitly considered. There is no doubt that longitudinal research is different from other forms of investigation, and this chapter therefore aims to offer some reflections on the particular perils and pitfalls, but also the unique advantages, of such an endeavour, in particular as they relate to the research that I have been carrying out since 1996 on Nicaraguan gang dynamics in *barrio* Luis Fanor Hernández. It begins by considering the idea of longitudinal ethnography, and what this actually means in practice, before then exploring how longitudinality can affect the research process, both negatively and positively, with regard to practical considerations as well as research practices. While some of the issues that I explore are common to all forms of longitudinal research, other concerns are specific to the study of gangs, including more specifically those relating to the changing experience and understanding of risk and danger.

LONGITUDINAL ETHNOGRAPHIC RESEARCH: "BEING THERE" AND "NOT BEING THERE"

In an article published in 2003 in the *American Journal of Sociology*, Michael Burawoy discusses the variable nature of what he terms ethnographic "revisits," that is to say, going back to places where research has previously been carried out. His central concern is to "disentangle the movement of the external world from the researcher's own shifting involvement with that same world" (Burawoy 2003, 646), and he argues that this is in large part a function of the type of revisit involved. Burawoy identifies four principal types of revisits: (a) the "focused" revisit (going back to find out something specific); the "rolling" revisit (going back from time to time, but without any definite plan); (c) the "punctuated" revisit (returning regularly over a long period of time to observe changes over time); and (d) the "valedictory" revisit (going back to report on previous findings). He particularly highlights how these all lead to different types of experiences and understandings of social change, insofar as different types of revisits place greater or lesser emphasis on either "the [changing] relation of observer to participant," "[new] theory brought to the field by the ethnographer," "internal processes within the field site itself," or "forces external to the field site" (Burawoy 2003, 645), but he also implicitly suggests that strictly speaking, only punctuated revisits can really be considered longitudinal research, as they are the only revisits that explicitly aim to explore long-term change from a realist perspective. Having said this, Burawoy also notes that it is rare for ethnographic studies to be started with a view to conducting such regular, punctuated revisits. Most of the time, different types of revisits combine serendipitously, and longitudinality develops over time.

My own longitudinal ethnographic research on Nicaraguan gangs is a case in point in this respect. It began with my spending a year in Nicaragua in 1996-1997, in order to carry out fieldwork for my doctoral studies. My pre-fieldwork doctoral project had aimed to explore how the economic survival strategies of the urban poor related to political ideology in a post-revolutionary context, and so my focus on gangs was largely accidental, contingent on the fact that during my first couple of months in Nicaragua I suffered several violent encounters with gangs and then subsequently moved—for completely serendipitous reasons—into a neighbourhood—*barrio* Luis Fanor Hernández[3] —that happened to have a particularly notorious local gang. Both of these experiences firmly fixed my attention on gangs as a topic of investigation and set the tone for my research. In particular, due to a series of perhaps somewhat unlikely events, within a few weeks of directing my investigative attentions towards gangs, I ended up actually being initiated into *barrio* Luis Fanor Hernández's local gang a couple of months after arriving in Nicaragua (see Rodgers 2007). As a result, during the course of the subsequent ten months, I was able to carry out extensive participant observation with the gang, spending significant amounts of my time hanging out with gang members on street corners and in their homes, smoking, drinking, chatting, as well as participating in a range of gang activities, both violent and non-violent.

Becoming a gang member obviously provided me with an incredible ethnographic research opportunity.[4] I was able to rapidly familiarise myself with gang norms, codes, and behaviour patterns, and it gave me extensive access to gang members, and allowed for open and frank interviews that were not clouded by fear or mistrust (on either side). I was able to hear from gang members what it was that had motivated them to join the gang, how they perceived themselves, as well as obtain extensive details about their delinquent activities. I was able to compare their discourses against their everyday practices, as well as observe individuals acting in a range of different circumstances, including some that would normally have been impossible for a non-gang member to observe. More generally, I engaged in what Loïc Wacquant (2004, viii) has termed "carnal ethnography," experiencing—obviously only up to a point, within the limits of my particular standpoint as a foreigner and an anthropologist—a "moral and sensual conversion to the cosmos under investigation."[5]

The fact that I joined the gang also provided the foundation for my longitudinal research. Although I formally "retired" from the gang when I left Nicaragua in July 1997, I was trusted as an "old timer" when I returned for my first revisit in 2002, and gang members—old and new—continued to be willing—indeed, eager—to exchange and to share details about their illegal activities. This continued to be the case during my subsequent revisits in 2003, 2007, 2009, 2012, 2014, and 2016. These revisits were of different natures, however. My 2002 revisit was both a rolling and a valedictory revisit. I had no agenda other than the very general intention to see if anything had changed since my first visit, as well as to "report back" to individuals who had contributed to my research in 1996-1997. My 2003 revisit to *barrio* Luis Fanor Hernández was similarly rolling in nature (indeed, it was completely opportunistic, as it was the result of my going to Nicaragua for a holiday). My 2007, 2009, 2012, 2014, and 2016 revisits were more focused in nature, motivated by the intention to investigate certain specific issues and processes. In 2007 and 2009, I returned to Nicaragua to study the political economy of Managua's urban transformation, for a project on "Fragile Cities" funded by the London School of Economics's Crisis States Research Centre (see Rodgers 2008; 2011; 2012). In 2012 I went back to carry out interviews on the evolution of firearm use by different generations of gang members, funded by the Geneva-based Small Arms Survey (see Rodgers and Rocha 2013). In 2014, I returned in order to carry out two specific interviews, one with an ex-gang member who had emigrated to Miami—where I stopped on my way to Nicaragua—and the other with an ex-gang member turned drug dealer who had been released from prison after having served four years of a seven-year sentence for drug-dealing (although I also carried out other interviews whilst in the *barrio*). Finally, in 2016, I returned explicitly to continue my individual gang member life history interviews (see below) and celebrate my 20 years of ethnography in the *barrio*.

Although my visits since 2007 have been focused in nature, I am effectively returning to Nicaragua more or less every 18 months, and I plan to continue this for the foreseeable future, most likely combining rolling and focused revisits. The regularity of my revisits is effectively transforming them into punctuated revisits, especially as every visit I engage repeatedly in a number of activities aimed at chronicling social change in *barrio* Luis Fanor Hernández: regularly re-interviewing a range of individuals about new developments, taking the same "transect" walk through the neighbourhood, taking the same photos over and over again to visually document changes, and so on. Having said this, the timing of my revisits has unquestionably been extremely important. As Raymond Firth (1959, 22) famously highlighted in his "re-study" of the Tikopia in Melanesia, a distinction has to be made between "dual synchronic" studies and "diachronic" studies when thinking about longitudinal research. The former represents the combined perspectives from research carried out "at two periods of time," while the latter constitutes an observation of "social change, as trends and not simple differences," that is to say, as it takes place. Only diachronic research is truly longitudinal, according to Firth. Strictly speaking, this is only really possible if the ethnographer is *in situ* during the whole time period that they want to study, which is of course rarely practical, so the next best thing is to engage in regular revisits, but these have to be appropriately timed in such a way to be able to observe trends rather than disparate "snapshots."

There are obviously significantly serendipitous aspects to this, both in relation to practical considerations as well as the need to be "in the right place at the right time." With regard to the former, for example, I would ideally have liked to return to *barrio* Luis Fanor Hernández within a year of my first stay there. As a doctoral student, I simply did not have the financial means to travel to Nicaragua in 1998, and I had to wait until I finished my PhD degree and was hired by the London School of Economics's Crisis States Research Centre in September 2000 until this became a practical possibility. Indeed, part of the reason for my recruitment was explicitly to send me back to Nicaragua in order to see what had happened since my doctoral investigations, and so I returned for three months in February 2002. The fact that my first revisit ended up occurring in 2002 rather than 1998 was extremely significant, however, as it meant that I was "in the right place at the right time." By all accounts, had I returned to Nicaragua within a year of my first visit, I would have encountered a situation not hugely different from the one in 1996-1997.

Gang dynamics, in particular, would have been very similar to the ones I had previously studied. Returning to Nicaragua in 2002, however, I found gang dynamics completely transformed. In particular, the *barrio* Luis Fanor Hernández gang had mutated from being a vigilante-style organisation that was principally concerned with identity issues and protecting the local neighbourhood to a more predatory drug-dealing gang. Principally as a result of this serendipitous time lapse, the major focus of my research has become the institutional evolution of gangs, something that has helped me avoid conceiving of gangs in either a static or a deterministic manner (both of which are hallmarks of much existing gang research).

This was not just a question of a longer lapse of time passing by, however. I would likely have missed this evolution had I gone back, say, 10 years after my first visit to Nicaragua, in 2007 instead of 2002. The *barrio* Luis Fanor Hernández gang had by then been supplanted by more professional drug dealing organisation known as the *cartelito* (little cartel).[6] Although I would likely have been able to glean something about the gang's institutional transformation during the preceding period from interviews, memories are notoriously fickle, and I would have had to reconstruct events rather than observe them. It is of course difficult to determine in advance how far apart revisits need to be spaced in order to enable a meaningful diachronicity, and hence there is very much a serendipitous element to this. At the same time, however, as David Mosse (2006) has pointed out, the notion that "the field" is a temporally and spatially separate and bounded location that we can only engage with *in situ* increasingly makes less and less sense. While distinguishing between "the field" and the "non-field" might have been feasible 100 years ago, when most ethnographers travelled to far-flung locations to study so-called "primitives" with whom they never had any contact outside of "the field" due to the lack of means of communication and the one-sidedness of travel, this is almost never the case nowadays. I am for example in constant contact with individuals in *barrio* Luis Fanor Hernandez, by phone, email, and Skype (and am being harried to open a Facebook account and download Whatsapp. . .). This means that I'm kept informed about new developments in the neighbourhood by email and text message, and regularly sent photos and video recordings — including some in "real-time" — all of which inform my understanding of how the situation in the neighbourhood evolves between my revisits.[7]

Certainly, such communications provide me with important reference points for my investigations when I revisit *barrio* Luis Fanor Hernández, to the extent that it is difficult to really make a strict distinction between "being there" and "not being there," something that also makes Firth's distinction between "dual synchronic" and "diachronic" research less meaningful. Having said this, although the increased intensity of my communication with people in *barrio* Luis Fanor Hernández has lessened the need to be "in the right place at the right time," this has also been a function of a shift in the principle type of research that I have been carrying out, which itself is related to the longitudinal nature of my research. Ethnographic investigation combines many different things, but one of the most important elements is "participant observation." This can be carried out in a more or less active way—some anthropologists privilege observation over participation, for example—and in a multi-layered manner—you can of course participate in different processes at the same time. Over the years, my participant observation in *barrio* Luis Fanor Hernández has for example included joining the local gang, living in the *barrio*, living with the Gomez family, running a local market stall, participating in political rallies, or hanging out and drinking on street corners, among other things. I have continued to engage in many such forms of participant observation, but as my gang research has progressed, I have however spent less time carrying out participant observation with the gang, particularly compared to my first two visits in 1996-1997 and 2002. Instead, I have increasingly focused on carrying out more purposeful one-on-one interviews, with both new and old gang members. From my first revisit onwards, I began to engage in regular "repeat interviews," initially with gang members whom I first interviewed in the 1996-1997, but subsequently with others whom I interviewed during later visits. As a result, in addition to carrying out one-off formal interviews with fifty-seven individual *barrio* Luis Fanor Hernández gang members between 1996 and 2016, I have repeatedly interviewed nineteen more, seven every time since my first visit in 1996-1997, two every time since 2002, two since 2003, two since 2007, three since 2009, one since 2012, as well as adding two more to my sample in 2016. I have also interviewed a further eight more individual gang members on multiple occasions, albeit more irregularly.[8]

CHANGING RESEARCH APPROACHES AND EPISTEMOLOGICAL HUBRIS

This evolution in my research practice has both practical and epistemological underpinnings. With regard to the former, the generally shorter durations of my revisits—the longest of which lasted three months, the shortest two weeks, with the median duration being a month, compared to the twelve months that I spent in Nicaragua in 1996-1997—has made meaningful participant observation of certain types of events and behaviours—those predicated on a repeated, long-term engagement—difficult. I have also become increasingly reluctant to engage in the risky behaviours associated with gang participant observation (see Rodgers 2007). On the one hand, this is due to the fact that as I have become older, I have also become (a little) wiser (or at least, outgrown the "folly" of my youth. . .).

On the other hand, it has also been a function of a particular evolution in a major gang member habit, and more specifically their drug consumption. Gang members become ubiquitously addicted to crack cocaine from the early 2000s onwards, which not only made them much more unpredictable, therefore rendering casual interaction more difficult and personally dangerous, but it also increased my social distance from them, as contrarily to the widespread marijuana smoking that gang members engaged in and that I was happy to partake in during the mid-1990s, I did not engage in crack consumption. This was all the more the case considering that while smoking marijuana had been an eminently communal activity for gang members, consuming crack was very much an individual one, and therefore did not act as "a social cement constituted of common emotions and shared pleasures" (Maffesoli 1997, 116) in the same way.

At the same time, there are also clear epistemological motivations that pushed me to adopt new research approaches. A major advantage of refocusing my research around the gathering of life histories through regular repeated interviews with a set of specific individuals is that these are inherently longitudinal data. Life histories are arguably fundamentally diachronic in nature, and they have been especially valuable in providing me with a more dynamic and nuanced picture of the gang's evolving social practices, more specifically with regard to the existence of continuities in practices and associations beyond the gang. I have also been able to explore the different types of trajectories that individual gang members can undergo, as well as trace what happens to them after they leave the gang. The fact that I have been able to record almost all my formal interviews since 2002 has furthermore also meant that I have also been able to play back past discussions to interviewees several years later, which has frequently provoked very interesting reflexive insights, particularly when their interpretations of past events differ significantly from the accounts previously recorded. Having said this, a potential problem with this particular sort of research strategy is that it does imbue the researcher with a sense of omniscience, especially when the individuals whose life histories are being gathered are people that I have known since the beginning of my research. More specifically, it has clearly fostered a sentiment that I have an enhanced, "total" knowledge about their lives and *barrio* Luis Fanor Hernández more generally, one consequence of which is that unusual events jar more as a result, as I experienced in February 2014, during an interview with a gang member called Bayardo.

I had been talking about the history of the drug economy in *barrio* Luis Fanor Hernández with him, and had rather vainly been displaying my detailed knowledge about it, in particular narrating how the marijuana-selling business run by an individual called *el Indio Viejo* that had existed in the mid-1990s became a fully-fledged cocaine-dealing economy in the 2000 as a result of his contacts on the Caribbean coast of the country, before then transforming into an international drug trafficking business in the late 2000s when he began collaborating with a Colombian cartel (see Rodgers [2018] for more details). Bayardo listened to me waxing on for a while, before interrupting a little exasperatedly:

> *Pues*, Dennis, you do know that cocaine isn't anything new in the *barrio*? *El Indio Viejo* wasn't the first guy to bring it here.

> OK, OK, it's true, I guess, there was that time the gang held up that *diplomático* and he had cocaine with him. . .

> No, no, Dennis, long before that, there was cocaine in the *barrio*, in the 1980s, and it was brought here by Pablo Escobar himself, you know, the Colombian *poderoso*.

> What? I know who Pablo Escobar is, but *no jodas, maje*, he never came here to the *barrio*, come on, stop shitting me.

> I'm not shitting you, *maje*, that's what they say. I was just a kid at the time, so I don't remember, but the guy who can tell you all about it is *el viejo* René Vargas, you should go and see him.

I immediately went to find *Don* René, who proceeded to tell me the most incredible story:

> Yes it's true, Pablo Escobar stayed here in the *barrio* in the 1980s. I think it was 1984-1985, something like that. He stayed at my mother's place— she rented rooms out, you see, and one day some people from the government came and asked whether she could put up four men. She said yes, and so Pablo Escobar came to stay, with a friend of his called Gustavo Gaviria, as well as a *Salvadoreño*, Raul Mata, and a Mexican, *como se llamaba, algo* Gacha (what was he called, something Gacha). . . They stayed for several weeks, and paid really well, and also became really friendly with people here in the *barrio*. I drank with them several times, but the person you should really talk to is Lucia, you know, the *suegra* (mother-in-law) of your friend Julio whom you're always hang-ing around with—*ella bailo por el narco*—she danced for the drug dealer (in the context, a euphemism to indicate that she had been a prostitute).

I decided for obvious reasons that it was perhaps best not to talk to Lucia directly about this, but cautiously approached her daughter, Marlene, who was married to my good friend Julio, about her mother's potential relationship with Escobar. Marlene began by telling me that according to her mother it was absolutely true, that she had slept with Pablo Escobar, and she regularly boasted about it when she drank too much, and she also confirmed that her mother had been a prostitute at the time. Still somewhat unconvinced that Pablo Escobar had really stayed in the *barrio* in the 1980s—it seemed to me at this point more likely that it was some random Colombian who had been transformed into Pablo Escobar by virtue of the latter's notoriety—I then asked Marlene whether she would be willing to show a picture of Pablo Escobar to her mother, but without saying who it was and asking her whether she recognized him. She agreed, and so I immediately went to an internet café to find a photo of Pablo Escobar via Google Images to print and give to her that very evening.

The next day Marlene came to see me and said that her mother had immediately exclaimed *"Ay, mi Pablito lindo"* on seeing the photo, and had confirmed that the person that she had slept with was indeed *the* Pablo Escobar. Slightly stunned by this development, I proceeded to do a bit more research via the internet. I focused especially on the names that *Don* René had mentioned and found that they were all names of know Escobar associates. But even more amazingly, I subsequently discovered that Pablo Escobar had indeed visited Nicaragua in 1984, and that there were photos of him, along with the Mexican Rodriguez Gacha, taken at Managua airport on 25 June by the undercover DEA agent Barry Seal.[9] Further research suggested that Pablo Escobar may have visited Nicaragua several times in the 1980s,[10] seeking a deal with the *Sandinista* regime to allow him to transport drugs freely across the country (which by all accounts, they refused, but at the same time without making any moves to arrest or extradite Escobar, perhaps wise to the huge potential of his cartel to be violent, as the Colombian state was to discover when he declared war on it in the late 1980s). It would make sense that Escobar might want to stay in a poor neighbourhood rather than a five-star hotel in order to avoid alerting the DEA, which he would likely have known to be trailing him, and to this extent, the story of Pablo Escobar staying in *barrio* Luis Fanor Hernández is not necessarily implausible.

It was however a major surprise to me, however, because I felt that I knew the neighbourhood, its history, and everything to do with the drugs business there very well, and I certainly assumed that nothing of this magnitude would be unknown to me. As such, this anecdote highlights the importance of never losing sight of the inevitable partiality of the research endeavour, all the more so when one is carrying out longitudinal investigations. It is all too easy to fall into the trap of feeling that we know it all, especially if we have accumulated a depth of knowledge about a particular context through longitudinal research, something that inevitably promotes a sense of omniscience and what might be termed "ethnographic hubris." Having said this, the story of Pablo Escobar in the *barrio* is a relatively innocuous one, and has effectively provided me with a rather unusual and somewhat comical anecdote when I discuss the drug economy in *barrio* Luis Fanor Hernández. The sense of omniscience and ethnographic hubris that can develop as a result of carrying out longitudinal research can however have much more dangerous consequences, particularly when the research is about dangerous topics or occurs in contexts of chronic violence.

BARRIO TRANSFORMATION, RESEARCH TRANSFORMATION

This has certainly proven to be the case during the course of my own research, where my particular trajectory as, first, a gang member, and then a respected "elder," meant that although the *barrio* Luis Fanor Hernández gang has evolved and changed over time, I have often felt that I had a good handle on it, as well as, more generally, of the political economy of insecurity in the neighbourhood. Indeed, for a long time, although the gang was a major source of insecurity for many, it was one over which I had a certain influence, and I therefore felt very much in control during my research. While this was without doubt the case during my revisits in 2002, 2003, and 2007, where it could be argued that I was effectively managing what—following Donald Rumsfeld, the US Secretary of State during the George W. Bush presidency—might be termed "known uncertainties," this changed subsequently. The neighbourhood gang's (temporary) demise between 2006 and 2012 led to the emergence of "unknown uncertainties" that were more difficult for me to appreciate due to my particular research trajectory, and changed my ethnographic experience substantially.

This transformation was related to the professionalization of the cocaine economy in *barrio* Luis Fanor Hernández, which had initially emerged in a rather organic and *ad hoc* manner around a single individual, *el Indio Viejo* in 1999-2000 (see Rodgers 2006; 2018). He had initially involved the local gang as street dealers and security apparatus, but by late 2005 had gathered a shadowy group referred to locally as the *cartelito*, who had muscled out local gang members. This led to the development of tensions—also linked to the fact that the *cartelito* did not want any potential challengers to its dominance in the neighbourhood—and after a series of violent confrontations in early 2006 that left several gang members critically injured and one dead—executed in cold blood "as a warning to the others," as his killer Mayuyu put it in an interview in July 2012—the gang effectively ceased to exist as a collective unit. The *cartelito* then sought to consolidate its domination over the neighbourhood through a campaign of intimidation against local residents. Unlike with the gang, local inhabitants could only identify a few individuals associated with the *cartelito*, as its membership remained a close-guarded secret.[11]

As a result, levels and feelings of insecurity had reached new heights in the neighbourhood during my 2009 revisit, as anybody was seen as a potential source of danger, and there were no clearly discernible patterns to the violence afflicting the neighbourhood, meaning that developing consistent avoidance strategies was difficult. Unexplained shootings were commonplace, including for example the one I experienced late one evening in November 2009, as the following extract from my field diary describes:

> Tonight I was helping Pablo, Adilia, and Argentina [two members of
> the Gomez family with whom I stay when I'm in *barrio* Luis Fanor
> Hernández] to bring a motorcycle into the house and lock the front
> door, when a motorcycle with two men suddenly surged out of dark-
> ness, and the man on the back seat pulled up a shotgun and pointed it
> at us. We all threw ourselves to the ground screaming, but the driver
> shouted "No, no, está no, la próxima" [no, no, not this one, the next
> one], and they drove on to the next house, into which they shot two
> rounds. Nobody has any idea who they were, or why they shot in into
> the neighbour's house, but it has left everybody involved—including
> myself—shaken and on edge in a way that past episodes of violence
> never did—including those perpetrated by the gang, even when they
> were highly brutal and predatory of local inhabitants. . .

It was very much the unpredictable nature of the violence that made it an
"unknown uncertainty," and which fundamentally changed the lived experience of insecurity in *barrio* Luis Fanor Hernández, as well as my
ethnographic experience. As a result of this, my 2009 revisit was much
scarier than the previous ones.

Having said this, it is not just the emergence of "unknown uncertainties" that can be complicated within the context of longitudinal research.
Much of the power of the ethnographic methods derives from its flexibility, and the ability that being both an insider and an outsider at the same
time gives to seize on contingency. An ethnographic approach inherently
leaves open the possibility of engaging with the new, the unexpected, or
even simply interacting on a basis that is not open to those who are from
this given context. There were certainly many moments during my initial
visit to Nicaragua where the fact that I did not know certain practices or
people very well allowed me to ask questions and engage in a range of
activities in a socially less constrained manner. Going back to Nicaragua
and engaging in long-term research has however changed the nature of
many of the relationships I have with people in *barrio* Luis Fanor
Hernández, and created expectations, both directly, in terms of material
or emotional demands, for example, as well as indirectly, insofar as I
cannot get away with "playing the idiot" in order to elicit information as
much as before, because people assume that I will know certain things
about the neighbourhood context.

While this of course has numerous benefits—increased trust, more
sharing, less lying—the flipside is that I have much less social flexibility
than I had at the beginning of my research. Sometimes this is also a result
of extraneous factors. For example, my relationship with older gang
members in *barrio* Luis Fanor Hernández has always been much stronger
than younger ones. During the 1990s, this was actually a significant advantage, as it provided me with an extra aura of authority vis-à-vis
younger gang members, who deferred to older ones. This particular relationship persisted into the 2000s, despite gang member generational turn-

over, with new gang members generally respecting older gang members. They were therefore always happy to talk to me and answer my questions. This generational deference has dissipated since 2012 and the post-*cartelito re*-emergence of a new gang, whose members often pick fights with older ex-gang members, partly "to prove themselves." This has particularly involved individuals who belonged to the gang in the early 2000s, but both the fact that I am associated with the 1990s iteration of the gang, as well as my being on good terms with most gang members from the 2000s, this generational conflict has sometimes made my researching contemporary gang dynamics more difficult.[12] At the same time, however, by 2016 the new gang wave in *barrio* Luis Fanor Hernández had once again mutated with the unprecedented rise of a female gang (see Rodgers, forthcoming), whose members I was able to interview surprisingly easily, clearly partly because I was a male foreigner (as well as the fact that I am well-known in *barrio* Luis Fanor Hernández as a vocal critique of *machista* social practices), so to a certain extent it can be argued that there are "swings and roundabouts" in this respect.

CONCLUDING REFLECTION

Longitudinal ethnographic research is often held up as a major aspiration, yet it is an investigative strategy that has a range of ramifications that are rarely considered, whether from a practical or an epistemological perspective. There are clearly numerous benefits to carrying out longitudinal research, whether from a "dual synchronic" or a "diachronic" perspective, although the latter is probably the most interesting, insofar as it allows a dynamic focus on trends and evolutions, and is therefore a much better reflection of the way the "real" world works. At the same time, a longitudinal approach also inherently pushes the researcher towards certain practices, and both opens up and closes off avenues for investigation. When the research focuses on a phenomenon such as gangs, it also creates a range of practical dilemmas relating to risk and danger. But this in many ways is simply on a par with research in general, where any particular approach, any particular focus, or any particular practice will inevitably both enable and inhibit. Research is by its very nature imperfect and limited, and this not only in terms of "the data," but also "the method," "the researcher," and "the context." Having said this, longitudinal research is clearly also imbued with a particular addictive quality. Certainly, in my case, partly as a result of the rather serendipitous nature of my initial research, and the way that "nothing was as expected," there is no doubt that I feel a compelling fascination to know "what happens next" in *barrio* Luis Fanor Hernández, and it is this that spurs me to return again and again, and will no doubt continue to do so for the foreseeable future. . .

REFERENCES

Burawoy, M. 2003. "Revisits: An Outline of a Theory of Reflexive Ethnography.' *American Sociological Review* 68, no. 5: 645-79.

Firth, R. 1959. *Social Change in Tokpa: Re-study of a Polynesian Community after a Generation.* London: George Allen and Unwin.

Maffesoli, M. 1997 *Du nomadisme: Vagabondages initiatiques,* Paris: Le Livre de Poche.

Mosse, D. 2006. "Anti-Social Anthropology? Objectivity, Objection, and the Ethnography of Public Policy and Professional Communities." *Journal of the Royal Anthropological Institute,* 12, no. 4: 935–956.

Rodgers, D. 2006. "Living in the Shadow of Death: Gangs, Violence, and Social Order in Urban Nicaragua, 1996-2002." *Journal of Latin American Studies* 38, no. 2: 267-92.

Rodgers, D. 2007. "Joining the Gang and Becoming a *broder*: The Violence of Ethnography in Contemporary Nicaragua." *Bulletin of Latin American Research* 27, no. 4: 444-61.

Rodgers, D. 2008. "A Symptom Called Managua." *New Left Review* 49: 103-120.

Rodgers, D. 2011. "An Illness Called Managua: Urbanisation and 'Mal-Development' in Nicaragua." In *Urban Theory beyond the West: A World of* Cities, edited by T. Edensor and M. Jayne, 121-136. Abingdon: Routledge.

Rodgers, D. 2012. "Haussmannization in the Tropics: Abject Urbanism and Infrastructural Violence in Nicaragua." *Ethnography* 13, no. 4: 411-436.

Rodgers, D. 2017a., "Of Pandillas, Pirucas, and Pablo Escobar in the Barrio: Change and Continuity in Nicaraguan Gang Violence." , in *Politics and History of Violence and Crime in Central America*, edited by S. Huhn and H. Warnecke, 65-84. New York: Palgrave.

Rodgers, D. 2017b. "*Bróderes* in Arms: Gangs and the Socialization of Violence in Nicaragua." *Journal of Peace Research* 54, no. 5: 648-660.

Rodgers, D. 2018. "Drug Booms and Busts: Poverty and Prosperity in a Nicaraguan Narco-*barrio.*" *Third World Quarterly* 39, no. 2: 261-276.

Rodgers, D. forthcoming. "Gang Rule(s): Towards a Political Economy of Violence and Domination in Gangland Nicaragua." In *The Civil Wars of Central America*, edited by A. Blazquez and R. Lecour Grandmaison. Cambridge: Cambridge University Press.

Rodgers, D., and J. L. Rocha. 2013. "Turning Points: Gang Evolution in Nicaragua." In *Small Arms Survey Yearbook 2013: Everyday Dangers.* Cambridge: Cambridge University Press.

Wacquant, L. 2004. *Body and Soul: Notebooks of an Apprentice Boxer,* Oxford: Oxford University Press.

NOTES

1. Preliminary versions of this paper were presented at a panel session on "Ethnographies and/of Street Violence in Latin America" at the Latin American Studies Association (LASA) annual meeting, Chicago, 21–24 May 2014, the conference on "Anthropologists at Work: Challenges and Dilemmas of Qualitative Fieldwork Methodologies in Sensitive Settings," Utrecht University, 3 July 2014, and to an Urban Sociology Lab brown bag research seminar at the University of Texas, Austin, 20 October 2014. Thanks to participants at all these encounters for useful comments and suggestions.

2. This name is a pseudonym, as are the names of all the neighbourhood inhabitants mentioned in this chapter.

3. This name is a pseudonym.

4. It is important to note that gang members knew that I was carrying out research about them.

5. There is obviously a gendered aspect to my research that should be kept constantly in mind, insofar that I am a male researcher investigating a phenomenon that is extremely gendered, and this clearly played a critical role in terms of the research possibilities open to me. Although female gang members are not unknown in Nicaragua, until 2016 all the gang members I encountered in *barrio* Luis Fanor Hernández were young men, and many of their social practices and behaviour patterns were intimately related to a *machista* way of being. As a result, I do not think I would have been able to have the same form of engagement with the gang that I did had I been a female researcher. On the other hand, my gender—as well as my association with the gang—also negatively impacted on the possibility of my exploring a number of other research avenues, including, for example, complicating my interaction with gang members' girlfriends, due to *machismo*-related notions of jealousy, for example.

6. The *barrio* Luis Fanor Hernández gang completely disappeared between 2006 and 2012, but has since reappeared following the demise of the *cartelito* (see Rodgers 2017a; 2017b).

7. This veritable plethora of communication has built up progressively, of course, and is very much a function of technological evolution. I actually lost touch with people in *barrio* Luis Fanor Hernández between my first and second visits, largely due to the fact that there were very few phone lines in the neighbourhood at the time—and these were moreover often only ephemerally connected—while postal services were extremely unreliable and letter-writing was not a common practice. Email use took off in the mid-2000s with the spread of internet cafés, while mobile phones only began to become common from the end of the 2000s, and smart phones—with cameras—only from the early 2010s onwards.

8. To these formal interviews must also be added eleven group interviews, as well as hundreds of hours of more informal conversation and interaction with gang members past and present, as well as over one hundred interviews about gangs with non-gang member inhabitants of *barrio* Luis Fanor Hernández.

9. See http://www.proyectopabloescobar.com/2011/05/pablo-escobar-en-nicaragua.html.

10. See http://www.confidencial.com.ni/articulo/3345/el-fantasma-de-escobar-recorre-nicaragua.

11. The group also involved individuals who were not from the neighbourhood and its membership moreover did not overlap with any collective category—such as "male youth," for example—that allowed local *barrio* inhabitants to adopt certain generic avoidance behaviour patterns.

12. It should also be noted that this current crop of gang members is also the first generation to have no direct knowledge of my initial involvement with the gang in the 1990s, and they clearly trust me less as a result.

TEN

Interpretation of Dreams and Humor in Affective Fieldwork on State Violence in Argentina

Eva van Roekel

INTRODUCTION

This inquiry on my role in the field and my own feelings during unexpectedly significant field encounters with alleged perpetrators and victims disclosed, to certain extent, prevailing local affective attitudes in Argentina towards state violence and suffering. In other words, my own feelings enabled me to grapple with disturbing feelings that lie beneath local transitional justice trajectories in Argentina. When you conduct fieldwork amongst informants that suffer from or are being prosecuted for crimes against humanity, there is often not mentioned during an interview. During my fieldwork it was often during these reflexive field moments that I learned a lot about people's less overt feelings, like shame, guilt, and revenge and contested memories about the perpetrated violence, which were often left unarticulated. As an alternative, exploring my own unexpected feelings provided worthy additional insights into self-inflicted amnesias and repressed memories of my informants. Thus instead of covering-up or omitting such "unprofessional" personal experiences, I suggest that we should examine them because they allow increasing transparency about the actual data gathering processes and subsequent interpretative processes that are important foundations for anthropological theorizing. In my view, the latter is especially relevant in times when validity and reliability of qualitative research is severely questioned, because of several "scientific scandals" in different disciplines of the social sciences. A reflexive inquiry on these personal field-work processes can therefore offer another "instrument" to safeguard scientific integrity and quality of anthropological work.

Consequently this chapter disentangles how important new insights on lived realities of justice in post-conflict settings emerge out of personal fieldwork serendipities. It first examines feelings of shame and guilt that emerged out of a disturbing dream that I had dreamt the night before. Yet instead of analyzing the dream from a researcher's viewpoint, I will contextualize the dream and how people in the field reacted upon this dream by means of a local interpretative framework of psychoanalysis. Second, it examines my own uncomfortable laughter about local practices of humor that subsequently revealed important everyday immoralities related to state violence that questions issues of responsibility and re-venge. Both personal moments in the field cracked important affective riddles and produced important new insights on the people under study. Nonetheless, in order to avoid annoying confessions from the field and unproductive navel-gazing, instead I employed a situated reflexive meth-od. This means that I explicitly mirrored and discussed these personal field experiences with informants and tried to interpret these unexpected, uncomfortable and surprising field moments by their cultural logic.

Before I turn to these feelings that emerged out dreams and humor, the chapter first provides a brief overview on how I did my fieldwork on people's feelings in Argentina and secondly it addresses previous anthro-pological work that explores the methodological value and validity of ethnographer's feelings in the field in order to understand the other.

AFFECTIVE FIELDWORK

During my fieldwork I learned that in urban Argentina, from an early age many people are socialized in a particular manner where feelings are easily expressed, highly valued, socially shared, and carefully analyzed on an everyday basis. Feelings, then, are not considered individual or inward. Instead feelings are vibrant social matters, and this may have simplified my fieldwork on feelings. Empirically accessing people's feel-ings by means of ethnographic fieldwork can be partially done through conventional ethnographic methods like informal conversations, semi-structured interviews, and participatory observations. During my entire fieldwork period in Argentina I therefore asked people to explain how they would define and explicate their own feelings and those of others regarding the perpetrated violence and the current official pursuit of jus-tice at the courts. Besides brief personal anecdotes and complex life histo-ries to explain their feelings, during these spontaneous or planned con-versations, people often spoke in metaphors or local aphorisms, which produced interesting insights.

Listening to people how they talk about feelings is one way to examine feelings in action. As Margaret Lock (1993, 141) in her anthropological work on the body rightly points out, the body is an active expressive forum that transcends speech. I learned for instance that bodily presence and bodily absence at the courts communicated people's cherished ideologies and strong sentiments. Likewise silence was another important resource to grapple with feelings in the field, particularly those feelings that people considered immoral and uncomfortable. Silences during interviews of informal conversations indicated for instance important moments of "conflicting" feelings (Sheriff 2000, 117) that provided important insights into repressed memories or self-inflicted amnesias. During my fieldwork I also gradually learned about the strong feelings attached to artifacts like the famous white scarf of the Mothers of Plaza de Mayo or the Argentine flag. The affective meaning of these objects was fluid and depended on multiple factors like the person who employed the artifact, the space in which it was employed, or other people that were present.

All these field practices that involve speech, bodies, social interactions, spaces, artifacts, and even silences are quite conventional in ethnographic fieldwork. I learned also about people's feelings through reflexivity about my own feelings in the field and empathic processes with informants. However, the clear-cut methodological value and scientific validity of your own feelings in the field has been issue of debate amongst several anthropologists. Francine Lorimer (2010, 100) and Tanya Luhrmann (2010, 213) explore for instance how ethnographers' feelings play a significant role in understanding the other during fieldwork and they mostly emphasize the intersubjective character of feelings, which would validate and legitimize reflexive methodologies. Andrew Beatty (2010, 433) instead has argued against this way of understanding the other, because he says that ethnographers' feelings lose their explanatory power away from home as they belong to too different narratives. Likewise, Ghassan Hage (2010, 144–149) also argued that there would always be fundamental differences between informants and fieldworker's feelings, which would delegitimize an inquiry into ethnographers' feelings in the field. In so doing, they seem to mystify feelings, which turns feelings into impossible phenomena to learn. In my view however, Beatty and Hage first underestimate the—at least temporal—transformative process of the ethnographer while submerging into a foreign context where different cultural logics regarding feelings can be learned. Renato Rosaldo's (1993) work on headhunter's rage and grief and the tragic loss of his wife is therefore still significant. Moreover, like any other cultural phenomenon an ethnographer studies, it is exactly within these differences of feelings of an informant and an ethnographer where knowledge can be found. Looking at how I position and interpret my feelings and how my informants do opens up a whole new space for understanding. Therefore I think that ethnographers that are interested in feelings should openly discuss their own feelings in the field with the people they study. I learned about specific cultural logics regarding guilt and revenge amongst survivors of detention and remorse and shame amongst military officers, partially by discussing my own feelings in the field with my informants.

Therefore, drawing from my own research in Argentina in the next two sections I provide an explanatory frame, based upon ethnographic "techniques" of empathy and reflexivity, which examines two personal field experiences of a dream and humor. Yet instead of explaining away the limits of ethnographic fieldwork with so-called new methodologies, as Hayder Al-Mohammed (2011, 134) has argued, I simply explored the tensions between what I saw and experienced in the field, and what I did not experience, and how this fed into my own life and that of the people I had come to know. In order to avoid annoying confessions from the field and unproductive navel-gazing, as said, I employed a situated reflexive methodology. This means that I explicitly mirrored and discussed personal field experiences with informants and tried to interpret these unexpected, uncomfortable and often surprising field moments by their cultural logic.

A DISTURBING DREAM AND LOCAL INTERPRETATIONS OF PSYCHOANALYSIS

During my fieldwork at the courts female survivors rarely testified about forced (sexual) encounters with their torturers, although it is widely known that rape and the so-called Stockholm syndrome between female victims and torturers occurred at the illegal detention centers during the civil-military regime in Argentina (CELS 2011,178–182). The few women I witnessed at court who did speak about it only addressed a few apologetic words to these disturbing memories. These few words resonated strongly amongst the people at the public gallery at federal court and often left a deeply uncomfortable atmosphere when the court session was over. Although I noticed that these uncomfortable moments at court were tremendously important in order to grapple with state violence and justice from a victims' viewpoint, these matters on sexual violence remained difficult to address in interviews and informal talks. Nonetheless, sexual violence became an important focal point in order to understand shame and guilt. Not that I deliberately started to examine shame and guilt in relation to sexual violence; it was a more unanticipated process of understanding.

Without claiming to be able to fully understand experiences like rape and other forms of forced intimacy, I do believe that enhanced understanding can partially rise out of triangulation between different field experiences grounded in empathic processes and reflexivity. In other words, besides listening to the testimonies, subsequently in a period of a few weeks fieldwork, I interviewed female survivors who spoke reluctantly about their guilt and shame, I read survivors' testimonies, I had confidential conversations with military officers, but I also had a dream where I had an intimate encounter with an indicted officer, which, through empathic processes, taught me to an important extent about guilt and shame.

Particularly by reading and listening to female testimonies I noticed the issue of guilt and shame, but it was often not explicitly related to sexual violence or intimate relationships between officers and detainees. When I met Elena Brodowski, a female survivor, during this same fieldwork period we spoke in more detail about her forced rendezvous in bars in Buenos Aires with one particular military officer and her torturer during her forced detention in the late seventies. Without addressing many words to these disconcerting memories I did grapple with her deep discomfort. Elena wrapped it up by saying that she had finally worked through her guilt of survival.[1]

Meanwhile I had informal get-togethers with often conservatively charming retired military officers at cafes, prison, and their homes to talk about their experiences of justice and state violence. This made Elena's experiences a bit more knowledgeable. The field relationship with these military officers was often casual and sometimes even family-like and although this intimacy and casualness troubled me, I saw no reason or possibility to alter it, because these men were providing important insights. During another testimony at court, when a female survivor explicitly addressed her feelings of guilt and shame regarding the forced relationship with her torturer, I learned again unexpectedly about feelings of guilt and shame. The witness's words triggered a flash of a disturbing dream I had dreamt the night before. It was a dream about an intimate encounter with one of the indicted officers of the corresponding trial. My body temperature rose immediately, and it felt deeply wrong, as if I had transgressed an important moral boundary, yet on an imaginary level. Having dreamt about such intimate encounter made me somehow more complicit and for a moment I felt deeply ashamed and guilty.

Empathy in the field can be another faithful intent shifting between nearness and distance to experience the world from another position, as empathy can be understood as the action of understanding, being aware of, being sensitive to, and experiencing the feelings, thoughts, and experience of another. Empathy during the fieldwork does not mean, however, homologous experiences between researcher and participant, nor is it a linear process, as Jason Throop (2010, 772) rightly pointed out. Moreover empathy is not a straightforward systematic procedure that you can design beforehand like an interview or survey. It happens or not. And although empathy in the field often seems to indicate new understanding, the value of empathy during fieldwork is often only implicitly acknowledged.

Although my first impulse was to silence the dream, I wanted to make this "empathic moment" more explicit and I decided to explore its meaning later on during my fieldwork. Obviously, memories about dreams and associative imaginings belong to the experiential flow of everyday life; yet the meaning people address to them differs greatly and need systematic examination of its local interpretations. Besides the dream and my feelings of shame and guilt about the imaginary encounter with the alleged perpetrator with people in the field, I also discussed other "troubles," like indifference and fear for moral blindness that I experienced going to court and listening to the testimonies of torture and disappearance too much. People I had come to know interpreted my dream, the feelings and anxieties as something normal or even a good thing. They interpreted that it clearly showed that I cared and I was taking my fieldwork and the traumatic past of my informants seriously. Likewise, several people told me in return that they were having disturbing dreams too and encountered a more general heightened state of anxiousness in their life while attending the court hearings too often. In order to deal with their troubles people limited their court visits. Others took (homeopathic) tranquilizers instead. But a great amount worked it through during their weekly psychoanalytical therapy or discussed it with relatives or friends, like a more informal form of therapeutic analysis.

During a casual talk, when an Argentine friend told me that he had a hard time ending his years' long therapy with his psychoanalyst, I suddenly understood that therapy means something quite different in Argentina then I was accustomed to. He explained me that he already had been trying for more than six months, yet his therapist interpreted his desire to end the therapy as a form of resistance that needed further analysis. Through all these casual "therapeutic" talks about previous dreams, anxieties, and discomforts, there emerged understanding about important everyday moralities in relation to the perpetrated violence and trauma amongst victims in Argentina that must be located in a local psychoanalytical culture.

Psychoanalysis is a social institution with long and meaningful roots in Argentina (Súarez-Orozco 1990, 369–370). Argentine scholars Mariano Plotkin (2009, 72–80) and Sergio Visacovsky (2009, 54–62) have argued that especially in the larger urban areas, an overall existing psychoanalytical practice has been very much internalized as a social language and adapted to its local context, which provides answers to difficulties, suffering, malaise, and injustices. This local form of psychoanalysis should not be mistaken with mere therapies between analyst and analysand. This therapy is shared and belongs very well to everyday social life. Words and social practices like "analysis," "working through," and "catharsis" fit well into this everyday life, as I had witnessed in the field and even partially internalized while discussing and interpreting my dream, subsequent feelings, and daily anxieties with substantial others in the field.

In my view, besides a form of social therapy to cope with trauma and everyday misfortune, this collective form of "working through" also characterizes a local morality, where the social sharing of traumatic experiences, daily troubles, misfortune, and hardship in general show that you care and should be analyzed in order to reach better comprehension of self. In other words, this form of social therapy constitutes a moral self in everyday fashion. How this situated local morality locates troubling feelings in everyday life of a heterogeneous group of relatives of the disappeared, survivors and activists is beyond the scope of this chapter though. In my forthcoming book I reflect in more detail about this local morality that I have called "A traumatic home" which culturally locates Argentine victims' feelings of pain and guilt regarding state violence. The epistemological value here is that by exploring your own feelings and uncomfortable memories of dreams in the field with informants provides an alternative reflexive procedure in order to unlock how people live with traumatic or troubling experiences on a daily basis.

A MUFFLED LAUGH AND LOCAL BLACK HUMOR

Cynical remarks in the court room, muffled laughs at the public gallery, embodied parodies during recess, and printed ironies between other forms of black humor turned out to be another important interface to further comprehend the lived experiences of state violence and justice in Argentina. Especially those aspects people considered difficult to address, because of painful memories or immoralities about how to judge and live on an everyday basis with a past of collective violence. At the beginning this humor was difficult to comprehend though. The first encounter with this form of humor was during my first short stint of fieldwork in Buenos Aires in 2009 when I worked briefly with a local research team on an evaluation project of the trials regarding the last dictatorship, with specific emphasis on a witness protection program. After the disappearance of witness Julio López, and the emergence of new threats against future witnesses, in 2007 the government initiated a program to protect witnesses in the trials on crimes against humanity. One day during a break one of my fellow researchers, Olivia, pointed to the López column in *Barcelona* and asked me, "Have you seen the latest Day by Day?" I told Olivia that I had not read the column or even seen the magazine yet. With a smothered laugh she replied that it would probably be too difficult for me anyway, to understand such jokes. Olivia had put it right; I had no clue what could be so funny about a recent disappearance.

Yet through long-term fieldwork I gradually began to decode these local humor practices, which discerned other, more uncomfortable, feelings regarding state violence, the memories, and the justice practices of the last thirty years in Argentina. More in general, I learned that black humor and printed satire was an important element in the daily struggle against inconsistencies and injustices in Argentina (Foster 1989; Pedrazzini 2010). Understanding columns like the López column at *Barcelona*'s should be located amid this local humor culture regarding the last dictatorship. In another article (van Roekel 2013) I have explored in more detail different forms of embodied and discursive humor that provide an alternative field instrument to explore alternative, often silenced feelings in (post) violent field settings that look beyond official versions and the morally accepted.

Besides multiple unexpected moments of wit in the field, during two interviews I spoke in more detail about the local meaning of black humor in relation to violence, trauma and the current trials. Laura Figueroa, a psychologist who has worked for long with victims and relatives of the disappeared, openly acknowledged that without black humor it would become impossible for her to work with survivors:

> Sometimes I just yell to my partner "enough, enough, I do not want to hear anything anymore from any victim-survivor!" Humor is a necessary exit . . . it has to do with the exhaustion while working on horror. I mean you need to get in and out of this horror if you want to do this work. [. . .] Also in psychological therapy, humor is often the only possible way to access this horror; it is way of translating it into something else. Above all [humor] is a way of entering and exiting . . . if you do not take sufficient distance you become carrier of the same [horror].[2]

When I interviewed one of the members of *Barcelona*, the satirical magazine, I did not understand at the beginning of my fieldwork, the junction of humor, violence, injustice and immorality became an explicit matter of inquiry instead of an unforeseen field moment. Surprisingly, the first thing Fernando Carrizo told me was that *Barcelona* was not a humorous magazine: "We are journalists." "We are an acid satirical magazine that informs against the media; we basically observe double discourses of the media and the ruling class." [3] Fernando and I also talked about the human rights organizations in Argentina and their intertwinement with the current government. A bit reluctantly he acknowledged their sinuous sides and said: "When you have a non-critical, idealized and clean vision of the human rights groups, there will definitely remain things [related to the human rights groups] that are difficult to accept." Mocking the sinuous sides of suffering, social injustices and responsibility is what they do at Barcelona, and in so doing, they show a mirror to members of the

Argentine middle classes in order to question their responsibilities regarding past and present immoralities and social injustices.

From a viewpoint afar, Frances Buckley (2003, 5) argues that endorsing certain humor implies complicity and belonging, because approving a joke is accepting a moral point of view on a certain matter and simultaneously constructs a sense of solidarity. In my view, humor in contexts of (past) state violence may also reflect the difficulty with defining boundaries of complicity and accountability in the grey areas of collective violence and state terrorism. In other words, this black humor exposes co-existing confusing everyday moralities. It is the latter that I want to explore in more detail through an unexpected personal moment of wit in the field that enabled me to understand more about living with the uncomfortable, or even the immoral, in everyday Buenos Aires.

After eight months in the field I had completely forgotten about the column on Julio López. Then, my eye accidentally fell on a copy of *Barcelona* in a kiosk. On the back page I read the headline, "August 2nd: National Son of a Bitch Day." Underneath were nine black-and-white photos of military officers involved in current human right trials, each captioned "Happy Son of a Bitch Day." I instantly thought this hinted at the commercial excesses of these contrived celebrations, like Secretary's Day and Teacher's Day, which both happen in September. Suddenly recalling what Olivia had said about the López column, I bought a copy of the magazine. After months of fieldwork and trying to understand what state violence and justice meant for survivors, family members of the disappeared and indicted and loyal officers, the faces of these military officers made me stifle an almost inaudible laugh. I felt a mix of discomfort and pleasure, as if I were not supposed to laugh.

Sharing talks, dreams, meals, worries, and laughter with people from rather opposite local morals worlds, where notions of state violence, suffering, guilt, and justice were interpreted quite differently, had created a deeply confusing moral field. I often worried that I was becoming morally blind or simply indifferent, especially because of my recurring close engagements with indicted and loyal officers and their families. The spontaneous morbid pleasure I then encountered looking at the cover of well-known local satirical magazine, ridiculing several military officers I had spoken to, for an instant eased my ambiguous research position, but at the same time troubled me. I believe that was the moment I started to grasp the complexity of *Barcelona*'s humor that Olivia had hinted at and Fernando explained me later on in the field. I somehow had started to acknowledge my dual fieldwork position by assuming and simultaneously relativizing my own responsibility in constructing an immoral field site. Like with the dream, the feelings of guilt and shame and my anxieties at court, I triangulated this wit with previous moments of humor I had encountered in the field and subsequently I talked about this uncomfortable laughter with some Argentine friends. They all thought it was a sound response to the uncomfortable disposition regarding responsibility, collective violence and social injustices many people in Argentine encounter on an everyday basis.

CONCLUSIONS

While I examined feelings in the field related to state violence and suffering in Argentina, I definitely needed an alternative practical engagement with the object of my understanding. Besides conventional ethnographic practices that in involve speech, bodies, social interactions, spaces, artifacts, and silences, reflexivity about my own feelings in the field and empathic processes with informants also produced new insights about victims' and perpetrators' underlying feelings that shape local transitional justice processes. However, merely reflecting behind a desk about personal feelings of guilt and shame that merged out of an empathic dream or uncomfortable morbid laughter in the field would not have been satisfactory and may have produced, as said, annoying confessions from the field and unproductive navel gazing. Instead in this chapter I have suggested a shared and situated reflexive procedure that involves, besides contextualization, discussion and debate about these personal experiences with substantial others in the field, which allows interpretation by other cultural logics. Then empathy and reflexivity can produce tangible procedures that clarify, to certain extent, how ethnographers can grapple with feelings in the field.

Furthermore, by describing, contextualizing, and analyzing explicitly these two personal field experiences enabled me to enhance transparency about how I gathered data in the field, which profoundly guided my thinking and theorizing in subsequent stages of my research about how feelings that lie beneath local transitional justice trajectories interact with important everyday moralities amongst two conflicting communities regarding state violence and the current pursuit of retributive justice in Argentina. Thus partially through the remembrance of a disturbing dream and subsequent uncomfortable feelings I gradually learned more about people's shame and guilt, which clarified lived experiences of state violence and justice. Likewise, my own unexpected laughter at a kiosk made me understand that humor, that at the beginning of my fieldwork seemed incomprehensible, can be a sound response in a morally confusing social world after state violence, where right and wrong, victim and perpetrator, and one's social responsibility is often ambiguous and indeterminate. Analyzing these so-called alternative hermeneutic resources of an ethnographer in the field is just not enough and needs to be discussed with others and interpreted by their cultural logic. Only then the ethnographer's own feelings are put to work in order to understand the other.

REFERENCES

Al-Mohammad, H. 2011. "Less Methodology More Epistemology Please: The Body, Metaphysics and 'Certainty." *Critique of Anthropology* 31, no. 2: 121-138.

Beatty, A. 2010. "How Did It Feel for You: Emotion, Narrative, and the Limits of Ethnography." *American Anthropologist* 112, no. 3: 430- 443.

Buckley, F. H. 2003 *The Morality of Laughter*. Ann Arbor: The University of Michigan Press.

CELS. 2011. *Hacer Justicia. Nuevos debates sobre el juzgamiento de crímenes de lesa humanidad en Argentina*. Buenos Aires: Siglo Veintiuno.

Foster, D. W. 1989. *From Mafalda to Los Supermachos: Latin American Graphic Humor as Popular Culture*. Boulder: Lynne Rienner Publishers.

Hage, G. 2010. "Hating Israel in the Field: On Ethnography and Political Emotions." In *Emotions in the Field: The Psychology and Anthropology of Fieldwork Experience*, edited by J. Davies and D. Spencer, 129-154. Stanford: Stanford University Press.

Lock, M. 1993. "Cultivating the Body: Anthropology and Epistemologies of Bodily Practice and Knowledge." *Annual Review of Anthropology* 22: 133-155.

Lorimer, F. 2010. "Using Emotion as a Form of Knowledge in a Psychiatric Fieldwork Setting." In *Emotions in the Field: The Psychology and Anthropology of Fieldwork Experience*, edited by J. Davies and D. Spencer, 98-126. Stanford: Stanford University Press.

Luhrmann, T. M. 2010. "What Counts as Data?" In *Emotions in the Field: The Psychology and Anthropology of Fieldwork Experience*, edited by J. Davies and D. Spencer, 212-238. Stanford: Stanford University Press.

Pedrazzini, A. 2010. "Absurdo, Bulo e Ironía: Pilares del humor escrito del suplemento argentino Sátira/12." *Perspectivas de la Comunicación* 3 no. 2: 84-106.

Plotkin, M. B. 2009. "Psicoanálisis y habitus nacional: un enfoque comparativo de la recepción del psicoanálisis en Argentina y Brasil (1919-1950)." *Memoria y Sociedad* 13, no. 27: 61-85.

Rosaldo, R. 1993. *Culture and Truth. The Remaking of Social Analysis*. Boston: Beacon.

Sheriff, R.A. 2000. "Exposing Silence as Cultural Censorship: A Brazilian Case." *American Anthropologist* 120, no. 1: 114- 132.

Suárez-Orozco, M. 1990. "Speaking of the Unspeakable: Toward a Psychosocial Understanding of Responses to Terror." *Ethos* 18, no. 3: 353-383.

Throop, C. J. 2010. "Latitudes of loss: On the Vicissitudes of Empathy." *American Ethnologist* 37, no. 4: 771-782.

Van Roekel, E. 2013. "Accessing Emotions through Humour in the Contemporary Argentinian Transitional Justice Trajectory." *The Unfamiliar* 3, no. 1: 24-33.

Visacovsky, S. 2009. "La constitución de un sentido práctico del malestar cotidiano y el lugar del psicoanálisis en la Argentina." *Cuicuilco* 16, no. 45: 51-79.

NOTES

1. Interview Elena Brodowski, 24-06-2010, Buenos Aires.
2. Interview Laura Figueroa, 02-07-2010, Buenos Aires.
3. Interview, Fernando Carrizo, 28-03-2012, Buenos Aires.

ELEVEN

Swimming with Former Combatants

Ethics and Pragmatics of Fieldwork in Post-War Zones in Sri Lanka

Ariel Sánchez Meertens

OVERTURE

April 1, 2010, around noon. The once terribly feared white van stops. I step out and stretch my legs on what used to be LTTE[1]-controlled territory. Earlier that morning we crossed the former eastern frontline of the decades-long Sri Lankan civil war. Suresh—a former LTTE as well as TMVP[2] combatant—shows me the Unnichchai Tank as he approaches one of the streams descending from this reservoir. I'm an ethnographic shadow behind a group of ex-combatants in the midst of their political campaign. They seek enough votes to obtain a seat in the Sri Lankan parliament for TMVP, and they are confident they can persuade enough people by going door-to-door in this area they know so well. But it's hot, very hot. All the passengers of the van remove their shoes as well as their shirts and follow Suresh into the water in a choreography of smiles and juggling hops. Then, suddenly it happened: "come"—they said in unison—inviting me to join them in a midday swim.

What I experienced that afternoon, I see now as a condensed instance of some of the dilemmas anthropologists recurrently face when doing research in war or post-war zones, particularly amongst (former) combatants. It's the embodiment, or rather the literalization, of our commonly used boundary metaphors in which issues of access, trust, intimacy; but also risk, partiality and compromise, come into play. That call to jump into fresh eastern waters became an encounter wherein externally and self-imposed protocols bumped into effective interaction and data collection. However, this chapter is less about such guidelines, standards, or premises and more about emotional reflexes, spontaneous responses; impulse. In other words, this is an ethnographic window into a fieldwork landscape in which ethics and pragmatics pushed each other for protagonism.

In this chapter I explore the challenges of doing ethnographic work in the midst of a political campaign led by former combatants, a situation which placed the research and the researcher in the grey areas between politics and intimidation; between the subjects' hospitality and the required critical detachment; but also between the potentials of anthropological analysis and the perils of political manipulation. The pragmatic complexity of determining the limits of what is professionally—but also emotionally-permissible is illustrated through and around this unexpected invitation to join former combatants in a jovial swim in the midst of their proselytist journey.

TMVP was formed as an armed organization in 2004 after LTTE's former military commander—alias Karuna—defected, together with thousands of fighters under his command. They soon entered mainstream politics while still engaged in counterinsurgency operations against their former rebel partners. By 2008 they obtained several political posts in Sri Lanka's Eastern Province, though they officially and only partially disarmed after being elected into office. TMVP has been accused of being responsible for multiple killings, disappearances, abductions, and the forced recruitment of hundreds of under-aged youths; crimes for which they infamously used their white vans, maybe even the white van in which I spent so many hours with some of them that April 1, 2010.

The broader academic purpose that brought me to Sri Lanka's eastern shores was to contribute to a theory on the dynamics of armed conflict based on the articulation of the two pillars of any social reproduction: *transmission* and *transformation,* processes in which I envisioned a permanent interaction between instrumental and epistemic power. To capture the intergenerational discursive transmission that helped sustain the civil war for so many decades, I traced the movements of knowledge about the conflict, navigating from the more institutional spaces of transmission towards the more informal or defiant ones. I did this in order to examine how the possibility of armed conflict is manufactured, transferred and refashioned throughout different bodies of knowledge—textual or otherwise—as well as how those comprehensions are inter-generationally and trans-locally reproduced. At the same time, to address the crucial transformations that provided the war with its dynamism, I took as a point of departure the defection of the military commander of the LTTE, the formation of his paramilitary organization—TMVP—and its transition into electoral politics, as a critical process in Sri Lanka's transition towards a post-war scenario. It's in the midst of my activities in pursuit of this latter aspect of my research that the matters we are concerned with here took place.

Like most ethnographically informed research, my journey commenced with systematically stalking people. Quite some time was devoted to reaching high-ranking members of TMVP with the aim of capturing their life histories and their perspectives on the civil war they participated in. Tracking them (as well as their victims) led to an "ethnography on the move," taking me to the intimacy of people's houses, the solemnity of religious temples, the solitude of the eastern beaches and the shelters of vocational centres. Yet, conducting fieldwork among an armed organization such as TMVP posed a serious methodological problem because it forced a certain degree of intimacy between its members and the researcher; although in this case, a rather unsympathetic one. This challenge echoes to some extent the concerns presented by Carolyn Gallaher in her work on US right-wing militias. She addresses the specific consequences of doing research among what she calls rather controversially "repellent populations," arguing that by associating in the social sciences critical thought with advocacy for sympathetic populations, research on unsympathetic groups has until recently been all but ignored (Gallaher 2009, 136).

So how does morality look like when studying "unsympathetic organizations"? What if anything—Gallaher wonders—does the researcher owe these groups as one crafts a representation of them? (2009, 137) And finally, how does one handle the emotions unleashed in this type of research with its ideological and moral clashes (Armbruster 2009, 4); or in the words of Nordstrom and Robben (1996), how is fieldwork affected when people not only ask ethnographers for compassion, but also for collaboration and even complicity? These questions structured this text, even though definitive answers remained rather elusive.

TMVP and I started our conversations seeing each other as truly others, with the inescapable reciprocal mistrust. Working through that mistrust implied a methodological challenge as it constituted some sort of *ethnographic aversion*; a daring task surely, but perhaps a valuable one as it prescribed a useful critical and reluctant proximity. At least, till that afternoon in the Unnichchai waters, that is, when a crucial move was made switching from this calculated deference to more overt *ethnographic seduction* (Robben 1996). The invitation to swim was in fact a double kind of seduction, one stemming from the actor (Suresh) seducing me to join and become one with them; and the other stemming from the moment itself, as the invitation was pushing all my "anthropological buttons," so to speak.

WHY IS IT A DILEMMA? FIELDWORK "AFTER THE FIRE"

What made the invitation to swim a fieldwork dilemma was of course that it's precisely these kinds of "off the record," everyday interactions escaping the rigidness of interviews that anthropologists look for: these are the ethnographic treasures, the not-so-holy grails. Yet, such encounters are also the setting for a misinterpretation of the construed proximity, shifting the actors' perception of the ethnographer's role from embeddedness, to complicity; it's the edge between being among them, and being seen as one of them. I had in fact struggled with this before as I came to realize soon after a series of interviews that they had hoped to have me as "their man in Amsterdam," helping TMVP to distribute their pamphlets and newspapers in the European continent, or as I persistently had to clarify and deny, becoming their leaders' personal biographer.

But the invitation to swim was a dilemma also because it touches upon common courtesy and social obligation, the more so given the stage of my fieldwork at the time, for I had already spent months building a rapport, earning (or bargaining) their trust and gaining thereby access to their own web of meanings. More importantly, they had by then already (in)vested countless days and hours humoring me, and as far as anyone's concerned, I was the sole beneficiary. After all, in all those days of approaching each other, I was getting something out of it, but they obtained nothing more than a chance to tell their stories (which may however not be as insignificant after all). Is it then too much to ask (I imagine them think) to expect your courtesy? Or simply a brief moment of complicity, not in their politics but in their humanity; maybe just in their "boyishness"?

In my response I had to weigh in issues of politeness and expectations; I had to consider what Chakravarty (2012) calls "impression management." The call to swim posed a dilemma because conflictive as it was, the invitation actually implied a significant fieldwork breakthrough. How could I expect to obtain the green light to record Suresh's life history—as I intended to do in that trip—if I reject his invitation to swim? How to say no to such occasions when you recurrently meet the same people asking their attention, encountering them in different settings; hoping to meet their parents, visit their birth place, hear them sing, watch them dance. . . . Suresh and the others' request was a dilemma because accepting would elicit further ethnographic opportunities beyond that moment of cool liquid social reciprocity. The situation evokes in a large degree Bosk's dictum: "No trust, no access; no trust; no consent; no trust, no data" (Chakravarty 2012, 3). But trust also carries intrinsically the risk of people acting contrary to one's expectations (Ingold 2000), so much so, I would argue, that one is forced to conceive the notion of trust itself as the mutual recognition of each other's incontrollability. In that sense trust functions as a "device for coping with the freedom of others" (Gambetta 2000, 219).

And yet, despite acknowledging the above, I couldn't claim to be agnostic about what those boys had been part of either—killings, extortion, forcefully conscripting and torturing other boys I had also interviewed—(how would I feel if one of them were to see me swim with his tormentors?) nor to ignore the hazards of opening the portal of camaraderie with its associated web of anticipated tradeoffs in the form of favors, gifts, connivance and other formulas of social expectations. The issue became indeed that the relation of trust we were building started to be configured in these kind of circumstances "as an engine of epistemic distance-compression: where knowledge, responsibility and mutuality collapse into an identical social form" (Corsín Jimémez 2011, 178).

At the same time, the fact was that no matter how much prudent distance I may have wanted to maintain, there was already some sort of intimacy developed. Being called to swim with them was in itself proof of that. As such that invitation became literally the moment in which the supposed immersion of the anthropologist was suddenly—yet very vividly—tested. It also immediately enabled the question of whether this art we claim as one of our greatest assets—the art of being and doing with and among *them*, but without necessarily *becoming* them—whether this art, I insist, is in fact emotionally, physically and morally feasible. This is of particular relevance in post-war settings—in fieldwork after the fire— because the constant check produced by one's own visible security concerns active in the midst of violence no longer operate automatically. Thus, under certain circumstances, doing fieldwork after armed conflict may become, at least ethically, more dangerous precisely because of the violence's sudden invisibility. Though survival is less at stake, morally perilous transgressions seem to be a postwar minefield.

Deciding whether or not to swim with former combatants was also a dilemma because I too, like all the other passengers of that white van, could use a refreshing splash.

"VOTE FOR THE BOAT"

I knew that going with TMVP's campaign team was a fundamental ethnographic moment, yet one that could be instrumentalised by them in claiming, for instance, that I—the foreigner—endorsed them as a political party. I categorically insisted that they could not refer to my presence as a political strategy of legitimization; and after long deliberations I opted for a middle solution: to tag along, but remaining inside the vehicle, behind its polarized windows when they participated in a rally or went knocking on people's houses. In case people noticed me, they were to refer to me simply as an international observer not associated with TMVP in any way whatsoever. This meant sacrificing the detailed documentation of the interactions between TMVP and the community, remaining thus unable to record both the wording of their campaign in their interface with the electorate, as well as the latter's vocal response. I was limited instead to the observation of body language, messages spoken aloud and the reflections and behavior of TMVP members back in the vehicle. These precautions provided me, nonetheless, with valuable ethnographic entries through the journey itself and offered me the chance to revisit former combatants' memory landscapes, as they recalled their battles or reminisced about their early childhood.

That crucial day, we left the TMVP Batticaloa office around 10 a.m. In the van were six TMVP members and one police officer. We passed Vavunativu and stopped pretty much in every house where they left some pamphlets, gave a short explanation and requested people to *"vote for the boat"* (TMVP's election logo). In between stops, they played a cassette conveying TMVP's political message, the soundtrack to this campaigning journey.

After a few hours of driving around, they showed me the Unnichchai tank and found the spot to take that critical bath. As I stood there making up my mind regarding their request to join in, I suddenly saw them just as playful boys, simply fooling around. Indeed, some of the tension I carried from being for hours in a van with six armed former combatants seemed to fade, though now replaced by the ethical dilemma we are concerned with here. Literature on conflict and specifically on child soldiering is replete with references to the lost innocence of children engaged in violent practices. However, what I saw that day was rather exemplary of the cohabitation of playful naiveté and deadly threat. We want to believe too eagerly that the one excludes the other; but it doesn't, not even after years of violence, nor in the transition into politics or the passage to adulthood. The multi-layered dimensions of experience allows a versatility in which oblivion is not even a prerequisite for both childish play, war memories and political engagement to operate at the same time within the same individual.

Electoral campaigning continued after the break, and at the end I was taken to Suresh's old home, where I met his mother, grandmother, father, and brothers. Somewhere under the shadows of a mango tree, we continued our interview and then we had lunch prepared by his mother. Just as I was covered in rice and curry, I realized that one of the shack's screens was an old sugar sack from Colombia, the land where I was born and raised. This serendipitous encounter produced a bittersweet smile as I understood that there are traces of home everywhere, even in the walls and souls of war-torn combatants living in the antipodes.

CLOSURE

After eating we jumped back into the van and returned through the Dambulla road. Suresh drove and sang all the way back. I on the other hand held my breath as I realized not guns, but the passing maneuvers of an overexcited young male former combatant could very well mean my death.

In case the reader was left wondering, I never entered the water. A thousand thoughts may have crossed my mind in the split second between request and reply, but what actually came out of my mouth was that I couldn't join because I needed to take pictures. My non-waterproof camera saved me from crossing what I impulsively experienced as an undesirable ethical borderline. "I will send you the pictures afterwards" I said.

I don't know if I would have made the same call if this scenario repeated itself. I will also never know what kind of ethnographic jewels may have emerged from such sprinkles of intimacy; but I do know that my emotional response of immediate rejection has given place to a fruitful reflexive debate on my limits, on our limits. To claim that it was a balanced, thought-through, rational, and ethically informed decision would, however, be a lie. I simply felt I shouldn't. Yet, two days before I was called to jump into the turbulent waters of ethical ambiguity, I had spent a couple of days in a vocational centre sharing and sleeping amongst former forcefully recruited child soldiers. Many had been conscripted by TMVP, meaning this situation in itself already posed a problem, for how far can you go into doing research simultaneously on perpetrators and their victims. But that's a debate for another occasion; the point I want to make here is that after some interviews in that vocational centre I played football with formerly conscripted child soldiers. There was indeed far more confidence and trust in their eyes, more smiles and jokes after the match. Why exactly did I experience playing football with them as something ethically acceptable whilst swimming with Suresh felt as taking professional practice over the edge?

My dissimilar response to these two instances suggests that though I theoretically rejected the clear-cut division between victims and perpetrators, morally—or rather instinctively—I still operated under such dichotomous value judgments. The critical detachment I considered myself capable of, appears now fragile; at best incomplete. Indeed as Armbruster observed, "ethically knowing the other may involve a personal transformation into someone one did not think one was before" (Armbruster 2008, 12). I actually learned this some months before I was asked to swim. It was during an interview with TMVP leader Pillayan, in which I caught myself laughing at some of his jokes and shaking his hand before leaving his office. How could I have done this knowing the crimes this man had committed? I asked myself sitting at home in Trincomalee, moments after the interview. I was completely taken aback by my reaction; in fact I was rather angry and disappointed with myself, before coming to terms with it, eventually accepting that it was fine—maybe even necessary—to laugh.

Ultimately these dilemmas expose concerns with purity and binary schemes, but also with trust-building. Norman offers a possible way forward when he states that "it's not accurate to speak of a single static trust that one either has or doesn't have, rather there are multiple trusts that may ebb and flow in the context of different individual and collective relationships" (Norman 2009, 27). Our ethical reflexes do indeed ebb and flow together with these "partial trusts," as Chakravarty (2012) would call them, which are partial both because they are incomplete and because they are subjective. At the end of the day, after carefully and persistently working on trust building, one must recognize over and over again the "reversibility of trust" (Corsín Jiménez 2011), which means acknowledging its perpetual instability and ambiguousness.

In seeking an answer to the questions posed earlier based on Gallagher, Robben, and Armbruster I bumped into a rather simple ethical discovery, obvious in theory, less graspable in the field. As anthropologists we are by now trained to unpack the vilification of those involved in violence, to dismantle the tyranny of labels such as "evil," "monsters," "animals," "terrorists"; we have in fact developed quite sophisticated analytical tools to unravel and expose such semantic and political constructs. But what I found was that we—or at least I—was insufficiently prepared for how mentally demanding, painful, and uncomfortable it can be to discover, acknowledge, and accept a perpetrator's humanity. Part of getting through that process is to overtly present to the general reader, to peers, to victims, but also to those that invited me to swim, these struggles when one crafts a representation of them. Our discipline has devoted quite a lot of attention to establishing parameters for us to better respond to methodological and ethical challenges of fieldwork. Perhaps it's time we devote more attention to how we deal with the responses we produce, to how we can handle them, to how we may reflect upon them and make them part of our analysis. Years after the facts I begin to suspect that rejecting the invitation to swim was part of my tortuous process of fully accepting the other's humanity; a desperate and somewhat incongruous attempt at restoring my own moral balance I felt I had lost with my perceived misplaced laughter one day in a TMVP office.

REFERENCES

Armbruster, H., and Lærke, A. 2008. *Taking Sides: Ethics, Politics and Fieldwork in Anthropology*. New York: Berghahn Books.

Chakravarty, A. 2012. "Partially Trusting: Field Relationships Opportunities and Constraints of Fieldwork in Rwanda's Post-Conflict Setting." *Field Methods* 24, no. 3: 251–271.

Corsín Jiménez, A. 2011. "Trust in Anthropology." *Anthropological Theory* 11, no. 2: 177–196.

Gallaher, C. 2009. "Researching Repellent Groups: Some Methodological Considerations on How to Represent Militants, Radicals, and other Belligerents." In *Surviving Field Research: Working in Violent and Difficult Situations*, edited by C. L. Sriram, J.C. King, J.A. Mertus, O. Martin-Ortega, and J. Herman, 127–146. London: Routledge.

Gambetta, D. 2000. "Can We Trust Trust?" In *Trust: Making and Breaking Cooperative Relations*, edited by D. Gambetta, 213–237. Oxford: University of Oxford, Department of Sociology (electronic edition). http://www.sociology.ox.ac.uk/papers/trustbook.html.

Ingold, T. 2000. "From Trust to Domination: An Alternative History of Human-Animal Relations." In *The Perception of the Environment: Essays in Livelihood, Dwelling and Skill*, by T. Ingold, 61–76. London: Routledge.

Lee-Treweek, G., and S. Linkogle, eds. 2000. *Danger in the Field: Risk and Ethics in Social Research*. London: Routledge.

Mazurana, D. E., K. Jacobsen, and L.A. Gale. 2013. *Research Methods in Conflict Settings: A View from Below*. Oxford: Oxford University Press.

Nordstrom, C., and A.C.G.M. Robben, eds. 1995. *Fieldwork under Fire: Contemporary Studies of Violence and Survival*. Berkeley: University of California Press.

Norman, J. M. 2009. "The Challenge of Gaining Access in Conflict Zones." In *Surviving Field Research: Working in Violent and Difficult Situations*, edited by C. L. Sriram et al., 71–90. London: Routledge.

Sanchez Meertens, A. 2013. "Letters from Batticaloa: TMVP's Emergence and the Transmission of Conflict in Eastern Sri Lanka." PhD diss., Utrecht University.

NOTES

1. Liberation Tigers of Tamil Eelam.
2. Tamil Makkal Viduthalai Pulikal (TMVP)/ Tamil People Liberation Tigers.

TWELVE

Ethical Issues Raised by Legal Anthropological Research on Local Dispute Settlement in Ecuador

Marc Simon Thomas

INTRODUCTION

Doing legal anthropological research on dispute settlement often involves digging into issues that are sensitive for personal, legal, or political reasons. For example, in cases concerning alimony in relation to sexual violence, the paternity question sometimes is resolved by a DNA test and this medical information forms part of that file. In cases concerning serious crimes, a great deal of sensitive and even disturbing information (e.g., like photos of bloody corpses, detailed witness declarations, extensive records of phone calls) forms part of the file. And, as I encountered during my recent research on dispute settlement in an indigenous community in the Ecuadorian highlands, underneath a lot of disputes concerning property, violent crime, or social norms, issues concerning local power play a significant role (Simon Thomas 2013).

Thus, while conducting archival research in files at courts, public prosecutor's offices, police stations, or even when reviewing handwritten documents that are not part of the official record, legal anthropologists are often given access to legal knowledge of great consequence for people. In line with Starr and Goodale (2002), this chapter states that the impact of publication of such sensitive knowledge on the people involved should be carefully considered on a case-by-case basis. This is because any dispute, whether it is in the pre-trial, trial, or post-trial phase, has an effect on the social environment. On the other hand, based on fieldwork experiences, this chapter also argues that a legal anthropological researcher should not turn a blind eye to such sensitive conflicts.

BACKGROUND

The research on which this chapter is based was conducted during three distinct periods of fieldwork in the years 2007, 2009, and 2010. Its overall aim was to provide an understanding of the daily practice of dispute settlement in an indigenous community in the Andean highlands, specifically in a situation of formal legal pluralism, and what could be learned from this in terms of Indian-state relationships. It was shown that, at the local level, the phenomenological dimension of legal pluralism is best characterized in terms of "interlegality." At a macro level, legal pluralism still appears to be seen as a dichotomy between customary law and national law. It was argued that, because ordinary Indians are not positively biased in favor of customary law *per se*, a heterogeneity of legal practices can be observed on a daily basis, which consequently undermines the commonly held view of customary law as a "counter-hegemonic strategy." At other socio-geographical levels, however, this latter strategy does seem to hold true. With regard to the Indian-State relationship, the research showed that constitutional recognition of legal pluralism has worked both in favor of and against the legal-political empowerment of indigenous people in Ecuador.

The locality of the research was the parish of Zumbahua, Pujilí canton, Cotopaxi province, Ecuador. The methods used include archival research in files at courts, at public prosecutor's offices and at lawyer's offices, as well as in so-called *libros de actas* (books of handwritten files) that are used in indigenous communities; collection of other primary and secondary written sources; participant observation; semi-structured interviews and informal conversations. For example, at the four criminal courts of the Court of Justice in the provincial capital Latacunga and at the Civil Court in the cantonal capital Pujilí, I examined more than 120 files. On the La Cocha-Guantópolo murder case of 2010, I read through a file which contained more than 600 pages. And in the communities of Tigua and Gauntópolo, as well as at the *teniente politico*'s office (the lowest juridical official in the countryside) in the town of Zumbahua I read through all *libros de actas* of the past 10 years. On numerous occasions during the course of my research, I came across highly sensitive legal and/or personal information which served as fodder for reflection on the ethical issues concerned with the subject of my research.

A stimulus to further reflection could be found in Ecuador's contemporary sensitive political relationship between the state and its indigenous population. In terms of the political and power structures in Ecuador, the indigenous population has been always subordinate. Things seemed to change, though, when after years of protest a new constitution was promulgated. This Constitution of 1998 marked a radical break with the past, in the sense that, for the first time, several collective and other rights for indigenous people were recognized—including the right of indigenous authorities to make use of customary law instead of national law in order to settle internal conflicts. In other words, a situation of formal legal pluralism came into being. However, with the formal recognition of legal pluralism, almost immediately a subsequent, fierce political and juridical debate emerged regarding the scope of customary law in Ecuador. From the very start, it was unclear when, where, and which cases indigenous authorities were allowed to adjudicate. Actually, the issue of legal pluralism was put on the agenda at the very moment the Constitution of 1998 became effective. This is because the Constitution stated (while remaining rather vague on the actual scope of the recognition) that the law should develop rules which would make both legal systems compatible. The law, according to the 1998 Constitution, should develop rules which would make both legal systems compatible.

Although this promise was repeated in the so-called Montecristi Constitution of 2008, no such coordinating rules have yet been developed by either politicians or jurists (Simon Thomas 2013). As a result, there is still no agreement on the proper scope to be granted to indigenous authorities for the administration of customary law, resulting in a situation of legal uncertainty (Simon Thomas 2012a). So, it seems as if the Ecuadorian state formally "endorsed" customary law for political reasons, while doing nothing to support it. At the same time, the indigenous authorities (at the local, a provincial, or national level) continued their struggle to assure that the formal recognition was actually applied in the real world. They did so by trying to get new legislation implemented, but also by attempting to set new precedents in the courts. Some of the more serious cases (e.g., the La Cocha-Guantópolo murder case) evidently served that latter purpose. And in order to form a serious front against the unwilling state and the judiciary, the indigenous authorities had to act and speak with one voice. The second moral dilemma I faced thus had to do with the question of whether writing about internal quarrels, fights and conflicts might do harm by shattering the external perception of indigenous unity at a time when they were involved in a struggle to establish one of their fundamental rights.

RIGHTS TO CONFIDENTIALITY AND ANONYMITY

Legal anthropology inherently involves a consideration of both anthropological ethics and legal ethics, which sometimes do not perfectly coincide. According to the AAA Code on ethical obligations and challenges,[1] participants in research have the right to privacy, meaning that the anonymity of the subjects of study should be protected as much as possible and that their rights to confidentiality are respected. This Code also addresses legal anthropological research on disputes. Basically this means that confidentiality and anonymity to the outside world must be ensured—the sociologist Tolich (2004) calls this "external confidentiality"— which can be for example done by using pseudonyms. Regarding the "internal confidentiality," on the other hand, one has to be aware of the fact that insiders may recognize other insiders often quite easily. Here, the researcher faces a conflict between conveying detailed accounts of social reality and protecting the anonymity of his informants. All one can do is to anticipate potential threats to confidentiality and anonymity as much as possible, and to be open to one's informants that full anonymity cannot be guaranteed (informed consent).

However, legal anthropology, as a social science, differs in this matter from legal research where, it should be noted, regional differences also exist. For example, with regard to lawsuits, in The Netherlands it is common not to mention full names of victims, defendants, and witnesses in law reports or annotations. Instead, criminal cases are always presented in an anonymous version (e.g., Mr. A, living in the town of B). This in contrast to many other countries like, for example, the United States, where important rulings are known by the names of the litigants (e.g., *Kramer vs. Kramer*) (Wagenaar et al. 1993).

A similar way of referring to court cases can be encountered in international legal bodies, such as the Inter-American Court of Human Rights. In Ecuador, where I conducted my research, socio-legal ethics hardly seem to exist. As an Ecuadorian lawyer once explained to me:

> In Ecuador the issue of protecting your interviewees is, in my opinion, completely ignored. Legal articles I have read usually mention the parties by name. Scholars in the social sciences are more careful, but I have read several papers from anthropologists and sociologists that also mentioned the interviewees' names. When I was in law school, we never, ever, received any course or even a class that explained how to address issues of our informants' privacy and safety.[2]

Despite these disciplinary and regional differences, it is fair to say that it is in the best interest of the subjects of legal anthropological research to protect their privacy as much as possible, and therefore that it is best practice not to mention their real names while publishing on their cases.

Why bother about the right to privacy, one could ask. After all, isn't adjudication a public affair in the first place? The fact of the matter is that the extent to which legal cases are matters of public record varies among different nations. Broadly speaking, in The Netherlands, legal cases are not public (with only the parties involved and their attorneys having access to court files), while most trials and the final decision of the judge are. In the United States, not only the trial and the decision are open to the public, but the case files can be looked into by anyone who is interested, apart from certain exceptions. In Ecuador, files are open after the preliminary investigation is concluded. The point, however, is not so much the formal rules. From a legal anthropological perspective, it is far more interesting what the actual consequences are of the right (or lack thereof) to privacy.

Legal anthropological research emphasizes that disputes encompass not only the initial grievance and the trial, but also the final outcome of the case and its after-effects (i.e., the so-called post-trial phase). That is why it is important to pay careful attention to future consequences of legal cases and the extent of their public exposure in all different phases of disputes. Building on the work of Snyder (1981) and Felstiner et al. (1980-1981),[3] Von Benda-Beckmann (2003) argues that the dispute process should not be considered as having concluded after the final ruling has been issued. She distinguishes among a pre-trial, trial, and post-trial phase. With this, she in fact takes up a point previously made by Felstiner et al. (1980-1981, 639), namely that "there is always a residuum of attitudes, learned techniques, and sensitivities that will, consciously or unconsciously, color later conflict." They also argued that any given dispute might continue even after a settlement, or that the end of one dispute might lead in turn to a new grievance. This means that the expectation that disputes be resolved can be entirely unrealistic (Colson 1995; Von Benda-Beckmann 2003), and this makes the preservation of confidentiality of the parties involved in lawsuits so important.

Although protecting anonymity as much as possible is the rule, there are some exceptions. First, when cases are a matter of public record, it does not make much sense to conceal the identity of certain people involved. When names of people involved in a lawsuit have been revealed in newspapers or on television, then there is not much need for the researcher to protect the privacy of those persons. Second, there is no point in protecting the confidentiality of people (e.g., "public figures" like well-known indigenous leaders) or institutions whose identity and activities are a matter of public record. For this reason, I have chosen to refer to public figures such as politicians, published authors, public officials (e.g., judges, public prosecutors, *tenientes políticos*), and the organizations that they work for by their real names in all my articles. Thus, subjects whose real names have previously appeared in other publications or are a matter of public knowledge can be properly identified. In such cases, there is no need to ensure external confidentiality.

All other informants and subjects, however, should be referred to by pseudonyms, or by generic descriptions like "an ex-*dirigente*." Readers familiar with the events and institutions described may be able to discern the identity of these individuals, which challenges the internal confidentiality. However, in most cases the scholarly writings of the researcher won't provide them any facts that they were not aware of before (Wagenaar et al., 1993). This, of course, cannot diminish the researcher's obligation to anticipate potential threats to confidentiality and anonymity, nor exempts this the researcher from his or her obligation to a continuous process of informed consent. Although according to the AAA Code of Ethics, any individual anthropologist must make carefully considered ethical choices, as soon as others have already revealed subjects' identities, there is no point in sustaining the pretense of protecting external confidentiality. With regard to the internal confidentiality, which in a way lies below the surface (Tolich 2004: 101), special attention of the researcher is needed at all times. Therefore, what the publication of detailed personal information means for the people involved must be considered on a case-by-case basis.[4]

FRAGILE POWER STRUCTURES

Given the fact that legal disputes, whether in the pre-trial, trial, or post-trial phase, have an impact to the social environment, the researcher has to treat the reporting of any such matters with care. This is especially true regarding knowledge that is intertwined with often fragile local (or even national) power structures. It is a fact that legal anthropological research tends to produce such knowledge (Starr and Goodale 2002). It is for this reason that, in reference to research on internal conflicts in indigenous communities in Ecuador, Becker (2010) asks whether highlighting divisions does harm to the struggle for equal rights and autonomy. Given Ecuador's heightened recent political sensitivity towards the recognition of indigenous rights, it would seem that his concern is justifiable. Roughly one-third of the population of Ecuador is considered indigenous, and the country has politically dealt with its diversity in a variety of different ways, alternately employing assimilationist, integrationist and (most recently) multicultural models (Simon Thomas 2013).

Struggles between indigenous peoples and power holders are nothing new, and it is only since the "National Indian Uprising" in 1990 that indigenous people have gained a place on the political stage. Among other things, this led to the promulgation of a new Constitution in 1998 in which several collective and other rights were recognized—including the right of indigenous authorities to make use of customary law instead of national law in order to settle internal conflicts (i.e., the recognition of legal pluralism). These rights were ratified in the Constitution of 2008. However, daily practice reveals a huge gap between formal and actual recognition. This is specifically shown in the ongoing political and juridical debates regarding the proper scope to be granted indigenous authorities for the administration of customary law alongside national law. Because the AAA Code on Ethics specifically addresses power differentials and vulnerable populations, one ought to be very careful when writing about case studies that can be linked to this ongoing struggle for autonomy, in order not to harm the vulnerable position of the indigenous people involved.

On more than one occasion, I have had to deal with the dilemma of whether or not to write about disunity among indigenous people within the above-described context. One such instance involved the publication of material on the La Cocha-Guantópolo murder case of 2010 (Simon Thomas 2012a; 2012b; 2013). This case involved five indigenous persons who were suspected of homicide initially adjudicated by local indigenous authorities, before also being named as suspects in a criminal investigation conducted by the national courts. The traditional punishment the five received (consisting, among other things, of a ritual cleansing with stinging nettles and cold water, followed by a whipping) provoked an outcry from many sectors of Ecuadorian society. Elements of the media, "ordinary" Ecuadorians, jurists, and the government condemned the punishment as "barbaric."

Specifically the brutality of the treatment and lack of due process were criticized, and there was even disagreement about the proper content of customary law among indigenous people themselves. This public outcry, combined with the internal indigenous debates, helped bolster's President Correa's stance against full recognition of legal pluralism. On the other hand, the fact that the legality of the indigenous trial was questioned through the criminal investigation fueled the indigenous movement's dissatisfaction with the continued lack of full recognition of their formal rights. Finally, the fact that the people directly involved have had to live until today with the uncertainty of the outcome of a case that still has not been closed, helped strengthen the indigenous movement's case for full recognition of legal pluralism. In sum, this La Cocha-Guantópolo murder case turned out to be very politically sensitive and its consequences clearly transcended the actual case.

The moral dilemma I faced in this case was largely resolved by the case itself. This is because I was technically not allowed to do research in the files because no ruling has yet been issued on the case. The fact that I nevertheless had done so (the judge, the public prosecutor, as well as a couple of attorneys involved in this case had no objections at all that I read through their files more than once) did not absolve me from my obligation to write only about facts that had been made public already. In my publications on the La Cocha-Guantópolo murder case, I provided no new facts that had not already been published on television, in newspapers and in journals. However, when I was publishing on other cases concerning indigenous people and their customary law (e.g., Simon Thomas 2009; 2103), I did face the question of whether writing about disputes might harm vulnerable communities, or if doing so might disturb the fragile power structures within these communities (and in their relationships with the national authorities). Despite Becker's (2010) justifiable concern, I always decided to tell the real story.

"The real story" in this sense, is not about the issue of "what happened" in terms of objective, "true" facts, it is about the question whether or not to "play up feuds and flaws of impoverished groups" (Colloredo-Mansfeld 2009, 146); it refers to the real daily practice. Legal pluralism, the topic of my research, forced me to talk to a wide range of people about closely related issues like customary law and national law, their interaction, and its political sensitiveness. I discussed these issues with persons form a wide variety of back grounds and education, from taxi drivers, market vendors, and hostel operators to scholars, attorneys, prosecutors, judges, and indigenous authorities. Proceeding in this fashion taught me two things. First, on an analytical level, it led me to understand that legal pluralism does not mean the same thing to all people. Second, on an emotional level, I realized that my opinion on customary law had changed. At first, I had been uncritically in favor of it, attracted by its emphasis on reconciliation, compensation and restitution, instead of on meting out punishment. Over time, however, I began to realize that customary law, like any legal system, has its drawbacks and is not immune for criticism. This taught me once again that the daily practice of legal pluralism in Ecuador is told by many voices, rather than being an objective one. In a similar way this counts for stories about local internal conflicts too: of course conflicts do occur, but different versions of causes and effects exist. Truth, and stories on it, comes in many forms.

Therefore, telling the real story of daily practice—that is, local internal conflicts *do* happen, although there are many sides to it—is, in my opinion, the only option a scholar has. Colloredo-Mansfeld (2009, 146) argues that "turning a blind eye to internal fights will not do." This is because, according to him, plurality rather than unity has not only been typical for indigenous communities, but has also been a key factor to the success of indigenous movements in Ecuador (Colloredo-Mansfeld 2009). In line with this argument, I decided to tell the stories about local internal conflicts and the political controversy some of these cases caused on a national level as fairly as possible. I decided to do so because I believe that the challenge of legal pluralism (the overall subject of most of my research so far, and the subject by which most of my informants are influenced, or are concerned with) should not be understood as primarily a jurisprudential process.

I think it important to describe, analyze and understand it as an empirical reality—a reality of which conflicts form a substantial part. After all, because "any indigenous community will be riddled with conflicts" (Jackson 2002, 120), its customary law is invariably contested within the community itself, and thus reflects local tensions (Sieder and Sierra 2010). The reality is more complex than essentialist (or sometimes politically driven) portrayals of indigenous communities as harmonious, and customary law as always just, would suggest. It therefore makes no sense to ignore these tensions just because of a paternalistic idea that hiding them would serve the indigenous people's agenda best. It is my strong opinion that the opposite is true. If one takes his informants, their internal disputes, and their political struggle for autonomy seriously (regardless of whether one takes a stance in that struggle or not), one has to picture daily reality as accurately as possible, even if this means reflecting conflict and discord.

CONCLUSION

According to both anthropological and legal ethics, the protection of people's privacy, and therefore withholding publication of their real names in writing about their cases, is in their best interest. One of the reasons for this is that there is always a post-trial phase, meaning that disputes are not over after they are resolved, and thus individuals' positions in this later phase should be influenced as little as possible. However, when subjects' names have become known already through earlier publications or because they are public figures, there is no longer any privacy to protect. However, a clear distinction here should be made between external confidentiality (i.e., regarding the outside world) and internal confidentiality (i.e., concerning insiders). That is why the implications of the publication of detailed information for the people involved must be considered on a case-by-case basis. This also applies when writing about communities or populations which are already vulnerable, or if doing so might disturb often fragile power structures. The AAA Code on Ethics specifically draws attention to this. However, this attentiveness does not mean that internal tensions among or between such groups should be hidden. Telling the real story, even when that story involves conflict, is the only option a scholar has.

REFERENCES

Becker, M. 2010. Review of *Fighting Like a Community: Andean Civil Society in an Era of Indian Uprisings*, by Rudi Colloredo-Mansfeld. *Bulletin of Latin American Research* 30: 106–107.

Colloredo-Mansfeld, R. 2009. *Fighting Like a Community: Andean Civil Society in an Era of Indian Uprisings*. Chicago: University of Chicago Press.

Colson, E. 1995. "The Contentiousness of Disputes." In *Understanding Disputes: The Politics of Argument*, edited by P. Caplan, 65–82. Oxford: Berg Publishers.

Felstiner, W. L. F., R. L. Abel, and A.Sarat. 1980–81. "The Emergence and Transformation of Disputes: Naming, Blaming, Claiming. . ." *Law and Society Review* 15: 631–654.

Jackson, J. E. 2002. "Caught in the Crossfire: Colombia's Indigenous Peoples during the 1990s." In *The Politics of Ethnicity: Indigenous Peoples in Latin American States*, edited by D. Maybury-Lewis, 107–133. Cambridge: Harvard University Press: 107–133.

Sieder, R. and M. T. Sierra. 2010. *Indigenous Women's Access to Justice in Latin America.* Bergen: Chr. Michelsen Institute.

Simon Thomas, M. 2009. *Legal Pluralism and Interlegality in Ecuador: The La Cocha Murder Case*, Amsterdam: CEDLA (Cuadernos del CEDLA # 24).

Simon Thomas, M. 2012a. "Legal Pluralism and the Continuing Quest for Legal Certainty in Ecuador: A Case Study from the Ecuadorian Andes" . Gipuzkoa: The Oñati International Institute for the Sociology of Law. https://www.mysciencework. com/publication/show/1e1afa196110f6eeb40ccc90ac5fa950.

Simon Thomas, M. 2012b. "Forum Shopping: The Daily Practice of Legal Pluralism in Ecuador." In A. Ouweneel, ed. *Andeans and Their Use of Cultural Resources: Identity, Space, Rights & Gender.*, edited by A. Ouweneel, 85–106. Amsterdam: CEDLA (Cuadernos del CEDLA # 25).

Simon Thomas, M. 2013. "The Challenge of Legal Pluralism: Local Dispute Settlement and the Indian-State Relationship in Ecuador." PhD diss., Utrecht University).

Snyder, F. G. 1981. "Anthropology, dispute processes and law: A critical introduction." *British Journal of Law and Society* 8:141–180.

Tolich, M. 2004. "Internal Confidentiality: When Confidentiality Assurances Fail Relational Informants." *Qualitative Sociology* 27(1):101–106.

Von Benda-Beckmann, K. 2003. "The Environment of Disputes." In W. van Binsbergen, ed. *The Dynamics of Power and the Rule of Law: Essays on Africa and Beyond*, edited by W. van Binsbergen, 235–245. Leiden: Africa Studies Centre.

Wagenaar, W. A., P. J. van Koppen and H. F.M. Crombag. 1993. *Anchored Narratives: The Psychology of Criminal Evidence.* Hertfordshire: Harvester Wheatsheaf.

NOTES

1. See http://ethics.aaanet.org/ethics-statement-0-preamble/ for the Code of Ethics of the American Anthropology Association (accessed June 4, 2014).

2. Personal e-mail correspondence on May 28, 2014.

3. Snyder (1981), for example, recognizes the pre-conflict or grievance stage, the conflict stage, and the dispute stage, as three phases of the dispute process. Felstiner et al. (1980-1981) went further, identifying what they call the naming, the blaming, and the claiming, as three important aspects of conflict preceding the actual trial.

4. In order to avoid any appearance of impropriety, it seems to make sense for the researcher to clearly indicate that the identities of individuals he or she has named have already been revealed in published or broadcast reports (and to reference those reports). This is the practice that I myself follow.

THIRTEEN

Security at Stake

Dealing with Violence and Public (In)security in a Popular Neighbourhood in Guadalajara, Mexico

Monique Sonnevelt

INTRODUCTION

Startled and still a little drowsy I look around me, and realize where I am. Despite the heat, the bumping and the shaking, I dozed off in the 639 bus, which leaves from near the San Juan de Dios market in downtown Guadalajara to Colonia Jalisco on the periphery.[1] Slightly uphill in front of me looms what I now call "my neighbourhood": Colonia Jalisco. The streets here, some paved, some not, are dusty, full of pot holes and large stones. They are lined with simple houses and occasionally a car wreck. Graffiti on the walls spells out the names of the youth gangs who are marking their territory in this part of the neighbourhood. There are a lot of these gangs here, with varying levels of infamousness. The bus turns a steep left at Totatiche Street, one of the few asphalted streets. We then turn into the direction of the central plaza of Colonia Jalisco, where the main church is located, as well as the *delegación*, the police station, and some small shops.

I get off the bus and walk the last couple of blocks to my destination. It is four o'clock, and a couple of street vendors are setting up stalls where they sell pirate CDs with *banda* and *reggaeton* and the latest Hollywood blockbuster. Others sell the regular popular snacks: hotdogs, hamburgers, and of course everything containing vitamin T, which comprises a wide variety of tacos, tamales, *tortas ahogadas*, and tostadas. Some older men sit side by side on one of the various benches on the central square, neighbors get together to exchange the latest

> gossip, families go for a snack, and groups of teenagers hang out and
> flirt. However, after dark it quiets down quickly in the *colonia* and the
> atmosphere in the neighbourhood turns grimmer, and the streets more
> dangerous.

The above extract from my field notes provides a brief impression of
Colonia Jalisco, a popular neighbourhood in Mexico's second largest city,
Guadalajara. It is an area with a bad reputation for violence and public
insecurity, a feature it shares with many other so-called *colonias populares*
in Mexico's cities. Yet it is also a place that many people call home and
therefore have to cope with the challenges that living there implies.

Violence and insecurity are of great concern to many Mexican citizens,
and the number-one concern for many people in Colonia Jalisco. The
ineffectiveness of the police, corruption, and widespread impunity provide spaces for non-state armed actors such as youth gangs and drug
dealers to emerge and to compete with the state for control over a certain
territory. As a result, a market for security opens up (see Bandiera 2003;
Elwert 1999; Shah 2006; Volkov 2002). Both legitimate and illegitimate
"violence entrepreneurs" (Volkov 2002) dive into the void to provide
protection and even forms of privatized justice. However, the market
process surrounding security is more complicated than the basic economic principle of offer and demand. Coercion by armed actors, but also the
social contextual dimension of the relationship between local residents
and violence entrepreneurs, who often originate from the areas they end
up protecting, influence the security market (see Rodgers 2006a; Sánchez
Jankowski 1991; Venkatesh 1997 for examples of examinations of the influence of gang–community relations on gang behavior patterns).

Various authors have dealt with the rise of alternative strategies or
parallel structures of public security in low-income areas in Latin America, a process that is sometimes also called the "informalization" of public
security because it occurs in the absence of effective and legitimate
government policies and actions (see, for example, Caldeira 2000; Goldstein 2004; Koonings and Kruijt 2007; Leeds 1996; Moser and McIlwaine
2004).[2] Few have explored how emergent markets of security actually
operate, however, and this chapter seeks to describe the ways in which
the residents of Guadalajara's low-income community of Colonia Jalisco
manoeuvre between formality and informality, legitimacy, and illegitimacy, in their quest for security.[3] The chapter is divided into three sections. In the first, I explore the theoretical framework of the market for
security. In the second section, I offer an overview of Colonia Jalisco's
security market, detailing the different actors within the neighbourhoods'
particular political economy of violence. The third section zooms in on a
specific fieldwork episode that sheds light on the complicated nature of
the relations between the local community, the local youth gang as a

source both of violence but also protection, and the local police in the context of the local security market.

THE STATE AND VIOLENCE ENTREPRENEURS

Brutal *narco* violence, one of the world's highest rate of kidnappings, and the widespread presence of youth gangs make public insecurity a dominant feature of everyday life in contemporary Mexico, especially in the larger cities. This reality is at odds with the assumption that it is the duty of the state to protect its citizens against basic dangers, both internal and external, real or perceived, legitimate or fabricated.[4] The state is normally supposed to monopolize and concentrate the means of violence (Weber 1995, 310, 311; Weber 1972, 121, 122; Tilly 1985). Although this monopoly of violence is seldom absolute in practice, violence by non-state actors is generally considered to be an exception, not the rule.

When the monopoly of violence disintegrates and the state does not adequately fulfill its protective role, spaces open up to violence, and so-called violence fields emerge (Elwert 1999). This opening generates (violent) competition among various armed actors for control, material benefits, or services, which also increases citizens' need to enhance their security. These services often end up being offered by the same protagonists that initially cause the increase in violence. Security in other words becomes a valuable commodity, and consequently, a security market with an array of both legitimate and illegitimate violence entrepreneurs emerges.[5] This is particularly obvious in low-income areas; as Sánchez Jankowski's (1991, 22) has noted, "low income areas [. . .] are organized around an intense competition for, and conflict over, the scarce resources that exist in these areas." Security is one of these scarce resources, as it is a basic condition for survival.

The provision of security as a commodity does not depend solely on the level of demand and available choices. "The marketing strategy of private enforcers, once called 'the offer one cannot refuse,' implies that the initiative all too often belongs to force-wielding organizations rather than economic subjects" (Volkov 2002, 20). This does not necessarily mean coercion, but rather the creation of a field of pregiven possibilities. The point is well illustrated by Bandiera (2003) and Shah's (2006) research, respectively, in Italy and India. The former focuses on land reform and the way the Sicilian Mafia acted both as an enforcer of security and an extorter. Shah (2006), for her part, illustrates how the "terrorist" Maoist movement in Jharkhand, India, did not simply offer protection from competing political groups, but also from itself. In both cases, however, the interaction of various armed actors also brought about a system that limited and governed the activities of violence entrepreneurs, creating relative order (Volkov 2002, 21).

The relationship between the community and illegitimate violence entrepreneurs is complicated. The entrepreneurs might provide some level of security to the community, within which they frequently live and where they have personal ties. However, it remains a relationship that in the end has a negative outcome for the wider community, a form of perverse social capital (see Moser and McIlwaine 2004, 158). Drug lords or (youth) gangs might offer some protection, but also remain a source of violence and social problems. For example, gangs and drug dealers can instill fear in a community that undermines democratic grassroots initiatives (Leeds 1996). Or else violence entrepreneurs might stop providing protection if it interferes with other (more profitable) interests, as illustrated by Rodgers (2006a, 2006b), who describes how a youth gang in Managua first protected local neighbourhood inhabitants against violence and crime, but over time became involved with drug trafficking and lost interest in protecting local residents, terrorizing them instead in order to protect their drug-related economic activities.

The police force occupies an ambiguous position within the security market. On the one hand the police force is formally the state institution bestowed with the legal and legitimate means to maintain law and order. On the other hand, as Denissen (2008, 29) points out, drawing upon the examples of Russia, the United States, and Brazil, police corruption and brutality is widespread, and the police force systematically operates in the margins of illegality and illegitimacy. The Mexican police force is widely viewed as incompetent, corrupt, and often involved in crime in order to supplement their meagre salaries (Suárez de Garay 2006, 13). Features such as corruption and the involvement in crime create a situation in which the boundary between the police and criminal activity becomes blurred, and consequently citizens no longer know whom they can trust. When a policeman is involved in corruption, he oversteps the boundaries of the legitimate power attributed to him as a policeman. One can wonder whether this policeman is still a representative of the legitimate state, or a criminal disguised as a state agent. On the other hand, this policeman invokes the power attributed to him by the state for his illegitimate business, and citizens will perceive this actor through his uniform as a representative of the state.

As Leeds (2007, 24) has pointed out in her study of the violence in Brazilian *favelas*, the permeable demarcation between unlawful and "official" violence has created a perverse dynamic whereby low income populations often perceive greater protection from the criminals than the police. In Latin America's socially divided societies, Kruijt (2008) describes how these practices enhance the gradual expansion of a gray zone between the formal and the informal, decency and illegality, respect for the law and criminality, civil society and "uncivil" society.[6] This zone of indifference and indefinition generates hybrid forms of injustice within legality, insecurity within the framework of the law, and informality within the institutions of order. Several scholars have therefore considered the continuity between the state and non-state actors of violence (see, for example, Leach 1977; Shah 2006; Sluka 2000; Tilly 1985).

This line of thought does not necessarily mean that the situation in *colonias populares* such as Colonia Jalisco is the result of a weak state, with the violence fields the result of "governance voids."[7] Corruption by policemen and other government officials, as well as random police arrests, are everyday events that remind the *colonia*'s citizens that the state is arbitrary but also powerful (see Rodgers 2006b). Legitimate and effective governance might be limited but is not absent in the *colonias*, and the state continues to be perceived as a strong entity. These limited levels of legitimacy and effectiveness do however strengthen other social actors, and allow for competition to emerge, as I elaborate in the next section in relation to Colonia Jalisco.

COLONIA JALISCO AS A SECURITY MARKET

Colonia Jalisco is a large *colonia popular* located on the periphery of the *Zona Metropolitana de Guadalajara* (ZMG). The community emerged in 1980 on the lands of *ejido Zalatitan* as an illegitimate settlement, at a time when shantytowns mushroomed on the periphery of many Latin American cities.[8] It was an era of economic crisis and restructuring through neoliberal reforms, and, consequently, poverty grew and the gap between the rich and poor became more pronounced. At the same time, violence rose significantly in Guadalajara and in Mexico generally. From the 1980s on, organized, professional, and effective gang activity increased in Guadalajara. Drug-trafficking activities proliferated and started to penetrate all social sectors and political institutions, especially following the rerouting of cocaine smuggling through Guadalajara. Together with the crime and violence, feelings of public insecurity increased dramatically among the general population (Ramírez Sáiz and Chávez Sevilla 1998, 198; Regalado Santillán 2001, 160).

Regardless of the initial privations and lack of public goods and services in Colonia Jalisco, residents believed this was the first stage of upward mobility for them. The community was seen as a place of hardship, but one in which improvements were possible and which would consolidate as an urban neighbourhood over time. During the administration of President Carlos Salinas (1988–1994), Colonia Jalisco was selected as a model neighbourhood for the National Solidarity Program (PRONASOL). "Solidarity" was presented as a poverty alleviation program directed at the urban poor, but was above all meant to establish a host of new relationships outside traditional patron-client mechanisms, and restore the legitimacy of Salinas and the ruling *Partido Revolucionario Institucional* (Institutional Revolutionary Part, PRI) party (Haber 1994,

278–279). Colonia Jalisco received several public goods and services under this program, such as running water, electricity, schools, and a police station. Previously, policing had been virtually absent in this community.

Despite these developments, the community never fully consolidated as an urban area. The urban goods and services were insufficient to cater to the whole population or turned out to be of low quality. To this day, many houses remain unfinished, and the Colonia remains an area where the urban underclass reside and which is stigmatized for its violence, youth gangs, drugs dealing, and social problems.[9] Indeed, it became very clear during my fieldwork that despite the presence of many other social and economic problems, violence and insecurity, most notably in the form of youth gangs and drugs related violence, were the main concerns of the people living in Colonia Jalisco.[10] Although the police post on the *colonia*'s central plaza ensured there was a round-the-clock police presence, it was no guarantee for effective policing.

Indeed, the inhabitants of Colonia Jalisco generally had a very critical view of the police whom they described as corrupt, involved in crime, incompetent, and not having the interests of the population at heart. They felt that they always deliberately arrived too late whenever they were called, once the real trouble was already over, and more often than not making up an excuse for not interfering usually by referring to an event as "a private matter" (something that was often said in relation to cases of domestic violence). It was universally reported that policemen were often visibly drunk or drugged on duty and generally displayed an arrogant attitude, frequently stopping and searching neighbourhood inhabitants without legal ground. Indeed, they would often randomly arrest people, in order to extract a bribe from them for their release (sometimes in the form of spot "confiscations" of items of interest such as alcohol, cigarettes, and the likes) or else to have some "fun" with them.

The absence of effective policing meant that the *colonia* was very much an Elwertian "field" open to all sorts of violence, as various armed actors competed for control, material benefits, or services within its territory. Apart from the criminalized police, there were also some 20 different youth gangs, four or five of which are considered particularly dangerous and violent.[11] These youth gangs fought each other and other "enemies." There were also various small-scale drug dealers, who all had their own territory for (local) retailing, which they defended with violence. They themselves usually worked for drug lords higher up the hierarchy who lived elsewhere, but also employed people in the *colonia* to work as "body guards" or traffic small quantities of drugs from one part of town to another. There were also elements of organized crime present, for example, in the form of older, former youth gang members who had joined more professionally organized criminal gangs. These violent actors were complemented by a range of small-time individual criminals such as thieves, pimps, and so on.

As if the mere presence of all these different competing armed actors was not confusing enough, they and the community's residents were linked to each other in a network of multiple, but opaque, relations. Certain gang members, for example, worked together with drug dealers, who could be older sisters or brothers of a gang member. A drug dealer could have an agreement with a pimp for exclusiveness of drug sales in his brothel, while at the same time ensuring that the pimp was not bothered by other dealers. Members of different youth gangs might put aside their battles to work together on a lucrative "business project," or fight the police together. Gang members and drug dealers could also have protection agreements with policemen.

At the same time, there were also big differences between the different actors. Drug dealers in Colonia Jalisco were, for example, usually not involved in the security market in the same way as described in some studies of Brazilian *favelas,* where they have been depicted as maintaining strong networks of regulatory control over entire communities (see Gay 2005; Leeds 1996; Leeds 2007; Zaluar 2004). Rather, they simply sought to ensure that nothing interfered with their business, although they did sometimes provide broader forms of protection to their friends and family in certain cases. Youth gangs, on the other hand, provided security to the residents of their territory much more broadly and regularly—although not always systematically. They did so especially from individual thieves and robbers, and did so in exchange for loyalty among local residents, whom they expected to look the other way whenever they became involved in some illegal business, or else not denounce them in case of trouble with the police. As a result of such loyalty, the police often stressed that their efforts to improve security in Colonia Jalisco were fruitless because the local population did not cooperate with them.

The police were clearly a particularly important actor within the Colonia Jalisco security market, operating along different stages of both the legitimacy—illegitimacy and legality—illegality continuums. There were policemen who would come to the rescue whenever residents call them, while others would only watch out for their relatives or neighbors. Others still perhaps kept a keener eye over a particular shop, because the owner regularly provided them with coffee or a snack for free. There were of course also the policemen who provided protection to criminals, in exchange for goods or money. This "service" was often forced upon illegal entrepreneurs in order to avoid prosecution. In most of these cases, the incentive for the policemen was economic, but in some cases the existence of a personal relationship was important. This was quite paradoxical considering that according to the police the population of Colonia Jalisco generally displayed a hostile attitude toward police officers. Indeed, many policemen argued that the residents of Colonia Jalisco tended to be "on the other side of the law" and talked about the security problems in the *colonia* as an "us vs. the people" stalemate. As a policeman I interviewed in Colonia Jalisco puts it, "We try to do our job and to improve things around here, but they [the residents] don't want to, they don't cooperate. So what can we do? You arrive at the scene, and no one has seen anything, knows about anything, nothing . . . Meanwhile they provide shelter in their houses [to the gang members]."[12]

It is the coexistence of multiple actors with complex sets of relationships on the security market that makes the situation in Colonia Jalisco opaque. It is hard to know exactly who is protected by whom, under what circumstances, and how effective this protection is. This situation leaves citizens very vulnerable in the face of violence and insecurity, as a resident of Colonia Jalisco called *Doña* Lupe described:[13]

> I sell tacos in front of my house every morning, here at the corner. At some point some gang members started to deal drugs here right at this same corner. It bothered me because it interfered with my business. I asked them a couple of times if they would take into account that I try to make a living here, but they kept coming back. I then called the police and denounced that drugs were being sold right here. A couple of days later the police came by. They were talking to the gang members. They seemed very friendly, and at some point I saw them [. . .] giving money to the police. The police left, but they told the gang member who had made the complaint. From then on they started threatening me. [. . .] For example, they would come and say to me that they exactly knew that my eldest daughter was attending school at night, what bus she took and what time she came back. They said they would wait for her and gang rape her between all of them.

The gang members in this example do not care about *Doña* Lupe or protect her as a neighbour living in their territory. She tries to solve her problem with them in an informal way by asking the gang members to take their business elsewhere, but they are unwilling to take her situation into account. When she tries to interfere with the lucrative business of the gang members by notifying the police, they start to threaten her and her family. *Doña* Lupe initially hoped to solve her problem with the gang members in an informal way. She did not complain about the drug dealing per se, even though she was not happy with that, but about the fact that it affected her business. When this strategy did not work, she notified the police, hoping that they would protect her. Instead, the police provided security to the highest bidder: the gang members.

Policemen in Colonia Jalisco readily admitted to this kind of protection deal (although such confessions of course always concerned other policemen, never themselves).[14] The fact that *Doña* Lupe notified the police also indicates that there was a chance that the police could have acted in her interest, however. Or, as another informant explained, you need to know a "good" cop, one that takes care of your interests. If you had such a relation, it did not matter whether the interests for which you sought their protection were legal or illegal.

Security in Colonia Jalisco was thus a complicated matter that left residents in a vulnerable position since policing was inadequate and their options to buy security were limited due to their limited resources. Any formal initiative among neighbors to develop alternative security strategies was likely to interfere with the interests of armed actors in the *colonia*, and many residents therefore preferred to simply mind their own business and avoid such initiatives because they were afraid of getting into trouble. The next section explores some of these fears and ambiguities relating to the workings of the security market in Colonia Jalisco by focusing on the local youth gang as a violence entrepreneur.

THE GANG AS A VIOLENCE ENTREPRENEUR

Participant observation provides the researcher with a unique opportunity to observe the subjects that are studied in their own environment. As such, research is not a controlled experiment; one is not able to fully control situations. This exposes the researcher to a certain risk and presents a range of ethical dilemmas in situations of chronic insecurity (see Rodgers 2007). Nevertheless, even though such participant observation can sometimes become a rather unpleasant experience it can be very insightful, as the fieldwork episode presented below illustrates well:

> It was a Thursday afternoon when I walked down to Maria's house in Colonia Jalisco. It was sunny and the streets were quiet. Some children greeted me. As I turned around the corner, a guy known as *el alacrán* [the scorpion] came walking towards me. I did not really know him, except from seeing him in the street. He was a drug addict who often hung around with the guys of the youth gang here. He was not exactly a teenager anymore, although his precise age was hard to guess. His body showed several tattoos. A large image of the virgin of Guadalupe, right in the middle of his chest, was the most striking one. He greeted me and stopped me in the middle of the street by blocking my way. He had a plastic cup in his hand and said that he wanted to give it to me. I told him that was very kind, but that it was not necessary. That he should keep it. I told him I had to go, but all of a sudden his mood seemed to change. It all happened so quickly and just when the alarm bells in my head started ringing, it was too late, and he grasped my arm firmly. He was surprisingly strong, and maneuvered me in such a position that I could not move anymore. I told him to let me go, but he just responded by twisting my arm further and further. He started to feel me up. "This is really running out of hand," I thought. "What do I remember from the self-defence class? Is he armed? I have to . . ."

"Hey, you son of a bitch, what the hell do you think you are doing! Let
her go!" shouted some very angry neighbors, who came running towards us. *El alacrán* was startled by the women who suddenly appeared and finally let me go. I was relieved when the women took me
by the arm, leading me towards their houses down the road, while they
were still swearing at my assailant and tried to comfort me at the same
time. How could this happen! What did he do? Was there no one
around to help you? You have to be careful! Questions and advice were
bestowed upon me. We all sat down in front of Martha's house and I
had to tell them precisely what happened. "It is such a disgrace!
Looked what happened to you! And we do not even know who he is.
He does not even live around here, that scumbag! And he is always so
dirty, hanging around in the street. Our children play here in the street
too. Today it is you, next thing you know he will do something to our
children! This has to stop, we need to do something."

Something needed to be done, that was for sure. All the women agreed
that action should be undertaken. It was not really up to me anymore if
I wanted something to be done, it was a decision already made. So we
deliberated on the options. It basically came down to two possibilities.
We could either inform the police and see if they would do something
about it or we could go talk to "the boys," the gang members, to see if
they would help.

The neighbors who saved me wanted to undertake action for two reasons. On the one hand, because I had good personal relationships with
several of them, and they felt responsible for my security in their community. On the other hand, action was also required because of what they
felt could potentially happen to them or to their children if nothing were
done. Security in this case thus proved to be a community issue, not just
something individual. Beyond these motives, the neighbors considered
two courses of actions to be potentially suitable means of dealing with
the incident. One was reporting it to the police, the second one was to
notify the local youth gang.

Discussions about these two options seemed highly paradoxical at
times. The neighbors clearly considered policemen to be incompetent
good-for-nothings, the "bad guys" whom they labelled "dogs," criminals
even. They considered that the police would not necessarily help because
they were "lazy," "afraid," "did not take an interest," or "had some kind
of deal with criminals." Indeed, there was a palpable fear that notifying
the police might even backfire. Going to the police would also mean
engaging in a bureaucratic procedure that would probably take up a lot
of time. Bearing in mind such attitudes toward the police, and the bad
experiences that many local residents of Colonia Jalisco had had with
them, it is remarkable that filing a complaint with the police was regarded a viable option at all. At the same time, however, the police were
clearly seen as having the legitimate power to arrest criminals, and for

this reason it was thought that they might perhaps be able to intervene. There was also a sense that there was little to lose in this particular case. Not only was it "the right thing to do," since it was the official and legal means of handling such issues, but *el alacrán* was also not likely to enjoy police protection, so there was little risk that notifying the police would be counterproductive.

This deliberation over whether to call the police in this case was not an exception, as I was able to ascertain later through individual interviews. Local residents all suggested that whenever a violent event occurred in the *colonia*, for example, a fight between gang members or a dispute among neighbors, witnesses always considered the option of whether or not to call the police, asking questions such as the following: "Should I call the police?" "Has someone called the police yet?" or "Why has no one called the police yet?" Even if the authorities were not called in the end, the option was almost always considered. Despite the low opinion people had of the police in general it is important that the police were not "out of the game," so to speak. They were always perceived as a potential player within the wider security market.

No decision had been reached in the case of *el alacrán* when by coincidence a police patrol showed up at the other end of the street:

> While still talking about the possibilities of both solutions, we saw a patrol car with four policemen coming around the corner on the far end of the street. In the house on the corner lives a policeman and the patrol car could often be seen parked in front of the house, while the policemen would go in to get a drink or something to eat. Since they were here now anyway, we might as well go talk to them about the situation, Emilia suggested. Two of the neighbors accompanied me to the police car. The cops had parked the car and just got out when we approached them.

> "Excuse me sir, we have a problem, maybe you can help," Martha said. The policeman stood there in front of us, his body straight up, his legs somewhat apart, and holding his machinegun across his chest with both hands. Dark sunglasses hid his eyes when he looked at us. "What's up?" he said, with a short nod of the head. His colleagues stood on the other side of the car, listening to our conversation. We explained to the policeman what happened. "Hmmm, so, but no one died, right? Nothing really happened, no crime was committed . . ." "He felt her up!" Martha exclaimed "Something did happen!" "Well, there is not much we can do now. Call us if you see the guy, or if something happens again. This is the phone number of the station," the policeman said while he handed out a small card. I tried to describe what *el alacrán* looked like, so maybe they could look out for him, but the policeman started laughing. "A large tattoo of the virgin of Guadalupe in the middle of his chest! That could be anyone!" As there was

nothing more the cops could do for us, we thanked the policemen for their attention and went back to the other women.

"We should have known! This was a waste of time! Who could have thought they would really do something? They are useless." Some swearwords followed out of Martha's mouth. She was worked up about the policemen's behaviour and their arrogant attitude; showing no compassion or interest in helping us. Maria took the situation somewhat calmer. It was the kind of disappointment we could have seen coming, she argued. We went back to the other neighbors and told them what happened with the police. Everybody agreed that this meant that we had to talk to "the guys."

Maria's reaction makes it clear that a fruitless outcome to their efforts was anticipated, but it nevertheless led to feelings of frustration, as expressed by Martha. When we joined the other women again, and told them about our conversation with the police, some words of disapproval were uttered, but as no one had had very high hopes that the police would act, we moved rapidly to consider the other option: notifying the gang members. These we could go and talk to right away, as they usually gathered on the very same street corner where the incident with *el alacrán* occurred, so it did not take long to get hold of one of them:

Panzas, one of the older gang members, came walking down the street. "He is the right guy to talk to," one of the women said to me. Martha called Panzas over, and said that we needed his help. He walked over, and she told him what happened this afternoon. "You know this guy right?" Martha asked, referring to *el alacrán*. "Yeah I do, I know who you are talking about." "So this time it is her," Martha said, pointing at me, "and what will happen next? We cannot tolerate this! He just a piece of dirt; he has been bothering us for a while hanging around in the street where our children play without us knowing what he is up to, looking all dirty and drugged up." "So what do you want me to do then? Should I hit him, or go talk to him first?" Panzas replied. "Well, maybe talk to him first," Martha said while she looked around to the other women who nodded in approval. "Ok, I will see what I can do, all right." Panzas then went off and we continued talking. We went in to Maria's house and spent the rest of the afternoon there.

The neighbours knew whom to approach among the gang members, they knew who was the right broker. Panzas could not be replaced by any other gang member. He was one of the "old" gang members, less active in the gang than previously, and trying to change his behaviour patterns—although not always succeeding—since becoming involved in the local church and settling down with a girlfriend. He nevertheless still had a lot of influence on more active current gang members, and was known as someone not to mess with. He had been involved in violent crime and murder more than once, and it was clear that he would do so again if the situation warranted. As a result, Panzas had a lot of leverage and was the best person to turn to about the issue of *el alacrán*.

The option of asking the youth gang to solve the problem might suggest a good relationship between the gang members and the neighbors. Certainly, the neighbors who approached Panzas addressed him in a familiar tone. This however fails to underline the ambiguity of the relationship between neighbourhood inhabitants and gang members. On the one hand, gangs were seen as a threat because of the violence that they were inherently associated with—as *Doña* Lupe's story underscored—and there was a generalized avoidance of conflict with the gangs precisely because they did not refrain from resorting to violence to sort matters out. Gang members were also considered especially dangerous when they were under the influence of drugs, as their behaviour often became unpredictable. Certain drugs—crack cocaine, for example—make their users very violent or extremely anxious, to the extent that they can end up attacking their friends and neighbors (see also Rodgers 2006a, 280). On the other hand, the individual gang members are generally not considered inherently bad people, but rather victims of the circumstances in which they grew up: poverty, family abuse, broken homes, and so on. They were more often than not the kids whom local neighbourhood inhabitants had seen growing up; indeed, they were often their own children or grandchildren, or the kids of a next-door neighbour or of a close friend or relative living around the corner. Most neighbors would greet the gang members in the street and vice versa, exemplifying a certain level of mutual respect and understanding. Gang members would also benefit from their good relations with the local community. If they got into trouble with the police, gang members could call upon help from the community or else a neighbour with some nursing skills might look after gang members wounded in fights and in need of medical care. Some neighbors also talked about the gang as "the boys" (*los muchachos*), implying a certain sense of affection.

At the same time, however, a significant part of the insecurity in the neighbourhood was clearly caused by the very existence of violent youth gangs and the fighting between them. Although gang members were often part of the security solution for local residents, they were also frequently the cause of the violence problem. Even if each youth gang was likely to offer some protection to neighbors living on their turf, and protected them from the violence of rival gangs, as Volkov (2002) has pointed out, it is the violent competition between the—in this case—youth gangs that enhances the need for protection, while their actions are also limited and governed by other armed actors such as rival gangs, drug dealers, and the police. The gang is approached not because they systematically fulfill an order-keeping task in the community, but as members of the community that help out the neighbors who see no other effective solution to their problem. If the police have been able to take

care of the situation in a satisfactory manner, there would have been no
need to involve the youth gang. To this extent, the state is not absent in
Colonia Jalisco, and the youth gang is not a local parallel power structure
that makes the law. Rather, it is the ineffectiveness of the police that
makes the neighbors turn to the gang.

This was something that was also clear from the way that the problem
with *el alacrán* was dealt with through Panzas. Contrarily to the police,
the gang members were considered accessible, the justice process was
quick, and there was some "democratic" deliberation about a suitable
punishment. Yet even this solution contained the seeds of a certain ambiguity, as became obvious a few hours later:

> A few hours later when it was time for me to go home, Martha and
> Maria decided to walk up with me, just to be sure. We were on our way
> when Martha said somewhat alarmed: "Oh, Gosh, there he is . . ." *El
> alacrán* came walking towards us. Maria grabbed me tighter by the arm,
> as if that would protect me. *Alacrán* said he wanted to apologize to
> Martha and Maria. He was sorry he had caused trouble and told them
> he would never ever bother them or their children; he had no bad
> intentions and was really sorry that he upset them. As for me, he saw
> the whole affair a little differently: "Who did you think you are? You're
> not even from here, you stupid foreigner, you stupid American or Ca-
> nadian or I don't care where you come from! I'm not finished with you
> yet, I'll get you, you're going to pay for this," he said angrily. The
> women looked at him angrily, took me each by an arm, and we quickly
> walked on: "Come on, let's go." They warned me: "You have to be
> careful Monique. Tomorrow if you come down, give us a call first, and
> we will come to pick you up, all right?" I agreed, and we said good-
> bye.
>
> The next day I was picked up by Maria and her grown-up daughter
> Lula. They told me what had happened after I left. Maria and Martha
> had been upset by the threats and had gone back to Panzas to tell him
> about what happened. The gang members consequently made clear to
> *el alacrán* that they were serious and warned him not to show his face
> again in the neighbourhood. *El alacrán* clearly took the hint this time.
> Martha had also told her husband, Antonio—who had a reputation for
> being a tough cookie—about the whole affair, and later that afternoon
> he told me how he had run into *el alacrán* in the street in the morning,
> and when he tried to approach him because of what had happened, *el
> alacrán* panicked and ran, shouting to that he would go away, that he
> knew they would kill him, and that he would not show his face again.
>
> *El alacrán* stayed away for the rest of my stay, but I didn't have to
> worry anymore. Later that afternoon Pascual, one of the gang mem-
> bers, came up to me and told me that I did not need to be concerned
> about my safety around the neighbourhood, because I was considered
> a friend of the people who live there. They were watching out for me, I
> was told, and they would be on top of things before anything would
> happen to me.

It was obvious that Panzas had acted on his word when *el alacrán* came to apologize to Maria and Martha. He was aware that he had crossed a line, but only in relation to them, however. From his point of view, I was an obvious outsider to the community and he therefore initially felt that the warning he had received referred only to the trouble he had caused the community, not me. However, the broader nature of the gang's warning became clear when both gang members and Antonio told him that he should leave me alone as well. *El alacrán* knew then that he was in trouble and did not take the warning lightly this time.

CONCLUSION

This chapter has discussed the complexities of the local security market that arose in Colonia Jalisco in the face of high levels of violence and the absence of adequate policing. The chronic public insecurity has led to the need for autonomous local forms of security service provision. Different violence entrepreneurs compete with each other and the state in these spaces, and alternative power structures can arise in a space left empty by the lack of universally protective state structures. As Volkov (2002, 20) has pointed out, the provision of security as a commodity does not depend solely on the level of demand and available choices. The provision of security is sometimes also forced upon the "clients" with varying degrees of coercion, insofar as not obtaining security can expose clients to threats of violence by violence entrepreneurs.

What the more economic approach to the security market of Elwert (1999), Volkov (2002), and Bandiera (2003) fails to take into account, however, are the influences of contextual social relations. As I hope is clear from the case study presented, coercion is not the only factor that influences the processes of offer and demand. The example of the youth gang in Colonia Jalisco shows the multiple complex relations between the residents and violence entrepreneurs, which are not only economic in nature, but also social. The gang members originate from the community and are the children, siblings, friends, and partners of local residents. The gang as a whole might be despised as a cause of violence and insecurity, but the individual gang members are integrated into the social fabric of the community. This condition makes it much harder to tackle the perverse relationship the gang maintains with the wider community, and places residents in a vulnerable position.

The residents need to manoeuvre between the police as a legal state institution for security, but with often illegitimately acting policemen and illegal social phenomena such as gangs that arguably constitute legitimate violence entrepreneurs within the context of the local security market. Within their territory, gangs can indeed enhance a sense of order by keeping out other youth gangs and individual criminals. However, at the same time their power is limited by the interaction of other armed actors, such as rival gangs, the police, and drug dealers. Moreover, there is no guarantee that the gang members will actually provide security to the residents. Certain economic interests can either have more importance, or become more important, than providing security services (see Rodgers 2006a), and the gang members are of course themselves sources of insecurity at a general level, even within their own territory. Such ambiguities make the relationship between local residnts and local gangs extremely difficult and volatile.

To this extent, it can be argued that the alternative security strategies and services of violence entrepreneurs that emerge in low income neighbourhoods tend to offer limited solutions for a real improvement in security and safer living conditions. This is perhaps the reason why citizens continue to hope for a state-based solution to their tragic predicament, even though the state institution of the police force has lost a considerable part of its legitimacy.

REFERENCES

Bandiera, O. 2003. "Land Reform, the Market for Protection, and the Origins of the Sicilian Mafia: Theory and Evidence." *The Journal of Law, Economics & Organization* 19, no. 1: 218–244.

Caldeira, T. 2000. *City of Walls: Crime, Segregation and Citizenship in São Paulo*. Berkeley: University of California Press .

Denissen, M. 2008. *"Winning Small Battles, Losing the War": Police Violence, the Movimiento del Dolor, and Democracy in Post-Authoritarian Argentina*. Amsterdam: Rozenberg Publishers.

Elwert, G. 1999. "Markets of Violence." In *Dynamics of Violence: Processes of Escalation and De-escalation in Violent Group Conflicts*, edited by G. Elwert, S. Feuchtwang, and D. Neuberts, 85-102. Berlin: Duncker and Humblot:

Gay, R. 2005. *Lucia: Testimonies of a Brazilian Drug Dealer's Woman*. Philadelphia: Temple University Press.

Goldstein, D. 2004. *The Spectacular City: Violence and Performance in Urban Bolivia*. Durham: Duke University Press.

Haber, P. 1994. "The Art and Implications of Political Restructuring in Mexico: The Case of Urban Popular Movements." In *The Politics of Economic Restructuring. State–Society Relations and Regime Change in Mexico*, edited by L. Cook, K. Middlebrook, and J. Molinar, 277-302. San Diego: University of California, Centre for U.S.-Mexican Studies.

Koonings, K., and D. Kruijt. 2004. "Armed Actors, Organized Violence and State Failure in Latin America: a Survey of Issues and Arguments." In *Armed Actors: Organized Violence and State failure in Latin America*, edited by K. Koonings and D. Kruijt, 5-15. London: Zed Books.

Koonings, K., and D. Kruijt. 2007. "Fractured Cities, Second-Class Citizenship and Urban Violence." In *Fractured Cities, Social Exclusion, Urban Violence and Contested Spaces in Latin America*, edited by K. Koonings and D. Kruijt, 7-22. London: Zed Books.

Kruijt, D. 2008. "Violencia y pobreza en América Latina: los actores armados." *Pensamiento Iberoamericano* 2: 57–70.

Kruijt, D., and K. Koonings. 1999. "Introduction: Violence and Fear in Latin America." In *Societies of Fear: The Legacy of Civil War, Violence and Terror in Latin America*, edited by K. Koonings and D. Kruijt, 1-27. London: Zed Books.

Leach, E. 1977. *Custom, Law, and Terrorist Violence*. Edinburgh: Edinburgh University Press.

Leeds, E. 1996. "Cocaine and Parallel Polities in the Brazilian Urban Periphery: Constraints on Local-Level Democratization." *Latin American Research Review* 31, no. 3: 47-83.

Leeds, E. 2007. "Rio de Janeiro." In *Fractured Cities, Social Exclusion, Urban Violence and Contested Spaces in Latin America*, edited by K. Koonings and D. Kruijt, 23-35. London: Zed Books.

Moloeznik, M. 2003. "Seguridad Pública, Justicia Penal y Derechos Humanos en el Estado de Jalisco (1995–2002)." USMEX 2003–2004 Working Paper Series, originally prepared for the conference on *Reforming the Administration of Justice in Mexico* at the Center for U.S.-Mexican Studies, May 15-17, 2003. http://repositories.cdlib.org/cgi/viewcontent.cgi?article=1034&context=usmex.

Moser, C., and C. McIlwaine. 2004. *Encounters with Violence in Latin America: Urban Poor Perceptions from Colombia and Guatemala*. London: Routledge.

Nuijten, M. 2003. *Power, Community and the State: The Political Anthropology of Organisation in Mexico*. London: Pluto Press.

Ramírez Sáiz, J. M., and A. Chávez Sevilla. 1998. "La seguridad pública, talón de Aquiles de los ayuntamientos panistas del AMG." In *Cómo gobiernan Guadalajara? Demandas ciudadanas y respuestas de los ayuntamientos*, edited by J. M. Ramírez Sáiz, 217-248. Guadalajara: Instituto de Investigaciones Sociales; UNAM Centro Universitario de Ciencias Sociales y Humanidades de la Universidad de Guadalajara.

Regalado Santillán, J. 2001. "Sociedad y Gobierno: La Seguridad Publica en Guadalajara." PhD diss., University of Guadalajara and the Centro de Investigaciones y Estudios Superiores en Antropología Social (CIESAS) del Occidente .

Rodgers, D. 2006a. "Living in the Shadow of Death: Gangs, Violence, and Social Order in Urban Nicaragua, 1996-2002." *Journal of Latin American Studies* 38, no. 2: 267-292.

Rodgers, D. 2006b. "The State as a Gang: Conceptualizing the Governmentality of Violence in Contemporary Nicaragua." *Critique of Anthropology* 26, no. 3: 315-330.

Rodgers, D. 2007. "Joining the Gang and Becoming a *broder*: The Violence of Ethnography in Contemporary Nicaragua." *Bulletin of Latin American Research* 27, no. 4: 444-461.

Sánchez Jankowski, M. 1991. *Islands in the Street: Gangs and American Urban Society*. Berkeley: University of California Press.

Secretaría de Seguridad Pública. 2005. *Estado y Seguridad Pública*. Mexico City: Fondo de Cultura Económica/Secretaría de Seguridad Pública.

Shah, A. 2006. "Markets of Protection: The "Terrorist" Maoist Movement and the State in Jharkhand, India," *Critique of Anthropology*, vol. 26, no. 3: 297–314.

Sluka, J. 2000. *Death Squad: The Anthropology of State Terror*. Philadelphia: University of Pennsylvania Press.

Suárez de Garay, M. 2006. *Los policías: Una averiguación antropológica*. Guadalajara: ITESO/Universidad de Guadalajara.

Tilly, C. 1985. "War Making and State Making as Organized Crime," In *Bringing the State Back In*, edited by P. Evans, D. Rueschemeyer, and T. Skocpol, 169-191. Cambridge: Cambridge University Press.

Venkatesh, S. 1997. "The Social Organization of Street Gang Activity in an Urban Ghetto," *The American Journal of Sociology*, vol. 103, no. 1: 82–111.

Volkov, V. 2002. *Violent Entrepreneurs: The Use of Force in the Making of Russian Capitalism*. Ithaca: Cornell University Press.

Weber, M. 1972. *Gezag en bureaucratie*. Rotterdam and Antwerpen: Universitaire Pers and Standaard Wetenschappelijke Uitgeverij (compilation by A. van Braam).

Weber, M. 1995. *Political Writings*. Cambridge: Cambridge University Press (compilation by P. Lassman and R. Speirs).

Zaluar, A. 2004. "Urban Violence and Drug Warfare in Brazil, in *Armed Actors: Organized Violence and State failure in Latin America*, edited by K. Koonings and D. Kruijt, 139-154. London: Zed Books.

NOTES

1. This chapter has previously been published as: Monique Sonnevelt. 2009. "Security at Stake: Dealing with Violence and Public (In)Security in a Popular Neighbourhood in Guadalajara, Mexico." In *Youth Violence in Latin America: Gangs and Juvenile Justice in Perspective*, edited by Gareth A. Jones and Dennis Rodgers, 45-62. London: Palgrave Macmillan. Reprinted with permission.

2. Despite the terminology, I want to stress that these structures intertwine and interact with the state and should therefore not be seen as completely separate from the state.

3. My research revolved around two contrasting case studies of two different communities in Guadalajara's Metropolitan Zone: a working-class *colonia popular* and a well-to-do gated community. I conducted extensive anthropological fieldwork in both during 2006 and 2007. The focus of this chapter is on the security strategies and the market of the urban poor in Colonia Jalisco, where I lived for eight months during my fieldwork in 2006. In 2007 my fieldwork had a stronger emphasis on the gated community, but I nevertheless frequently visited Colonia Jalisco.

4. According to Article 21 of the Mexican constitution, public security is a task of the state (Moloeznik 2003, 2). Public security is described by the Mexican Ministry of Public Security as the primary obligation of the state and as presently the most important resource of a society, claiming that with security, citizens have the possibility to develop their complete potential and to freely exercise their rights (Secretaría de Seguridad Pública 2005, 9).

5. The idea of the security market is derived from the model of "markets of violence" as presented by Elwert (1999) and the "market of protection" used by Volkov (2002) and Shah (2006). Volkov (2002) uses the market of protection in reference to his study of the proliferation of armed actors, especially extortion, in the context of market reforms and the emergence of private businesses in Russia.

6. Uncivil society consists of "agents or groups that force their interest upon the public domain on the basis of coercion and violence, in such a way that the legitimate aspirations of other groups or sectors in civil society are jeopardized and the rule of law is fragmented or shattered" (Koonings and Kruijt 2004, 7).

7. I use this notion after Koonings and Kruijt (1999; 2004). Governance voids can be defined as "spaces or domains in which the legitimate state is effectively absent in the face of armed actors that abide by the rule of force—but also in the internal erosion of the capacity and willingness of state agents themselves to abide the rule of law" (Koonings and Kruijt 2004, 2).

8. The *ejido* constitutes a form of land tenure that was established as a result of the Mexican Revolution (1910–1917) in which landless peasants demanded "land and liberty" from the state (Nuijten 2003, 4). Right holders in the *ejido* community could use the lands assigned to them for agriculture, but they were not the legal owners and as a result were not entitled to sell these lands.

9. This stigma is, for example, illustrated by the fact that residents of Colonia Jalisco see their chances of obtaining a job or a loan decrease steadily when they use their original address on an application form.

10. It has to be noted, though, that many residents stated that the current violence is a little less intense than a few years ago. Although it goes beyond the extent of this chapter to discuss why violence has become less intense, I want to point out there is no clear indication that there is a general, perceptible trend of the area becoming structurally safer over time, but the situation is somewhat calmer after an explosion of violence.

11. These were the ones that had the largest territories and had been around for a while.

12. Protecting people from the police is, particularly with reference to youth gang members, something that is widely recognized among the local population, with neighbors, in fact, often criticizing each other for doing so. At the same time, however, it is a very understandable act, because gang members and neighbourhood residents generally have close personal ties with each other. They are each other's' relatives, friends, or friends' relatives.

13. The names of informants are pseudonyms.

14. On January 22, 2008, local radio announced that two policemen in Colonia Jalisco had been reported to the PGR for protecting a local drug dealer who had his business in a seedy bar called *El Dessierto* in Colonia Jalisco. Such reports are rare, however, because the police usually deal with these kinds of affairs internally. A corrupt policeman will generally be transferred to another department rather than punished (interview with police officer Colonia Jalisco).

FOURTEEN

Among Comrades

*(Dis)trust in Ethnographic Fieldwork with Former
Salvadoran Revolutionaries*

Ralph Sprenkels

INTRODUCTION

What happens when a former revolutionary activist returns to work with
his comrades from before only now in the role of the political anthropologist? Indeed, contacts and revolutionary credentials come in handy. In
my case, it helped me to perform fieldwork inside a major political party,
in meetings and conversations normally closed-off to outsiders. However, this level of access did not mean that I was always trusted. The revolutionary circles I formerly participated in had become increasingly divided among competing factions. Not only did my informants have
doubts about my work (what is this guy actually going to write about
us?) but also about my political preferences and loyalties (what faction
does he work for or sympathize with?). Such interpellation forced me to
think what it means to perform ethnographic fieldwork in a setting rife
with distrust.

Far beyond their possible impact on fieldwork, trust and distrust have
increasingly become acknowledged as central feature of social, political
and economical life. (Dis)trust is best understood as a dynamic compo-
nent of the negotiation of interpersonal relationships, consisting "of placing valued outcomes at risk to others' malfeasance, mistakes, or failures"
(Tilly 2005, 12). One way in which it is operated or manipulated is
through storytelling practices that indicate "whom we can trust, and

whom we should mistrust" (Tilly 2010, 388). By definition, trust comes in degrees, as does its antipode. Moreover, the performance of trust is not the same as trust itself. For example, as the Filipina anthropologist Anna Guevarra has pointed out, when her research became politically delicate, the participants' vocal claim to trust her was "essentially about their distrust of what [she] would do with the knowledge [she] gained about them" (2006, 539). In my own fieldwork among former participants in El Salvador's revolutionary movement I found that, rather than uncritically claiming trust based on my previous years of revolutionary militancy, it might be more fruitful to look at how my former comrades actually claimed, contested and negotiated trust with me and others, and to explore how this correlated to "the subterranean logics of the exercise of power" (Chabal and Daloz 2006, 262) among those concerned.

EL SALVADOR'S FMLN: DISILLUSIONMENT AND POST-WAR ASCENDENCY

I became involved with the El Salvador's revolutionary movement in 1990, while studying in Mexico. First I participated in a small FPL collective in the city of Guadalajara. The FPL stood for "Fuerzas Populares de Liberación" or "Popular Liberation Forces," the largest of the five political-military organizations that integrated the FMLN,[1] the united guerrilla front engaged in a full-on battle with the Salvadoran military and its US patrons since 1981. Early 1992, shortly after the signing of the Peace Accords, I was transferred from Mexico to El Salvador, and assigned to work the FPL structures in Chalatenango, a stronghold area during the war. In 1995, the FPL formally dissolved to become integrated within the FMLN as a legal political party.

During my four years of participation within the FPL I was involved in a range of tasks, such as fundraising, propaganda, education, and research into the human rights violations perpetrated by the military and the death squads during the war. With the FPL falling apart and the FMLN dedicated to electoral politics, I continued to work in human rights research and activism in El Salvador for many more years. I met and eventually married a Salvadoran woman whose family had also been heavily involved in the revolutionary movement. Up until the present day I have remained closely connected to circles around El Salvador's former revolutionary movement.

Thus, in 2009, when I started ethnographic fieldwork on the post-war developments in what remained of the Salvadoran revolutionary movement, for me personally it meant re-entering familiar turf, but in a new role. I wanted to understand better why the FMLN had developed the way it had, including the impact of the war on the movement and its participants. I was keenly aware that, in spite of the eventual successes of the FMLN as a political party, for many involved in the revolutionary movement the transformation from the guerrilla groups to a political party was difficult and even painful. As I had witnessed up close, the 1995 dissolution of the FPL qualified as an unsettling experience for many of its integrants. FPL affiliation meant to be part of a community of people with extraordinary levels of internal cohesion and solidarity. Its only horizon was revolutionary triumph (Kruijt 2008). For many revolutionaries, the movement had been their live project. Shared history and purpose created very strong interpersonal ties. The revolutionary organization was the militants' most priced possession, to be protected at any cost. Stories of audacity and sacrifice imbued the organization with an almost mythical stature. At the same time, it was also true that the FPL had accumulated significant wear and tear, associated with deep losses, missed opportunities, and internal abuse or internal strife. Furthermore, the way the leadership handled the transition process after the war also resulted in discontent among many former cadres and rank-and-file. The demobilization process, the meagre benefits of the post-war reintegration projects and the dissolution of the FPL generated many questions among militants regarding the worth of revolutionary endeavours (Sprenkels 2014a).

The FMLN first post-war years as a political party were highly conflictive, including several important splits and purges, which contributed to further distress among the militancy. In 1994, for example, two out of the five historical guerrilla groups left the FMLN to set up their own political party. Meanwhile, the factions remaining within the FMLN engaged in an increasingly polarized dispute between so-called *renovadores* and *ortodoxos* over the control of the political agenda and the party apparatus. At the same time however the FMLN was still able to gradually consolidate its position as main opposition party, and eventually win the presidential elections in 2009, 17 years after the Peace Accords. In 2014, the FMLN retained the presidency, albeit with a tiny margin over the rival candidate of the right-wing ARENA party (Colburn and Cruz 2014).[2]

The FMLN's electoral success has to be understood at the light of its decades-long power struggle with ARENA. The main and most radically opposed contenders during the war continued to be the country's dominant political forces until present days. These two blocks recur to wartime antagonisms and rhetoric to polarize the political landscape. Thus, Salvadoran democracy has been characterized as "the continuation of war through other means,"[3] and has been accompanied by the recycling of non-democratic political tools, like clientelism and fear mongering, including some fleeting political violence (Montoya 2012; Sprenkels 2014b). Together with poverty and endemic violence, the above contributed to widespread "democratic disenchantment" in post-war El Salvador (Moodie 2010, 145).

At the light of post-war developments, many former revolutionaries became disillusioned and questioned whether their struggle and sacrifices had been worthwhile.[4] Nonetheless and at the same time, electoral politics gradually opened new opportunities. As a result, a significant amount of former revolutionaries over time found employment in the public sector. After the FMLN won the 2009 Presidential elections, this tendency was strengthened further. Electoral success also translated in intense internal competition over access to public office, often fuelling new internal disputes (Allison and Martín Alvarez 2012). Thus, somewhat contradictorily, during the two post-war decades, El Salvador's former insurgents experienced both widespread disillusionment as well as increased political ascendency.

SETTING UP FIELDWORK

My fieldwork with guerrilla veterans started in 2009, just after the FMLN won its first presidency. I visited the FMLN's main office in San Salvador in order to ask the FMLN party secretary, a former FPL *comandante*, for permission to perform ethnographic fieldwork inside party structures, particularly with the veterans' sector. In the first two years after the war, when the FPL was still functioning, this office, known as "1316," functioned as the FPL headquarters. When the FPL dissolved, the building, a former upper-middle class residence that had been gradually transformed into an office, was donated to the FMLN. I had visited 1316 regularly during my years with the FPL, but only sporadically afterwards.

What struck me in 2009 was how much the office had changed. Before, there had only been security at the entrance. Once you were inside you could go wherever you wanted. In the evenings, portable mattresses were pulled out, and comrades would use the floors to lie down and spend the night. Now, the inside of the building had become much more orderly and formal and included three visible security parameters. At the entrance, at the door from the waiting room into the rest of the office, and finally, an electrical gate to the second floor, which was opened for me from upstairs. This was where some of the most important party members now had their offices. An appointment was required, which three people had to verify before all the doors were opened.

As several veterans pointed out to me, the stronger security measures at 1316 were not so much connected to political threats, but rather functioned as an attempt to prevent uncontrolled constituent access to leadership. Many veterans would look up the comandantes they knew from before in order to obtain some kind of assistance for dealing with their most pressing problems; hence, the importance of the waiting room and the metal gate to the second floor. When the FMLN won the elections in

2009 it became worse, and 1316 was flooded with FMLN veterans looking for employment opportunities.[5]

In retrospect, my enthusiasm for ethnography led me to underestimate the complexity of the political and ethical dilemmas I would come across in the course of fieldwork. Even though I explained to all informants that my research project was motivated by academic interests — and not political ones — my historical ties to the FPL were instrumental to arranging different aspects of fieldwork in and around the FMLN. Setting up meetings with people I knew from previous years I had the benefit of personal consideration. My activist years helped me to gain a level of access that would probably have been much harder to obtain for a researcher without previous affiliations. I was often introduced as someone with revolutionary credentials, someone that could be trusted.

POST-INSURGENCY: A DIVIDED SOCIAL FIELD

But did the fact that some said I could be trusted also mean that others trusted me? The problem was that the FMLN veterans did not trust each other very much either. Many were wary of the politics of others. For example, several important former FPL members had left the FMLN in the post-war years, and some had become outspoken critics of the party. On the other hand, some of those who remained loyal to the FMLN did not hesitate to label these critics as "traitors." Other comrades resented the fact that former members of the Communist Party were now often better positioned within the FMLN than members of other guerrilla groups, and denounced what they saw as nepotism or worse.

As I confirmed throughout my fieldwork, post-insurgency[6] was a contentious and divided field, in which different groups of former insurgents often saw others as rivals, and frequently said terrible things about each other behind each other's backs. They engaged in different forms of "malicious gossip and character assassination," (Robben 1995, 94) regularly referring to or insinuating their former comrades' involvement in corruption, intimidation and other unsavoury plots. Thus, even though my former affiliation with the FPL provided me with a solid basis for informed conversation on the internalities of the FMLN and its post-war adjustments, it did not necessarily mean that mutual trust was a given, and that there were no apprehensions with regard to what could be said, both by my informants and by myself.

I first realised that I had put myself in a difficult position after a few weeks of fieldwork, while visiting the toilet in one of the FMLN offices in the centre of San Salvador. Outside, in the roofed patio, the weekly Monday evening meeting of the "official sector" of FMLN war veterans was taking place. I could clearly hear everything that was being said, while temporarily absent from the meeting, and invisible for the rest of the participants. The walls of the bathroom had been painted, not very long ago, in the red and white, the FMLN colours. On the inside of the door someone had scribbled with a blue permanent marker the phrase "Opportunists out of the FMLN." Below, standing out in thick black ink, was written "Treason Is Paid with Blood," the word "blood" triple underlined.[7]

This last phrase threw me off. How can treason still be a salient concept, with military structures and discipline long dissolved? Why do contemporary political disagreements give rise to such violent passions? These questions were more painful at the light of the details that had recently been revealed about purges within the guerrilla groups.[8] If correlated to the fact that several hundred revolutionaries had been executed during armed struggle at the hands of their comrades as a result of (false) accusations of treason and infiltration, the threat on the bathroom door acquired an even sinister tone.

Then a feeling of wariness overcame me. I slipped into pondering my own personal situation. How does this group of veterans actually see me, as I take notes in their meetings? To what extent do they actually trust me? Could I be labelled at some point as an opportunist as well, as someone who no longer had any legitimate business there? Was I not there in service of social science or myself (depending on the perspective) and ultimately not (or not necessarily) for the benefit of the FMLN? Worse, could I be called a "traitor" if my writing disclosed things that some wanted to keep hidden or voiced opinions some did not want to hear?

And how would it make me feel if I were to be referred to as a traitor? I sensed that my personal identification with the FMLN—especially with friends and loved-ones circulating in and around the FMLN—was large enough to make me not only uncomfortable, but also hurt, by such an accusation. Could this sentiment potentially influence my research? Would I allow myself to write freely, even if some of my informants might not like some of my findings, and might then even claim a violation of trust, which some could then propel into the troublesome semantics of treason? To what extent could I or should I (still) be subjected to the moral discipline of the revolutionary movement?

These five-plus minutes of intimate seclusion turned the implicit idea I had of myself as a trusted insider to FMLN politics on its head. I frequently and sometimes involuntarily returned to the admonitions on the FMLN bathroom door throughout the remainder of my fieldwork. I concluded that the best way to avoid being drawn into the contentious dynamics of post-insurgency was by documenting and analyzing these dynamics as thoroughly as I could. I sought to make myself more immune to self-censorship by including and interpreting the politics of distrust as one of the features of post-insurgency.

It proved to be a fruitful approach. Throughout my fieldwork, I was recurrently confronted with the peddling of distrust. In particular, my willingness to work with several different veterans' groups with different political and ideological positions raised quite a few eyebrows. In one meeting, someone handed me a detailed document concerning alleged fraud committed by the orthodox line of the party in the 2003 FMLN internal elections. He told me: "don't show this to anyone, they could kill you for this." Perplexed because of this comment, I asked him: "do you really think that they would be capable of doing something like that?" He replied: "Of course they are. Do you know [he mentioned a former revolutionary military cadre]? This man is really dangerous. He is the one who does their dirty work for them."[9] A few months later, a different veteran handed me a 10 page handwritten report labelled "confidential" with details of the FMLN leadership's alleged involvement in acts of corruption and intimidation. Again, discretion and secrecy were requested of me, particularly with regard to making the information traceable. I asked what use it might have then for my study. His answer was: "see for yourself."[10]

Clearly, my level of access to different groups of veterans did not mean that I was trusted by everyone; quite the contrary. Everybody knows that trust can be violated or betrayed, and that this happens all the time, especially when stakes are high and polarization is rife.[11] Many veterans were furthermore keenly aware that their political practice did not always resemble the ideals they voiced. While presenting my research project and working with the FMLN veterans that figure in this study, I could almost "see" some of them thinking: very well that he has taken an interest in us, but what will this guy actually write about us? As Wolcott observes, to the informers "the *real* mystique surrounding ethnography . . . is not in doing field work, but in subsequently organizing and analyzing the information one gathers and in preparing the account that brings the ethnographic process to a close" (1997, 155-6).[12]

In effect, the fact that I was a relative insider to the FMLN, its people, and its political environment, rather than inspiring assuredness, also potentially turned me into a greater liability, since it provided me with more access to the kind of information that some people might not want to share outside their own personal circles (Ergun and Erdemir 2010, 17). It also plausibly supplied me with interpersonal contacts with people that might want to lay a hand on this type of information to use it against their political contenders.

AN ANATOMY OF POST-INSURGENT DISTRUST

Where does all this post-insurgent distrust come from? I identified three interrelated ingredients: the history of the revolutionary movement, the ongoing struggle with ARENA, and the internal dynamics of FMLN party politics.

The first ingredient is intimately related to guerrilla warfare. During the cold war, while the US attempted to tighten its grip on Latin America through political and military support for conservative regimes and counterinsurgency efforts, including massive covert action, Marxist guerrillas like those in El Salvador relied on clandestine organizing and secret support from Cuba, Vietnam, and, to a lesser extent, the Soviet Union. The guerrilla organizations organized while in strong military disadvantage and under siege of persecution, a situation "superseded through iron discipline, discretion and extreme distrust" (Hernández 2011).

Without heavy reliance on conspiracy methods organizing the insurgency in El Salvador would not have been possible. Before and during the war, the guerrilla organizations had to use strict security measures in order to minimize the chance of success of enemy intelligence work, and thus to be able to survive repression. Enormous levels of trust were needed to penetrate the inner circle of the guerrilla organizations. Distrust towards outsiders was fomented almost as a second nature.

Extreme distrust in order to avoid infiltration and persecution further contributed to sectarianism among the different revolutionary groups, also fuelled by internal power struggles and ideological differences between the different groups, even when they had become united in the FMLN. Salvadoran insurgents

> turned conspiracy into a way a life. Most members of the FMLN had to lie about everything in order to survive. They gave themselves new names, made up cover stories, they misled their families, indeed they re-invented almost everything about themselves. This, they all accepted, was perfectly normal in the situation, and naturally they expected everyone else to be doing the same. Worst of all, everyone was always looking for enemy spies and infiltrators. This was especially true of the leadership, . . . [since] lack of vigilance would cost them dear. (Gibb 2000, 223)

Some of this suspicion lingered on after the war, as evidenced for example in the constant references to infiltrators. Also, some veterans claimed that some comrades used conspiracy methods to strengthen their internal position within the FMLN within the post-war context.[13]

A second key ingredient of post-war distrust is the ongoing and virulent power struggle between ARENA and FMLN. ARENA, born out of anti-communist death squads, won the presidency during the last years of the war and continued in power until the FMLN won the presidency two decades later. It was the ARENA government that negotiated the Peace Accords with the FMLN. Roberto d'Aubuisson, the infamous death squad leader and founder of ARENA, died in 1992, and most of the post-war ARENA leadership had not played a prominent role in the dirty war.

Even so, distrust between FMLN and ARENA has remained very high during the post-war period. ARENA sympathizers have controlled the country's main newspapers and television channels, and these have campaigned strongly against the FMLN before each election. Both ARENA and the FMLN have often recurred to heavy-handed wartime rhetoric, as well as slander and other forms of dirty campaigning (Sprenkels 2011).

Mutual distrust between ARENA and FMLN thus continues to be extremely high. Political incidents have often resulted in mutual accusations that fuel further distrust.[14] Militants tend to see the rival party not only as unreliable, but also as actively involved in conspiring against their party. Such (imagined) plots take place on different levels, varying from municipal employees that secretly sabotage the efforts of the other party in that municipality to nation-wide conspiracies to manipulate the elections or cover up scandals from the war. Furthermore, a significant part of the FMLN and ARENA militancy depend on electoral success for employment opportunities, which means the personal stakes of campaigning are high.

Finally, as we have already seen, the internal dynamics of the post-war FMLN, with all its internal tensions, constitutes a final important factor correlated to the matter of trust and distrust in the field of post-insurgency. Apart from the infighting and the political purges, another source of post-war distrust is the growing distance between different participants of the revolutionary movement. Many veterans complained about internal inequality and lack of solidarity. In their view, those former comrades that were able to obtain well-paid positions should share with other veterans that were less fortunate. Many also considered that certain FMLN leaders marginalized the veterans in order to avoid them becoming potential competitors for public office. When engaging in political initiatives, veterans were often wary that certain leaders might manipulate them to garner benefits only for the leaders and not for the veterans.

SV-FMLN: INFILTRATION, CONSPIRACY, AND FIELDWORK DYNAMICS

It must have been difficult for some of the veterans, and in particular for their leadership, to have someone like me present at their meetings. They must have been aware that in my fieldwork I was bound to stumble across some of the weaknesses and contradictions of their organizing efforts. In effect, the former comandante who led the official FMLN veteran's sector (Sector de Veteranos del FMLN or SV-FMLN) was clearly uncomfortable with my presence, imposed because the higher-level FMLN leadership had granted me permission. When I asked him for an interview, he agreed only on the condition that it would not be recorded and even then his answers to my questions remained evasive.

It also took weeks of persistent requests to get him to pass me a copy of the sector's work plan. When he finally did, he indicated that I would be allowed to read it and take notes, but not to make a photocopy. I was to return the document to him after the meeting. The matter of infiltration and betrayal within the FMLN featured prominently in the document. As I hand copied into my notebook

> These leaders . . . no longer had either principles, ethics nor revolution-
> ary morals and they furthermore created divisions within the party, . . .
> organizing groups around their personal interests, . . . trying to move
> the party to the Right. . . . In order to do this . . . they blackmailed and
> tricked party members. It is important to point out that many of these
> leaders, over the years, became traitors who are now working with the
> Right, . . . however, like it or not, remnants within the party are still left,
> only to be eliminated over time. [15]

The document indicated that the veterans' sector should be seen as "the historic-moral reserve" that functions as a counterweight against such negative influences within the party. [16] But, I wondered, weren't the dissidents also almost invariably seasoned war veterans, with years of struggle and many personal sacrifices on their slate? How to determine what qualified as "truly" revolutionary, what constituted "treason" and what was simply a disagreement on a political topic? And what to think of the announced purging of emerging "traitors" within the party?

References to traitors and infiltrators were also frequent during the veterans' meetings I attended. The veterans talked about the FMLN as certainly infiltrated, and about their own sector being prone to infiltration. Referring to supposed ideological disputes inside the FMLN, they made references to the "next traitors" that had already sold out and were to be purged from the FMLN somewhere in the near future. [17] These references were used to justify or explain processes of political inclusion and exclusion. In the minds of the veterans, infiltration and the breeding of treason were tools that the Right used to influence the development of the FMLN with the ultimate aim of weakening and destroying the party. The SV-FMLN veterans saw the Right as a force that was permanently manipulating and conspiring against the FMLN. On occasions, elaborate conspiracy theories would be discussed and validated during the meetings. For example, after the devastating Haiti earthquake (January 12, 2010), different comrades argued at the meeting that the US had in fact secretly provoked the disaster in order to establish a stronger military presence in the Caribbean in order to close in on Venezuela. [18]

My previous FPL affiliation did not help my integration in SV-FMLN. Though the group claimed to represent veterans of the five different guerrilla groups, most participants were former members of a group called the Resistencia Nacional (RN). The former RN comandante that led the group had previous ties with most participants from back then. Other than previous RN affiliation was scarce. A former member of the Communist Party told me that the reason for his presence in SV-FMLN meetings was mainly to make sure that the RN leadership would not start doing anything unwarranted according to the Communist Party line.[19]

Wartime sectarian identities played an important part in veteran organizing also in the other groups I worked with. And historical sectarian disputes were often evoked to qualify the trustworthiness of specific individuals or groups. While the different veterans' groups I worked with sometimes engaged in ideological debates, it was clear that their main concern was how to position the members of their group to get access to government employment or other benefits, such as agricultural supplies or health care, dispensed through government agencies or municipalities. In these efforts, different veteran groups sometimes cooperated, but mostly competed with each other. While some veterans were reluctant to discuss the clientelist dynamics of veteran organizing with me, others vocally defended the privileged access to state benefits in my presence. They saw this as the historical debt the FMLN had accumulated with them during the war, and that now that the FMLN was in power, had become a moral duty for the FMLN to fulfil.

CONCLUSIONS: THE HEURISTICS OF DISTRUST

Leaning on Geertz, it is often assumed that successful anthropologists are highly skilled in establishing trust and complicity with their informers, deeply penetrating the communities they study. However, in real life, "people are 'insiders' or 'outsiders' by degree in any named group" and "membership in any community or category comes in shades of gray" (Schatz 2009, 6-7). Out- and insiderness are "ever shifting and permeable social locations," that are "negotiated and renegotiated in particular, everyday interactions" (Naples 1996, 84). For the ethnographer, insider status is relative at best and problematic at worst.

During my fieldwork, not trust but familiarity was the main benefit of previous involvement. In essence, ethnographic familiarity is not about insiderness or accumulated trust, but about the capability to generate historicized understandings of communities and the individuals within them (Scheper-Hughes 1992, 29). In my case, familiarity helped to capture and understand the possible meanings and interpretations protagonists attached to unfolding social and political developments from the historical perspective of previous experiences and positions. It allowed me to witness, and probably also to benefit from, the relative disorientation caused among my informants by my own changing role from activist to anthropologist.

Once I was able to harness personal vulnerability and to suppress moral discomfort, I found that the study of distrust provided a valuable heuristic tool during fieldwork. For former Salvadoran revolutionaries, the post-war years were characterized by strong tensions between political disillusionment and electoral ascendency. Historical distrust associated with clandestine warfare and sectarianism then became partially re-mobilized in the emerging arena of electoral politics. The post-war power struggle between FMLN and ARENA, as well as between different factions and subgroups of former revolutionaries, contributed to a political landscape particularly susceptible to slander and disqualification, and to finding new roles and uses for wartime categories like "traitor" and "infiltrator."

As Tilly points out, the structuring of trust in insider's networks is particularly important when it comes to risky collective enterprises, such as politics or revolutions (2005). However, I suspect that claiming, contesting and negotiating trust is part and parcel of how power is produced in any social field. This process, which could be seen as an ongoing interpersonal manipulation of trust, is shaped by many factors, including contemporary disputes and historical baggage. When entering or re-entering a particular social field, the anthropologist also becomes enmeshed in such dynamics. This is tricky, and it can be unsettling. It also one of ethnography's exciting intellectual challenges.

REFERENCES

Allison, M., and A. Martín Alvarez. 2012. "Unity and Disunity within the FMLN." *Latin American Politics and Society* 54, no. 4: 89–118.

Aretxaga, B. 2000. "A Fictional Reality: Paramilitary Death Squads and the Construction of State Terror in Spain." In *Death Squad. The Anthropology of State Terror*, edited by J. A. Sluka, 46–69. Philadelphia: University of Pennsylvania Press.

Auyero, J. 2010. "Patients of the State. An Ethnographic Account of Poor People's Waiting." *Latin American Research Review* 46, no. 1: 5–29.

Chabal, P., and J. P. Daloz. 2006. *Culture Troubles. Politics and the Interpretation of Meaning.* Chicago: University of Chicago Press.

Colburn, F., and A. Cruz. 2014. "El Salvador's Beleaguered Democracy." *Journal of Democracy* 25, no 3: 149–158.

Ergun, A., and A. Erdemir. 2009. "Negotitating Insider and Outsider Identities in the Field: 'Insider' in a Foreign Land, 'Outsider' in One's Own Land." *Field Methods* 22, no. 1: 16–38.

Galeas, G., and B. Ayalá. 2008. "Grandeza y Miseria en una Guerrilla. Informe de una Matanza." https://www.scribd.com/doc/12950803/Galeas-Marvin-Grandeza-y-Miseria-en-Una-Guerrilla.

García Dueñas, L., and J. Espinoza. 2010. *¿Quién asesinó a Roque Dalton? Mapa de un largo silencio.* San Salvador: Indole Editores.

Gibb, T. 2000. "Under the Shadow of Dreams. El Salvador's Revolutionaries" (unpublished book manuscript).

Guevarra, A. 2006. "The Balikbayan Researcher: Negotiating Vulnerability in Fieldwork with Filipino Labor Brokers." *Journal of Contemporary Ethnography* 35, no. 5: 526–551.

Hernández, M. 2011. "La experiencia de guerra y el impacto en la idiosincrasia del veterano combatiente revolucionario." Unpublished paper, Universidad de El Salvador.

Kruijt, D. 2008. *Guerrillas. War and Peace in Central America.* London: Zed Books.

Ladutke, L. 2008. "Understanding Terrorism Charges against Protesters in the Context of Salvadoran History." *Latin American Perspectives* 35, no. 6: 137–150.

Montoya, A. 2012. "The Violence of Cold War Polarities and the Fostering of Hope. The 2009 Elections in Postwar El Salvador." In *Central America in the New Millennium: Living Transition and Reimagining Democracy*, edited by J. Burrell and E. Moodie, 49–63. New York: Berghahn.

Moodie, E. 2010. *El Salvador in the Aftermath of Peace. Crime, Uncertainty and Transition to Democracy.* Philadelphia: University of Pennsylvania Press.

Morales Carbonell, J. A. 1999. "El suicidio de Marcial ¿Un asunto concluido? Salvador Cayetano Carpio." In *Nuestras montañas son las masas. Documentos y escritos de la revolución salvadoreña.* Vienna: Der Keil.

Naples, N. 1996. "A Feminist Revisiting the Insider/Outsider Debate: the 'Outsider Phenomenon' in rural Iowa." *Qualitative Sociology* 19, no. 1: 83–106.

Robben, A.C.G.M. 1995. "Seduction and Persuasion." In *Fieldwork under Fire: Contemporary Studies of Violence and Survival*, edited by C. Nordstrom and A.C.G.M. Robben, 81–104. Berkeley: University of California Press.

Schatz, E. 2009. "Ethnographic Immersion and the Study of Politics." In *Political Ethnography. What Immersion Contributes to the Study of Power*, edited by E. Schatz, 1–22. Chicago: University of Chicago Press.

Scheper-Hughes, N. 1992. *Death without Weeping: The Violence of Everyday Life in Brazil* Berkeley: University of California Press.

Silber, I. C. 2011. *Everyday revolutionaries. Gender, Violence and Disillusionment in Postwar El Salvador.* New Brunswick: Rutgers University Press.

Sprenkels, R. 2011. "Roberto d'Aubuisson versus Schafik Handal. Militancy, Memory Work and Human Rights." *European Review of Latin American and Caribbean Studies* 91: 15–30.

Sprenkels, R. 2014a. "Revolution and Accommodation. Post-insurgency in El Salvador." PhD diss., Utrecht University.

Sprenkels, R. 2014b. "Arena, FMLN y los sucesos del 5 de Julio de 2006 en El Salvador: violencia e imaginarios políticos." *Trace* 66: 62–81.

Tilly, C. 2005. *Trust and Rule.* Cambridge: Cambridge University Press.

Tilly, C. 2010. "The Blame Game." *The American Sociologist* 41, no 4: 382–389.

Wolcott, H. 1997. "Ethnographic Research in Education." In *Complementary Methods for Research in Education.* Edited by R. Jaeger, 187–249. Washington: American Educational Research Association (second edition).

Zamora, R. 2003. *La izquierda partidaria salvadoreña: Entre la identidad y el poder.* San Salvador: Facultad Latinoamericana de Ciencias Sociales (FLACSO).

NOTES

1. FMLN stands for "Frente Farabundo Martí para la Liberación Nacional."

2. ARENA stands for "Alianza Republicana Nacionalista."

3. The quote is from leading Salvadoran jounalist Carlos Dada in his editorial comment after the 2014 presidential elections; available at http://blogs.elpais.com/dadaistmo/2014/03/un-pais-a-la-mitad.html, consulted on 20-06-2014.

4. See for example Silber (2011) and Zamora (2003).

5. Fieldnotes (28-05-2009). For outstanding ethnographical reflections on the power dynamics of waiting, see Auyero (2010).

6. Drawing on the sociology of Pierre Bourdieu, I define post-insurgency as a historically constructed space of relationships between multiple social agents that were previously connected through participation in the insurgency.

7. Fieldnotes (07-09-2009).

8. Descriptions of internal purges can be found in García Dueñas and Espinoza (2010), Morales Carbonell (1999), and Galeas and Ayalá (2008).

9. Fieldnotes (17-08-2009).

10. Fieldnotes (11-03-2010).

11. For an anthropological reflection on this matter, see Aretxaga (2000).

12. Italics in the original.

13. Interviews with José (15-12-2009), Rafael (01-12-2009, 08-12- 2009, 11-12-2009, 16-12-2009, 06-01-2010, 14-01-2010) and Tino (29-05-2009, 16-07-2009).

14. The most dramatic staging of this so far took place during and after the events of the July 5, 2006, when a gunman identified with the FMLN killed two police officers during a student protest. See Ladutke (2008) and Sprenkels (2014b).

15. Fieldnotes (31-08-2009).

16. Fieldnotes (31-08-2009).

17. Fieldnotes (30-11-2009).

18. Fieldnotes (25-01-2012).

19. Interview with Rafael (06-01-2010).

FIFTEEN

Embedded Ethnography

Conflict Research through an International Peace Mission in Colombia

Floortje Toll

INTRODUCTION

In February 2011 I attended one of many paramilitary truth-telling-sessions known as *versión libre* (literally "free account") that were part of the Colombian transitional justice process after the demobilization of the paramilitary United Self-Defense Forces of Colombia (AUC). These truth-telling-sessions were held in Public Ministry Offices in large cities like Bogotá or Medellín where the demobilized paramilitaries were imprisoned. To enable participation of the related victims,[1] a fundamental right encoded in the Justice and Peace Law that framed the process, the Public Ministry had decided that all sessions should be broadcasted in the area where the paramilitary had operated so that local victims could attend and ask questions (either directly or via their public defender).

In practice this meant that temporary facilities had to be set up in remote villages, generally in schools or other public buildings, to enable live on-screen broadcasting of the sessions and victim participation in them. Furthermore, the institutions responsible for the transitional justice process had to travel and stay in these villages for the duration of the event to organize and direct it. Part of my fieldwork consisted of accompanying the related institutional officials as they travelled from their offices in the regional capital to the different villages where the sessions were set up and observing the confession sessions as they unfolded.

That day in February I was in a small Andean town in Nariño, a department in the far southwestern corner of Colombia where my field-work took place. Former members of the local paramilitary structure were to render their account of cases occurred in or near the village. The transmission was set up in a local primary school. As I arrived, the screen was already up and the Public Ministry technician was checking the sound system and satellite connection. Other officials were discussing the setup of the event. Conditions were, as always, not ideal: the venue was a single space room just off the village main street, about eight meters square, with a single door and window. The climate was hot and without air-conditioning the options were to close the metal shutters, turning the room into an oven, or allow some air but risk interference of street noise and curious passers-by. The officials settled on a compromise: the shut-ters were half closed and three ventilators set up to mitigate the heat.

Meanwhile the victims started to arrive. Most took a seat in plastic chairs set up in front of the screen; others went through papers with their Public Defender, and some just sat and waited for the event to begin. Shortly after, the satellite connection went up: six confessors appeared on screen sitting behind a table in the hearing room in Medellín. The ad-journing public area appeared empty; all the related victims were gath-ered in the hot classroom on the other side of the country. The presiding Public Ministry official in Medellín took the microphone to ask everyone to take a seat and formally opened the session. All institutional represen-tatives in both locations introduced themselves followed by the confes-sors who shortly related their position and trajectory in the local paramil-itary structure. Then the session proceeded to the first scheduled case: the homicide of a local shop owner.

This is a typical start of the various transmission sessions I attended. I recall this particular one because after having spent about a year in the field and attending several sessions I felt I was getting a grasp of the full content of the event: I was familiar with the mechanisms of the transition-al justice process; not only the institutions and technical language but also the state representatives involved and how some of them felt about the process. I had attended previous sessions of some of the participating confessors and knew their trajectories and pseudonyms as well as those of other paramilitaries mentioned in the session. Most importantly, this particular session took place in the area where I spent most of my field-work. I had heard about several of the scheduled cases during earlier visits and had spoken to some of the victims; I was able to place the overwhelming judicial details of the session within the local context.

During my fieldwork, the paramilitary confession sessions were a source (one of many) of data and knowledge on the local conflict past. The endeavor of finding "the truth" about that past was taking place in front of my eyes in a dialogue between paramilitary and victims. I was aware that this dialogue was hampered in many ways: the precarious conditions of the make-shift venues and the technical failures in the satellite connection; the palpable fear and anxiety of the victims when confronting the perpetrators and their version of the truth; and the sometimes calculated answers of the paramilitary, conscious of the judicial consequences of every word. In spite of these deficiencies, the transitional justice process for me was a valuable window onto the past and for most of my time in the field I considered it just that: a way to gain material on my research topic, the conflict dynamics in Nariño. It was only after returning from the field that I realized how unique the access to these processes had been and that the process *itself*, with all the complexities implied in the implementation of such a comprehensive project in an area still affected by conflict and violence, was a valuable research angle.

The reason I had access to the transitional justice procedures, the confession sessions being a primary constituent, was the fact that I worked for the international Mission to Support the Peace Process in Colombia (Misión de Apoyo al Proceso de Paz, Mapp/OEA), a special mission of the Organization of American States (Organización de los Estados Americanos, OEA) created in 2004 to verify and accompany all aspects of the peace process with the paramilitary.[2] Monitoring the transitional justice proceedings, being present at local transmissions of confession sessions among other thing, was part of the mission's mandate.[3] I was thus present at these confession sessions not as an anthropological researcher but as a Mapp/OEA monitoring official: a role I maintained throughout my entire fieldwork and that defined my fieldwork activities.

The reason I opted for this somewhat unconventional arrangement was initially mostly an instrumental one: I wanted to gain access to the intended research area of Nariño, a region still immersed in conflict in spite of what the term "peace process" might suggest. The Mapp/OEA was one of the few institutions that extensively travelled the former paramilitary areas to monitor the process. At the time I was, of course, aware that such an arrangement would have consequences for my methods and role in the field but I could not foresee the scope of its implications beforehand. I thus started my fieldwork as somewhat of a methodological experiment, one that I now refer to as "embedded ethnography."

Eventually the choice for embedded fieldwork had far-reaching consequences not only during my fieldwork but also beyond, not in the least with regard to my identity as a researcher. This chapter will zoom in on this identity aspect; it analyzes the praxis and ethics of managing a double role in the field from the perspective of the respondents as well as that of myself as a researcher. The aim of the chapter is to render a methodological account of this particular fieldwork experience and to provide insights into the perks and pitfalls of "embedded ethnography" as a fieldwork strategy for those who consider a similar endeavor. After all, safety considerations will continue to hamper ethnographic research in conflict areas.

THE FIELD AND THE ARRANGEMENT

In 2009 I travelled to Colombia to explore Nariño as a fieldwork-site for my research on conflict dynamics after the demobilization of Colombia's paramilitary forces. Nariño had caught my attention because it was something of an enigma: initially known as a backward but quiet region, used by Colombia's guerilla movements as a zone of retreat, the violence had flared up around the turn of the century when paramilitary forces arrived in pursuit of the emerging coca cultivation. The conflict subsequently spiraled after 2005, following the demobilization of the local paramilitary structure, when a myriad of armed groups appeared to fill the power vacuum. By the time I started my PhD, Nariño had become a center stage in a new phase of Colombia's conflict the dynamics of which I planned to research.

During my exploratory fieldwork the possibility of operating as an independent researcher in the former paramilitary areas soon proved unfeasible. The readjustments following the demobilization were still in full fling and the volatile and unpredictable nature of the conflict meant that travelling to and through these areas could entail risks for myself and for those who cooperated, especially considering that the topic of the research was precisely the conflict itself. I was cautiously considering a change of fieldwork-site when, during one of my exploratory talks, I was presented with an alternative. Discussing my research plans and safety concerns with the Mapp/OEA regional office in Pasto (Nariño's capital) the team offered me an internship.

The Pasto field office was considerably understaffed at the time, with four employees (two officials, a driver, and a secretary) covering an entire department. Their proposal was that I would support the team in all its activities and in turn would be allowed to use the material gathered as input for my dissertation (with the restriction of internal or classified documents). As soon as we worked out the details with the Mapp/OEA head office and my University, I started a six-month internship (from August 2009 to February 2010) which was followed by a position as a Mapp/OEA observer for another twelve months (from June 2010 to July 2011).[4] In total I thus spent eighteen months in the field working for the Mapp/OEA.[5]

Of course such an arrangement implied practically handing over the reins of my fieldwork but I had good reasons to do so. In the first place, as said, I needed a vehicle (in the almost literal sense) to safely enter the aspired research area. The Mapp/OEA was one of few organizations in Colombia that disposed of the infrastructure to thoroughly and safely cover conflict zones (a substantial infrastructure involving field offices, equipped cars, experienced drivers, satellite phones, and a safety department).[6] The reputation of the mission in the region was sound according to consulted external informants. Furthermore, my position as Mapp/

OEA official gave me a clear role and purpose in the field: I was directly identifiable as part of a mission whose mandate and character were grossly known to armed groups and locals alike. Possible risks induced by ambiguity or questions regarding my identity, a common issue in anthropological fieldwork (see Walker 2009), were thus mitigated.

The third reason I accepted the Mapp/OEA terms was that the content and character of the work fitted my research aims: part of the mission's mandate was to monitor and report on conflict dynamics and security issues in former paramilitary areas and a great deal of my work would thus consist of field missions throughout the region. Furthermore, the methods used to perform this verification were largely derived from the ethnographic toolbox: they involved participant observation, open interviews, informal conversations and focus groups with demobilized combatants.

There was one last aspect that made me decide embark upon this "embedded fieldwork": the Mapp/OEA did not pose substantial limitations on the content of my analysis. After ending my contract I would have full ownership of the raw data gathered as an official. The only agreement was that, first of all, the Mapp/OEA itself would not be the object of analysis and, secondly, I would make clear that the analysis was the sole responsibility of the author, not a reflection of the institutional position of the Mapp/OEA. I fully agreed with both aspects: I wanted to write an independent dissertation on Nariño's conflict and had the work of the mission been part of the analysis, my position within the team would have been compromised.

MANAGING A DOUBLE ROLE? IDENTITY AND VISIBILITY IN THE FIELD

Let me start by stating that pursuing some form of institutional alliance to facilitate research in conflict areas is, though unusual, not unprecedented. Access and safety are central issues for anthropologists in any violent context (see Robben and Nordstrom 1995; Sluka 1995 and 2007; Smyth and Gillian 2001; Theidon 2001; Warren 2000; Wood 2006). In first instance, the term "embedded" might invoke associations with the strategy of "embedded journalism" used during the 2003 United States' invasion of Iraq when news reporters temporarily attached themselves to military units to report on the war. Anthropologists also have sought institutional alliances to enable research in dangerous or inaccessible conflict areas; Carolyn Nordstrom (1997, 41), for example, "hitchhiked" flights of relief organizations to access frontlines in Mozambique, a strategy she referred to as "runway anthropology."

Though in some ways similar to these endeavors, there is one aspect which distinguishes the "embeddedness" elaborated here: as a researcher

I was not temporarily *attached* to an organization (I did not "hitchhike" the Mapp/OEA car to then operate as a researcher on site); for the duration of my fieldwork I was an *integral part* of the Mapp/OEA as one of its field officials. My "embeddednes" was more intrusive and comprehensive. In that sense the term "embedded" here builds more on the original concept as introduced by economic historian Karl Polanyi (1944) who used it to explicate how economic exchanges were entangled with and conditioned by cultural values such as religion and kinship (thus contesting the rational choice theories predominant at the time).[7] To use Polanyi's words, I was not a "separate sphere" from the organization that facilitated my field access; I was an integral part of that organization and its mandate conditioned my activities in the field.

My role as Mapp/OEA official thus not only determined my access to the field but also my role in it. The Mapp/OEA identity was always manifest and visible, in the first place because I was required to wear a Mapp/OEA *chaleco* (institutional vest), I travelled in a Mapp/OEA car, and I carried around Mapp/OEA notebooks. Furthermore, I was performing Mapp/OEA tasks: my actions in the field were given in by the mission's mandate which induced whom I talked to, what I talked about and how I reported on it. From the perspective of my informants, therefore, this official identity was the only visible one. My role as academic researcher was inherently (though not consciously) hidden: it was overruled by the visible markers of my Mapp/OEA status.

Specifying my secondary identity as a researcher was complicated in many contexts, such as the collective and formal settings of confession sessions. Furthermore, when I *did* specify my double role, for example in individual interviews, informants generally did not mind whether their information was input for Mapp/OEA reports only or also (possibly) for an academic thesis. Over time I settled on the inevitable predominance of my Mapp/OEA identity also because I did not want to make things needlessly complicated. There was confusion at times about the precise role of the mission alone; to then clarify that I also worked for a Dutch university would have added to the confusion.

Most of my contacts in the field were thus unaware of my identity as researcher, and my relationships in the field were thus almost exclusively built on my institutional role. It was this formal role which had provided most of the contacts in the first place: the Mapp/OEA had an extensive contact network throughout the department to which I was personally introduced by a colleague on several introductory trips. The fundament of my rapport with these contacts was initially the reputation and trust that the mission had built up with them over the previous years. Some of these over time relationships acquired a more personal foundation but their character was undeniably an institutional one.

This "a priori" institutional trust, of course, was of a different nature than the kind established in most ethnographic fieldwork: gradually and mutually constructed on a personal basis (DeWalt and DeWalt 2002; Powdermaker 1967). Over time I came to value this a priori trust particularly given the polarized and volatile setting in which I was working: a more personal relation could have created loyalty (and safety) issues for those involved and would have limited my maneuverability in and perspective on the field: travelling between areas controlled by competing armed groups would have been complicated, for example, as would returning to a certain area after a competing group had taken over.

Of course the formal character of my field relations also influenced the kind of material they yielded. It would be counterfactual to speculate on what people would have told me had I been an independent researcher (or if they would have talked to me at all). What I can say is that, in general, the interviews and informal conversations with people in the field were "on topic," that is, we talked about Map/OEA-related issues. For one thing because I asked questions in that direction as my work required, but also because people automatically assumed that that was what I was interested in. My interviews and most of my informal conversations thus followed a certain path bound by my role as an official.

Clearly one of my roles in the field was manifest and official while the other was inevitably hidden and subservient (in that sense the term "double role" used in the title of this paragraph is slightly misleading). There was one obvious ethical issue induced by the inequality of these roles: that of informed consent. Informants knew their information would be used for publication purposes: I publicly took notes and informed those I talked to that their information served as input for internal or public Mapp/OEA reports (in which anonymity was, of course, guaranteed). However, due to my hidden researcher identity informants were generally unaware that the material might be re-used for academic purposes in a later stage. The informed consent was thus inevitably indirect or two-staged.

SELF-IDENTIFICATION AND FIELD PERSPECTIVE

The prevalence of my Mapp/OEA identity was not only evident from the perspective of my informants; it was also, and increasingly as my time in the field progressed, an issue of self-identification. While in the beginning of my fieldwork I still had to get used to my official role, over time the Mapp/OEA identity "took over." I gradually became familiar with the work and assumed more responsibilities especially when, after six months as an intern during which I could incidentally take a back seat and just observe, I was formally contracted as an official and thus bound to fulfill the role that came with it. Furthermore, the Mapp/OEA identity was the one constantly confirmed and addressed in the field and it determined most of my activities. My academic identity naturally took a back seat.

This shift in identity was gradual and mostly unconscious. When re-reading my field notes I came across only two scribblings on the "role-shifting" issue. In November 2009, three months into my internship, I wrote: "I am still acting too much a researcher, observing and taking notes. I need to act more like an official, it's a bit of a switch." This note was taken after an Entrega de Restos Óseos, a ceremony in which ex-humed remains of disappeared persons are handed over to their families to be buried. Apart from family members and institutional representa-tives there was always some press at these events. To guarantee the pri-vacy and safety of the victims journalists were bound to certain rules: their presence should not disturb the ceremony and the families could not be recognizably filmed or photographed. That day several reporters overstepped these boundaries and while I was taking notes on the cere-mony (including the attitude of the press) a colleague stepped in to ad-dress them which, I realized, was what the mandate required.

The second jotting was made as an official in September 2010, about a year later. I was in Pasto trying to write out a conversation I had during a transitional justice event two days earlier. In the middle of my field note it said: "Damnit, I have already forgotten half of it. I should be writing these kinds of stories down instead of report after report." Apart from these two notes, there we none on the double-role-issue nor on any other methodological or ethical dilemma in my notebooks: they were Mapp/OEA notebooks in every sense of the term. The two notes convey, first of all, that the balance between the identities had shifted by the time I was an official. The *number* of notes, furthermore, reveals that this shift was something I was only incidentally aware of (or frustrated by) in the field. I was hardly conscious of the issues implied in combining both roles because I mostly *didn't* combine them: I fulfilled my Mapp/OEA respon-sibilities and trusted that once back home the material gathered would be usable for my dissertation. I thus also did not monitor the content and character of the material gathered or in which direction it was taking me.

I do not intent to create a complete contraposition of the researcher versus the official here. The roles are not mutually exclusive; as a matter of fact, the whole experiment of embedded fieldwork was based on the assumption that both roles overlapped and they *did*. However, they also represented a different perspective on the field. For the Mapp/OEA I was meant to gather specific material relevant for Mapp/OEA purposes and write it up in a report-style manner. At the earlier mentioned confession session, for example, I would report on the institutional presence, the number of attending victims, the content of the cases, and possible irreg-ularities. There was no need to take notes on the setting and atmosphere of the event, the interactions between victims and state officials, or the informal conversations I had with victims. As a researcher I would have looked at such an event differently and my notes might have included aspects and details not relevant for the Mapp/OEA but interesting from an anthropological point of view.

Before I started my embedded fieldwork I was convinced I could do both at the same time: gather my official material and report on it while preserving my anthropological perspective and taking ethnographic field notes at the same time. In practice that turned out to be slightly overambitious first of all because I gradually internalized the Mapp/OEA perspective and my perception of the field thus changed. Furthermore, even when I did scribble additional notes down in the field, there was hardly time (or energy) to elaborate them once back in Pasto as the second note indicates. The Mapp/OEA work simply overtook me: it was intense and time-consuming (especially the field missions and report writing) and, not unimportantly, the Pasto team was small and close-knit: I felt very much part of that and we shared the field experience.

While "becoming" a Mapp/OEA official (in the broadest sense of the term) had been a natural and mostly unconscious process; its reversal was all the more deliberate and conscious for it. Practically, of course, the change was abrupt: at some point my arrangement with the Mapp/OEA simply ended and I went home to start working on the thesis. For most anthropologists this transition from fieldwork to writing is challenging; Wood (2006, 384) touches upon this as she notes the necessity to "reaffirm a sense of engagement with one's academic community" after fieldwork. In my case the "embeddedness" added an extra dimension to this challenge as I had not only been disengaged with my academic community but also with my "academic self."

Reinventing myself as a researcher ("unbedding" myself if you will) proved to be the most difficult part of the embedded experience, one that was conscious and hard-fought. I decided to start with elaborating and reengaging with my raw material since I had hardly monitored its content in the field or in which direction it was taking me. I needed to detach the material from the institutional aim for which was initially gathered and re-appropriate it as research material. This was a time-consuming and difficult process first of all because of the sheer volume of activities and data but also because I was slightly reluctant to reengage with since it had already served its main purpose: the institutional reports. I thus started to work through my notebook-jottings from beginning to end, simultaneously creating an overview of all activities and interviews to make the material more accessible and to create a reference for going back and forth between the notebooks and the institutional reports which added depth.[8]

I now had a grasp of my data and had detached it somewhat from the goal for which it had been gathered. The next challenge was to find a relevant and feasible research angle among the wide range of material. One thing that stood out in the overview of field activities was the amount of time I had spent accompanying state institutions responsible for the justice and peace process as they implemented various aspects of the process in Nariño's rural areas. The transmissions of confession sessions were and important part of these activities but the institutions also travelled to conflict areas to register victims, take DNA samples, and hand over reparation payments, among other things. The intensity of the travelling and working in conflict areas, not to mention the complexities of implementing a process of truth, justice, and reparation in the middle of an ongoing conflict were striking.

My access to the transitional justice proceedings had been entirely based on my Mapp/OEA role. As an official, however, they were an inherent and self-explanatory part of my work and I had considered them an interesting byproduct at most. Reviewing my activities with some distance from the field (rediscovering my researcher-perspective), however, I started to see the value of these proceedings themselves and the enormous institutional effort that went into realizing them in remote areas still immersed in conflict violence. Ultimately, my embeddness thus resulted in a change in focus: rather than analyzing Nariño's conflict dynamics after the paramilitary demobilization, I would analyze the implementation of the transitional justice framework *within* this context.

CONCLUSION: EMBEDDED ETHNOGRAPHY AS A FIELDWORK STRATEGY

The decision to embark upon "embedded fieldwork," in my case to enable research into Nariño's recent conflict dynamics, was a carefully considered one. The initial motivation was quite straightforward: working for the Mapp/OEA was a means to access my aspired research area. This rather instrumental inducement was followed by a careful consideration of the arrangement to ensure it was (likely) to yield the material I needed for my dissertation. When considering a strategy as intrusive and comprehensive as the embedded fieldwork presented here, this phase of discussing and revising the arrangement before formalizing it is crucial.

The main arguments to embark upon the experiment were that the content of the work (partially) overlapped with my research aim (the mission's mandate included monitoring conflict dynamics in former paramilitary areas) and that the methods used to perform this mandate were largely derived from the ethnographic toolbox. Furthermore, the reputation of the Mapp/OEA in the region was sound, a crucial consideration since my field relations would be built on its track record. A last important aspect was that the mission did not pose substantial limitations on the content of my analysis: I would have full ownership of the raw data gathered as an official and I was free to use them for an academic thesis (providing that the Mapp/OEA would not be the object of analysis and that I would make clear that the dissertation was the sole responsibility of the author).

Naturally I also intended to anticipate possible disadvantages at least to the extent in which I could foresee it at the time. I was aware that the Mapp/OEA work would determine my role and activities in the field although I initially expected to be able to also explicate my identity as a researcher but this resulted impractical and frequently impossible in the field. As for my activities, I assumed the time and opportunity to pursue a research agenda outside my formal role would be limited; I simply trusted (based on the earlier considerations) that the work would yield the material I needed. Furthermore, I was aware that the mandate of the Mapp/OEA was broader that my research aim and I would thus inevitably yield material that was not (or only indirectly) related to my focus. The intensive monitoring of the transitional justice proceedings, for example, was an aspect I considered and interesting byproduct at the time. I accepted these drawbacks as tradeoffs for the advantages I expected the arrangement to offer.

One aspect I had not been aware of beforehand was the issue of self-identification explicated here: the fact that the Mapp/OEA identity would overrule the researcher not only from the perspective of my informants but also increasingly for myself. In the field I was only marginally aware of this identity-transition but it was all the more apparent once the arrangement ended and I returned to academia. This, in the end, was the most important lesson learned from the experience: the fact that an arrangement as comprehensive and intrusive as embedded fieldwork inevitably determines ones identity in the field and that his has consequences beyond the fieldwork itself, most of all regarding the relationship and engagement with one's data.

The biggest challenge of embedded fieldwork might thus ultimately lie in the post-fieldwork period, not only in my particular case but for the method in general. In some ways this is not alien to the "normal" ethnographic experience: as a researcher one starts with a certain idea, a research plan, and methods and the field regularly turns out to have a dynamic of its own with players, incidents, and data that overrule this plan and lead to its reconsideration in hindsight. Embedded fieldwork adds an extra dimension to this challenge because in this case field data are a byproduct of fieldwork activities, not their primary goal. Analyzing such data requires not only a careful reconsideration but an actual rediscovery and re-appropriation in hindsight.

For me re-processing my material and separating it from the purpose for which it had been initially gathered also enabled identifying the strengths and weaknesses of the embedded endeavor. My position a Mapp/OEA official had opened up worlds that I would not have had access to or even been aware of as an independent researcher, most notably the transitional justice proceedings taking place in Nariño's conflict areas at the time. It was going through my notebook scribbles and sys-temizing my activities that I realized that this self-explanatory part of my formal role was actually a valuable research angle as a researcher.

All in all embedded fieldwork can be a valuable strategy to enable research into places and realities that would otherwise remain hidden or only accessible in hindsight. I am not the first and will probably not be the last ethnographer to embark upon some form of embedded field-work; after all, conflict and violence will continue to hamper the possibil-ities of ethnographic research in such areas. The challenge ultimately lies in seeking out the strength of the arrangement, the added value of the embedded perspective, while being explicit and transparent about the methodology that induced it.

REFERENCES

Dewalt, K. M., and B. R. DeWalt. 2002. *Participant Observation: A Guide for Fieldworkers.* Lanham: Rowman and Littlefield Publishers.

Nordstrom, C. 1997. *A Different Kind of War Story.* Philadelphia: University of Pennsyl-vania Press.

Polanyi, K. 1944. *The Great Transformation.* New York: Farrar and Rinehart.

Powdermaker, H. 1967. *Stranger and Friend: The Way of an Anthropologist.* London: Secker and Warbug.

Robben, A.C.G.M., and C. Nordstrom. 1995. "Introduction: The Anthropology and Ethnography of Violence and Sociopolitical Conflict." In *Fieldwork Under Fire: Con-temporary Studies of Violence and Survival,* edited by C. Nordstrom and A.C.G.M. Robben, 1-23. Berkeley: University of California Press.

Sluka, J. A. 1995. "Reflections on Managing Danger in Fieldwork: Dangerous Anthro-pology in Belfast. In *Fieldwork Under Fire: Contemporary Studies of Violence and Survi-val,* edited by A. C. G. M. Robben and C. Nordstrom, 276-294. Berkeley: University of California Press.

Sluka, J. A. 2007. "Fieldwork Conflicts, Hazards, and Dangers: Introduction." In: *Eth-nographic Fieldwork: An Anthropological Reader,* edited by A. C. G. M. Robben and J. A. Sluka, 137-142. Oxford: Blackwell.

Smyth, M. and R. Gillian, eds. 2001. *Researching Violently Divided Societies. Ethical and Methodological Issues.* Tokyo and London: UN University Press and Pluto Press.

Theidon, K. 2001. "Terror's Talk, Fieldwork and War." *Dialectical Anthropology* 26: 19–35.

Walker, M. 2009. "Priest, Development Worker, or Volunteer? Anthropological Re-search and Ascribed Identities in Mozambique." *Anthropology Matters* 11, no 1. http://www.anthropologymatters.com/index.php/anth_matters/article/view/20/29.

Warren, K. B. 2000. "Death Squads and Wider Complicities: Dilemmas for the Anthro-pology of Violence." In *Death Squad: The Anthropology of State Terror,* edited by Jeffrey A. Sluka, 226-247. Pennsylvania: University of Pennsylvania Press.

Wood, E. 2006. "Ethical Consequences of Field Research in Conflict Zones." *Qualitative Sociology* 29: 373–386.

NOTES

1. The term "victim" is used in a judicial/administrative sense: those individuals registered as victims of conflict within the justice and peace process. Through their

registration, these victims are connected to certain cases, paramilitary structures, and sometimes individual paramilitary. When their case is scheduled to be clarified by related paramilitaries in a versión libre, the registered victims are invited to attend.

2. The Mapp/OEA was formally created in February 2004 (through resolution 859 of the Permanent Council) after an agreement between the OEA and Colombian president Álvaro Uribe. Its initial five-year mandate was extended with several periods. The mission resorts under the Secretariat for Political Affairs, Department of Sustainable Democracy and Special Missions.

3. It is worth noting that there is certain ambivalence at the core of this mandate. On the one hand the Mapp/OEA is presented as an independent actor, funded by external donors, overseeing the peace process between the Colombian government and the AUC. On the other, it is created by and thus bound to a formal agreement with that same government. This ambivalence is also represented in its two, slightly contradictory, functions: verification (implying an independent position) and support (implying a certain alliance) of the peace process.

4. And after completing the formal application procedure through the OEA head office in Washington, DC.

5. Both the internship and the position were based on full-time contracts. This was a condition of the mission since any informal or partial relation would create ambiguity as to who was responsible for my safety in the field; as an employee the mission assumed full responsibility. Furthermore, the mission wanted to prevent being held accountable for the actions of an independent researcher that would inevitably be associated with the mission in the field but whose action they did not completely control.

6. The only other institutions with comparable field coverage were the various Unites Nations agencies; their work, however, involved the implementation of projects and thus answered to a different field logic and presence. When I started my internship in 2009, the Mapp/OEA had a head office in Bogotá and fourteen field-offices throughout Colombia.

7. Neoclassical economics assumed that economic exchanges were determined by the logic of rational action. Polanyi instead argued that most (local) economies were governed to a large extent by cultural values and environmental circumstances that did not necessarily involve utility maximization. His so-called "substantivist approach" was subsequently embraced by anthropologists.

8. The institutional reports consisted of the Monthly Agendas (with all planned activities), *Notas Internas* (short notes on meetings and other singular activities), *Informes de Misión* (reports of field missions), *Informes Mensuales* (monthly reports of the field office), *Relatorios de Grupos Focales* (notes on focus groups with demobilized combatants), *Formatos de Versión Libre* (reports of attended confession sessions), and *Informes Especiales* (special analyses that the Mapp/OEA head office incidentally requested on a specific topic, armed group, or subregion).

SIXTEEN

Fieldwork Frontiers

Danger, Uncertainty, and Limitations during Research with Former Combatants in Mozambique

Nikkie Wiegink

INTRODUCTION

One of the first ethnographies I read as an undergraduate was Douglas Raybeck's (1995) *Mad Dogs, Englishmen, and the Errant Anthropologist: Fieldwork in Malaysia*. At the time, my fellow students and I found Raybecks's beginner's mistakes, such as befriending the local lunatic and trying to visit people around noon in the blistering Malaysian sun when only mad dogs were out in the streets, highly amusing. When I started my own fieldwork among former combatants in Maringue, a rural district in central Mozambique, I often thought about Raybeck's reflexive anecdotes, as I also stumbled my way into the field making numerous mistakes, such as eating with my left hand, thinking that the sound of drums meant a party (while drums are mostly used during spirit exorcisms and religious services), and trying to visit people in cool early mornings when they were busy on their fields.

But I also made less innocent errors. During the first month of fieldwork, my research assistant and I arrived at the house of a woman I will call Olivia, who I presumed was a former government soldier. My research assistant, Beatrice, was the daughter of a prominent member of FRELIMO (*Frente de Libertação de Moçambique*, Mozambican Liberation Front), the governing party. After a brief and stiff conversation we left Olivia's house, as an interview was clearly not going to happen. I was puzzled about the reasons for "our failure," until Beatrice, also irritated by the bad conversation, said, "you cannot expect much, she is with the confused people." It was only then that I understood that Olivia was a former combatant of RENAMO (*Resistência Nacional de Moçambique,* Mozambican National Resistance), the rebel movement that fought the FRELIMO government for over sixteen years. This error was a reminder that my stumbling was not to be taken lighthearted, as in Maringue political affiliations were a sensitive and sometimes dangerous matter, and I was dealing with people who had experienced, witnessed, and perpetrated violence.

In this contribution I will address some of the challenges of doing fieldwork in a conflict-ridden post-war context by focusing on what I have called "fieldwork frontiers." By this I mean the ambiguous, subjective moments, in which I decided *not* to go further into unknown territory, may it be physically or socially, because it would risk putting the research participants, the research project, or myself in danger. In this paper I will analyse three fieldwork moments that reveal some of the limits I set for myself while doing fieldwork with former combatants in Maringue. These were fairly everyday fieldwork decisions that included to whom (not) to talk to, where (not) to go, and what questions (not) to ask. Yet in the context of political tension, incidents of violence, and fear of retaliation, these seemingly simple considerations were fraught with uncertainty and moral ambiguity. The decisions I eventually made were highly contingent on the social and political context, the moment in time, my personality, and even ecological circumstances. These moments convey a great deal about how I conducted fieldwork in Maringue and the nature of the data I gathered. But moreover, I want to show that these moments of doubt and of contemplating the next step to take or not to take, provided also a valuable source of analysis for understanding what it means to live in a politically polarised and sometimes violent world.

In the following sections I will present three moments in which I found myself at a "fieldwork frontier" and I decided not to go further. First, however, there is a need to provide some background information on the research location and my research.

MARINGUE: THE KINGDOM OF CONFUSION

I chose Maringue district as my research location because of its intense war history and the presence of large numbers of former Renamo combatants. At the time of research, Maringue was known for "trouble" (*confusão*) and had the dubious honour of being a RENAMO bastion, as sometime during the mid-1980s the rebel movement established their main military base in the district's dense forests. When the peace accords were signed in 1992, an estimated three thousand RENAMO *desmobiliza-*

dos settled in the area that is now the main village, and many have stayed until this day.

They live among a population that experienced violence, repression, and terror at the hands of both the government armed forces and RENAMO rebels. Since the war, Maringue has been one of the most pro-RENAMO areas of the country, also because one of RENAMO's remaining military bases is located in the district, housing an unknown number of "presidential guards" and a stockpile of weapons. In response to RENAMO's military presence, the government installed a riot police force allegedly under strong FRELIMO control. During fieldwork there were several near-confrontations between RENAMO combatants and riot police officers.[1] Small-scale violent incidents, such as beatings of party members and raising fire to huts, happened frequently but were often perpetrated FRELIMO and RENAMO party members. As a result political affiliations marked a central social divide within the village, and while many inhabitants would probably have preferred to stay "neutral," most were to some degree associated with one of the parties.

Maringue was an excellent place to research the war and post-war social navigations of former RENAMO combatants. My interlocutors were these ex-combatants but also their relatives, traditional authorities, church members, healers, political leaders, and so on. I mainly conducted semi-structured interviews and drew up life histories, which were complemented by countless hours of small talk and by "being there," hanging out in people's houses, in bars, political party headquarters, and local government buildings. I spend a total of fourteen months in the district, mainly in Maringue town, that is small enough to know all the main political players and large enough to avoid certain people when I wanted to. However, for this paper it is important to note that the small size of the town meant that my comings and goings were observed publicly (especially in wintertime when the bushes were dry and burned and did not provide any privacy) and subject to rumours and speculation. Most people invited me happily in their homes, but over time my association with RENAMO turned problematic in my relationships with several FRELIMO supporters. This paper conveys some of the balancing I did in order to maintain good ties with opposing "sides" and the choices I made in this process not to delve into certain aspects of Maringue-life.

A PERSON I COULD NOT TALK TO: JOÃO

The political tense situation in Maringue influenced who I could talk to and which places I could visit. As Feldman (1991,12) wrote in the introduction to his ethnography on Northern Ireland, "in order to know I had to become expert in demonstrating that there were things, places, and people I did not want to know." Although the situation in Maringue posed different challenges to those faced by Feldman, I found myself doing exactly that: emphasising by word and deed that there were some areas, people, and topics I was not going to familiarise myself with.

This is exemplified by a conversation I had with my research assistant Adão, who was one of my main links to RENAMO, and accompanied me to interviews. "You know who is also a *desmobilizado* [a demobilised person]? João from the hospital." he said one day. I was slightly surprised. I ran into João almost on a daily basis, as I lived next to the hospital. "But we cannot talk to João in the hospital," Adão said. This indeed seemed the most practical place for a meeting, but Adão explained: "People cannot see that you speak to him because he is from RENAMO. That does not look good and can be difficult for him." Apparently Joao's employer, the local ministry of health, did not know he was a former RENAMO combatant, as well as a member of the RENAMO party. This was crucial as public servants were expected to be FRELIMO members. A few people openly switched from one party to the other, but others carefully hid their political preferences and membership. There was a small possibility that João could lose his job by talking to me in public, as it was widely known in the village that I talked to RENAMO veterans. Additionally, the identity of my assistant also played a role in this, as Adão was a well-known RENAMO politician.

Adão said it was perfectly fine to talk to João at his home, but I felt also apprehensive about doing this, as the entire neighbourhood would quickly know about a white woman's visit. This was all the more the case as it was August, the dry season when the grass and bushes were low and leafless, meaning that everything that happened outside people's huts was visible. I did not want to risk putting João in a difficult position. Therefore, I never talked to him, at least no more than polite greetings.

Many anthropologists protect their interlocutors in writing by providing pseudonyms, which I used for João and Adão as well, as well as by omitting certain data from their publications, which I also did as João was not really working at the hospital, but in another public institution. But as this case shows, the protection of people during research may already begin in the selection of interlocutors in the field. My intentions to maintain good relationships with both RENAMO and FRELIMO members might have worked for me, but for the people participating in the research project this "neutrality" did not apply. For them, participation in my research could have unforeseeable and undesirable consequences.

A PLACE I DID NOT VISIT: RENAMO'S MILITARY BASE

A place I did not visit was RENAMO's military base. In the 1992 peace accords it was stipulated that RENAMO could maintain a certain number of "presidential guards" to protect the RENAMO leadership. This *de facto* elite force of RENAMO combatants was never demobilised and sixteen years after the war had ended, RENAMO continued to maintain several military bases throughout the country. RENAMO's largest base was said to be in Maringue. It was located within walking distance, somewhere southwest from the main village. At least that was what people told me, as I never visited the base.

Sometime during my second period of fieldwork I apparently had gained the confidence of the district's RENAMO leaders, as I received an invitation from the RENAMO general to visit the military base. Adão my research assistant told me the general had approached him saying that he would be delighted to receive me in "the bush" as his guest. I felt honoured and very much tempted to accept the invitation, as I had been secretly waiting for an opportunity to see what was "out there." All the more, because of frequent exclamations of several militant RENAMO members that I could not understand RENAMO if I had not seen the base. Nevertheless, I resisted my curiosity and politely declined the invitation. I felt that a visit to the base would have jeopardized my research project, as the base was a sensitive security issue and it would have given the local government a very good reason to expel me from the district.[2] Moreover, such a visit could also cause difficulties for the FRELIMO members who had become my friends and research participants. When at one point during fieldwork in 2008 rumours circulated that I was planning to visit the base, several of my "FRELIMO" research participants came to me in distress, urging me to deny these claims openly, which I did. The "base" thus remained a blind spot in my description of Maringue.

I sometimes wonder if a visit to the base would have deepened my relationships with RENAMO veterans and would have generated access to other hidden parts of RENAMO I can now only imagine. But it is also likely that just as with other kinds of "secret information," a visit to the base would not have enhanced my understanding of the everyday social practices of ex-combatants in Maringue, as for most of them, "the base" was an equally enigmatic matter.[3] For sure, it would have made it difficult, if not impossible, for me to return to Maringue, at least as long as political configurations would remain more or less the same. That was a risk I was not willing to take.

This example shows some of the balancing that I deemed necessary to be able to do research on a highly sensitive matter, in a politically divided context, which was at least bureaucratically controlled by the FRELIMO government. It were government officials who had provided me the research permit that allowed me to stay in Maringue. Several times government officials and FRELIMO party politicians warned me not to study "politics," to which I replied that I was focusing on culture and history, and needed to hear the stories of "many sides." I was never dishonest about the topic of my research, but on several occasions I used "impression management" (Goffman 1959) to mitigate certain suspicions (see also Berreman 1963; Sluka 1995) by presenting the research in less politicised terms. This was reluctantly accepted, but also meant that there were aspects of Maringue-life that I felt would be too "political" to delve into, and RENAMO's military base was one of them.

A TOPIC I COULD NOT (DIRECTLY) TALK ABOUT: SEXUAL VIOLENCE

A third frontier I encountered was the topic of violence in the conversations I had with former combatants (but also others) in Maringue. Much has been written about the particularities of narrating violent experiences and while I had made myself familiar with themes such as the inability to express violent experiences (Coulter 2009; Scarry 1985), narrations as cultural productions (Nordstrom 1997), their ability to create order and continuity in an otherwise chaotic and discontinuous world (Linden 1993), the role of the ethnographer (Robben 1996), and the contingency of narratives (Igreja 2007), I felt ill-prepared when I was confronted with silence.

This is well illustrated by my conversations with Ana, a former RENAMO combatant who I met on my first day in Maringue, and henceforth I made a habit of visiting her house weekly. We would spend the morning or afternoon sitting outside in the shade of a tree, chatting while her children played with my bicycle. Over countless conversations, she regaled me with anecdotes about her life. She became one of those key informants whom I could turn to for the (apparently) trivial and "thick" aspects of my research. I asked her many hundreds of questions, both crucial for my research and trivial. Often she answered them, but sometimes, especially when I believed the questions to be crucial, she did not. So while I felt we had established "rapport," or what I would rather call a bond of trust or friendship, there were topics she would explicitly refuse to get into. These included her deceased husband, her relationships with men during the war, and her personal experiences of violence. Once, I asked Ana directly about forced sexual relationships with male combatants during the war, and she simply replied that she was not going to talk about this topic. We sat in silence for a while, then she said quite matter-of-factly: "sometimes we wanted soap." I tried to probe this statement, but without much success. My interpretation was that she suggested that sexual relationships with male combatants were a way to obtain certain goods during the war, such as soap. Which reveals not only some of the terrible, mundane suffering of being a RENAMO combatant, but also seems to suggest a certain degree of agency, as Ana situated herself as in control of these relationships, using them to make life with RENAMO less harsh.

In writing my dissertation it was not my aim to analyse the psychological consequences of violence, nor did I have the therapeutic skills to delve into these subjects. Therefore, I mostly did not probe people's accounts about the perpetration and witnessing of (sexual) violence. Rather, I let my interlocutors define the limits, and I made an effort interpreting the things that were said, while also grasping what was unsaid. Some people talked very candidly about atrocities that they had experienced or else perpetrated, while others reduced their war experiences to a few sentences, referring to recruitment and demobilisation, and largely skipping over their experiences of combat or other forms of violence. Other conversations resulted in "meta narratives" about the war—why it started, what it was about, why they were fighting—and accounts of the experiences of others, which may have been a way for people to talk about themselves. I found these meta-narratives and the silences were not necessarily symbolically "thin." Meta-narratives, for example, often involved defining moments, post-facto legitimisations, and conceptualisations of suffering. Additionally, the things that were unsaid, were in some cases very present. I concur with Nordstrom (1997, 24) that "people define themselves in narration, but they equally constitute themselves in the silent space of the unsaid." Silence is not necessarily a sign of fear, resignation, indifference, or trauma. As Jackson (2004, 56) argues, silence may comprise respect and possibilities for healing and coexistence (see also Coulter 2009, 17).

One way of interpreting Ana's silence, and the silence of most female veterans about sexual violence, was that they were unable to convey these experiences into words. This might have been heightened by taboos about sex and sexual violence, but it could also be related to political taboos particular to Maringue, as it was rather unusual to hear RENAMO supporters criticise RENAMO. Yet another (not necessary mutually exclusive) reading of female veterans' silences might be that by omitting sexual violence from their narratives and simultaneously highlighting their roles as *militares*, female veterans created a story of themselves that underlines their professionalism, their courage, and their agency. Seen this way, their narratives are part of a strategy for, as Nordstrom (1997) argued, "creating a more survivable world."

Thus while I struggled with the question whether or not I was to probe experiences of violence, which most of the time I did not, I found that these conversations in which the limits were explored, but not touched, were in fact a rich source of analysis. In his fine-grained ethnography on a war-town area in Uganda, Finnstrom (2008, 21) wrote that narratives are always negotiations through dialogue and contextualisation in which both the ethnographer and the research participant are implicated. I would add that especially in the context of post-violence, the silences of both the ethnographer and his or her interlocutors are just as integral to these negotiations.

CONCLUSION

In this paper I have explored three frontiers I encountered while doing research on former combatants in a politically tense and sometimes violent context of a rural town in Mozambique. I have found it useful to reflect on the things I did not do, as these moments were decisive in how I dealt with issues that generally preoccupy ethnographers of violent, politically unstable, and conflict-ridden contexts. These included the protection of research participants, the balancing between opposing parties, the (im)possibilities of "taking sides," and the interpretation of narratives about violent experiences. All in all the frontiers I encountered (and did not cross) defined in many ways my position within Maringue, they limited access to some areas of community-life, but also deepened my insight in others. Being explicit about the places, people, and issues I did not want to know enhanced my rapport with FRELIMO members and not probing into the taboo and hidden spheres of conversations may also have strengthened my relationships of trust with Ana and others.

I can only speculate on what I have missed out on by not talking to João, by not visiting the military base, and by not probing the topic of violence. Each of these decision had probably a different impact on the data I was able to gather and the extent to which I could and can reflect on social and political processes in Maringue. Talking to one former combatant more or less probably did not make significant difference in my understanding of former combatants life trajectories. Not probing the topic of violence was a far more structural decision, which most likely influenced my understanding of people's suffering of the war. I can only hope that I have interpreted the said and unsaid in respectful ways. I do sometimes regret not having visited the RENAMO military base, as this would have provided a unique opportunity to understand RENAMO's post-war military wing. The potential relevance of such data for understanding RENAMO became all the more apparent in its recent remobilisation. As there was and is still little known about RENAMO's "presidential guards," its weapons stockpiles, and military capacity in general. In fact, it is this side of RENAMO that is the topic of one of my next research projects.

It is only logical that most ethnographic accounts are based on the events that we observed and participated in and that they are about the people we meet and about the things we heard people say. But as I have tried to show in this paper, there is a lot to be learned from the moments that we did not get access (or did not want to get access) and the stories that were not told to us. Therefore, I want to close by advocating the analysis of vulnerable moments of doubt and the decisions one made *not* to do something, as these may form an interesting lens for understanding the ethical and practical challenges of conducting fieldwork in "risky" areas. And even more, these moments may be valuable for analysis, as they may, even if only slightly, enhance our understanding of what it means to live in volatile and oppressive social and political environments.

REFERENCES

Berreman, G. D. 1963. "Behind Many Masks: Ethnography and Impression Management." In *Hindus of the Himalayas: Ethnography and Change,* edited by G. D. Berreman, xvii–lvii. Berkeley: University of California Press.

Coulter, C. 2009. *Bush Wives and Girl Soldiers: Women's Lives through War and Peace in Sierra Leone.* Ithaca: Cornell University Press.

Feldman, A. 1991. *Formations of Violence: The Narrative of Body and Political Terror in Northern Ireland.* Chicago: University of Chicago Press.

Finnström, S. 2008. *Living with Bad Surroundings: War, History and Everyday Moments in Northern Uganda.* Durham: Duke University Press.

Igreja, V. 2007. "The Monkey's Sworn Oath: Cultures of Engagement for Reconciliation and Healing in the Aftermath of Civil War in Mozambique." PhD diss., Leiden University.

Jackson, M. 2004. "The Prose of Suffering and the Practice of Silence." *Spiritus: A Journal of Christian Spirituality* 4: 4–59.

Klungel, J. 2010. "Rape and Rememberance in Guadelope." In *Remembering Violence: Anthropological Perspectives on Intergenerational Transmission,* edited by N. Argenti and K. Schramm, 43–62. Oxford: Berghahn Books.

Linden, R. R. 1993. *Making Stories, Making Selves: Feminist Reflections on the Holocaust.* Colombus: Ohio State University Press.

Mahmud, L. 2012. "'The World Is a Forest of Symbols.' Italian Freemasonry and the Practice of Discretion." *American Ethnologist* 39, no. 2: 425–438.

Nordstrom, C. 1997. *A Different Kind of War Story.* Philadelphia: University of Pennsylvania Press.

Raybeck, D. 1996. *Mad Dogs, Englishmen, and the Errant Anthropologist: Fieldwork in Malaysia.* Long Grove: Waveland Press.

Robben, A.C.G.M. 1996. "Ethnographic Seduction, Transference, and Resistance in Dialogues about Terror and Violence in Argentina." *Ethos* 24, no. 1: 71–106.

Scarry, E. 1985. *The Body in Pain: The Making and Unmaking of the World.* Oxford: Oxford University Press.

Sluka, J. A. 1995. "Reflections on Managing Danger in Fieldwork: Dangerous Anthropology in Belfast." In *Fieldwork Under Fire: Contemporary Studies of Violence and Survival,* edited by A. C. G. M. Robben and C. Nordstrom, 276–294. Berkeley: University of California Press.

NOTES

1. In 2012 a low-intensity war started between RENAMO combatants and the FRELIMO government, during which it was reported that the RENAMO military base in Maringue was under multiple attacks. But as these events happened after my fieldwork I leave them out of the analysis.

2. A foreign nun who had allegedly visited the base, when RENAMO combatants had imprisoned a government official in 2003, was expelled from the district.

3. Mahmud (2012) stresses that "secret knowledge" is often alluring, also for the ethnographer, but such information may be just as—or even less—important as public knowledge for ethnographic interpretation.

Appendix 1

Doctoral Dissertations Defended within the Utrecht Research Program

Table 16.1.

Author*	Graduate degree in:	Year#	Dissertation title (translated by the editors when not originally in English)
Chris van der Borgh	Political science	1999	Reconstruction in Chalantenango: Development Organisations in a Post-War Society
Marieke Denissen	Social sciences	2008	"Winning Small Battles, Losing the War": Police Violence, the Movimiento del Dolor, and Democracy in Post-Authoritarian Argentina
Ingeborg Denissen	Political science	2014	Negotiating Urban Citizenship: The Urban Poor, Brokers and the State in Mexico City and Khartoum
Tessa Diphoorn	Conflict studies and human rights	2014	Twilight Policing: Private Security in Durban, South Africa
Mirella van Dun	Anthropology	2009	Cocaleros: Violence, Drugs, and Social Mobilisation in the Post-Conflict Upper

			Huallaga Valley, Peru
Mario Fumerton	Anthropology	2002	From Victims to Heroes: Peasant Counter-Rebellion and Civil War in Ayacucho, Peru, 1980–2000
Henri Gooren	Anthropology	1998	Rich among the Poor: Church, Firm, and Household among Small-Scale Entrepreneurs in Guatemala City
Marie-Louise Glebbeek	Anthropology	2003	In the Crossfire of Democracy: Police Reform and Police Practice in Post–Civil War Guatemala
Christien Klaufus	Anthropology, urban studies	2006	The Cities and the Builders: Changes in Popular Housing and Social Change in Riobamba and Cuenca, Ecuador
Jacobijn Olthoff	Anthropology	2006	A Dream Denied: Teenage Girls in Migrant Popular Neighbourhoods, Lima, Peru
Elisabet Rasch	Anthropology	2008	Representing Mayas: Indigenous Authorities and the Local Politrics of Identity in Guatemala
Simone Remijnse	Anthropology	2003	Memories of Violence: Civil Patrols and the Legacy of Conflict in Joabaj, Guatemala
Eva van Roekel	Latin American and Caribbean studies	2016	Phenomenal Justice: State Violence, Emotion, and the Law in Argentina

Ariel Sánchez Meertens	Conflict studies and human rights	2013	Letters from Batticaloa: TMVP's Emergence and the Transmission of Conflict in Eastern Sri Lanka
Wim Savenije	Social psychology, philosophy	2009	Maras y barras: Gangs and Juvenile Violence in Central American Marginal Neighbourhoods.
Marc Simon Thomas	Latin American studies	2013	The Challenge of Legal Pluralism: Local Dispute Settlement and the Indian-State Relationship in Ecuador
Ralph Sprenkels	Latin American studies	2014	Revolution and Accommodation: Post-Insurgency in El Salvador
Nikkie Wiegink	Conflict studies and human rights	2014	Beyond Fighting and Returning: Social Navigations of Former Combatants in Central Mozambique

* Italicized names are contributors to this volume.

#Year in which PhD dissertation was completed and successfully defended. We include only the fully funded internal PhD positions.

Index

About the Contributors

Chris van der Borgh is assistant professor and consultant in the Centre for Conflict Studies at Utrecht University. He specialises in issues of peace and security, political order, and international intervention. He has published on parallel governance and the resistance against international state-building in Kosovo and about the conflicts and negotiations about security provisioning in Libya and South Sudan. He has extensive field experience—both as a practitioner and a scholar—in El Salvador. His PhD thesis (1999, Utrecht University) deals with the role of external donors in processes of local development and peacebuilding in El Salvador and was published as *Cooperación Externa, Gobierno Local y Reconstrucción Posguerra. La Experiencia de Chalatenango, El Salvador* (Governance, Foreign Assistance, and Reconstruction in El Salvador), Amsterdam: Thela Latin American Series, 2003. His recent publications deal with street gangs and government responses to deal with gangs in El Salvador.

Ingeborg Denissen holds an MA in political science from Amsterdam University (2002) and a PhD in social sciences from Utrecht University (2014) in the Netherlands, titled *Negotiating Urban Citizenship: The Urban Poor, Brokers and the State in Mexico City and Khartoum*. She has been working as a diplomat for The Netherlands Foreign Service for the past 15 years and has served at The Netherlands Embassy in Sudan and (on shorter assignments) in Poland and Ethiopia. Currently she is the deputy head of the Political Section at The Netherlands Embassy in Washington DC. Based on her research and on her diplomatic experience, Ingeborg Denissen has taught at various universities in The Netherlands (Amsterdam, Leiden, Groningen, Utrecht) and internationally (El Colegio de Mexico, New York University, George Washington University, and American University) on doing fieldwork in conflict areas, on urban and international security, and on international negotiations.

Tessa Diphoorn is assistant professor in the Department of Cultural Anthropology at Utrecht University. In 2016, her book based on her PhD about private security in South Africa—*Twilight Policing: Private Security and Violence in Urban South Africa*—was published by the University of California Press. In May 2017, she started a new research project titled "Policing the Police in Kenya: Analysing State Authority from Within," financed by the Netherlands Organisation for Scientific Research (NWO).

Kees Koonings is associate professor of anthropology and development studies in the Department of Cultural Anthropology at Utrecht University and Professor of Brazilian Studies at CEDLA, University of Amsterdam. Together with Dirk Kruijt he has published on political violence and dictatorship, political armies, and urban violence. He has also published on political militarism, urban politics, and violence public security in Brazil. Currently he is working on a book about the politics of war and peace in Colombia.

Dirk Kruijt is professor emeritus of development studies in the Department of Cultural Anthropology at Utrecht University. He is also an Investigador Incorporado at the Centro de Estudos Internacionais, Instituto Universitário de Lisboa, and a Research Fellow at the Centre for Military Studies, Stellenbosch University, South Africa. Together with Kees Koonings he has published on political violence and dictatorship, political armies, and urban violence. He also published on war and peace in Central America (2008) and on Cuba's influence on the Latin American Armed Left (2017). Currently he is preparing a co-edited volume on Latin American guerrilla movements.

Elisabet Dueholm Rasch is associate professor of anthropology of Development at Wageningen University. In 2008 she defended her PhD thesis *Representing Mayas: Indigenous Authorities and the Local Politics of Identity* at Utrecht University. In her current research she looks at how (activism towards) mega projects of natural resource extraction and energy production transform practices and meanings of citizenship and democracy. The research is rooted in the observation that the properties of resources (and how they are extracted) shape the ways people organize around them and (re)negotiate their relation with the state on the one hand, and that democratic institutions inform the ways that power relations transform in the field of energy production and subsoil natural resource extraction on the other. Her regional focus is Latin America (Guatemala and Colombia) and Europe (The Netherlands).

Simone Remijnse has been working for 13 years at PAX (the Dutch Peace organization, www.paxforpeace.nl), working in conflict regions worldwide. Her PhD thesis at Utrecht University was published as *Memories of Violence: Civil Patrols and the Legacy of Conflict in Joyabaj, Guatemala* (Amsterdam: Rozenberg Publishers, Thela Latin American Series, 2002). Initially she worked mainly on Colombia and Cuba, but the last three years she has been working more thematically as an expert on Dealing with the Past (DWP) and Local Governance and Peacebuilding at PAX. She has worked in different (post)conflict regions such as Kosovo, Srebrenica (BiH), South Sudan, Iraq, and Congo supporting local peace dialogues between warring ethnic or religious groups, work on memorialization and memory activism, work with victims and perpetrators of violence, storytelling by victims as a way of connecting, and supporting social contract (between citizens and local governments). In her work she tries to integrate some of the principles of non-violent communication (NVC). Aside from working with partners in conflict areas, she also lobbies and does research, both directly related to the work on the ground. She also give guest lectures at universities and presentations at conferences, to try and bridge the gap that still exists between university research and the work of NGOs.

Dennis Rodgers is research professor in the Department of Anthropology and Sociology at the Graduate Institute of International and Development Studies, Geneva, Switzerland, and visiting professor in International Development Studies at the University of Amsterdam, the Netherlands. A social anthropologist by training, his research focuses broadly on issues relating to the political economy of urban development, including the dynamics of conflict and violence in cities in Latin America (Nicaragua, Argentina) and South Asia (India). He was recently awarded a European Research Council (ERC) Advanced Grant for a 5-year project on "Gangs, Gangsters, and Ganglands: Towards a Comparative Global Ethnography" (GANGS), which aims to systematically compare gang dynamics in Nicaragua, South Africa, and France (2019-2023).

Ariel Sánchez Meertens holds a PhD in social sciences (Utrecht University), obtained with the dissertation *Letters from Batticaloa*: *TMVP's Emergence and the Transmission of Conflict in Eastern Sri Lanka (*Ipskamp Publishers*)*. Between 2015 and 2017, he held a postdoctoral fellowship at the Universidad Nacional de Colombia, which led to the book *Saberes de la Guerra: Memoria y Conocimiento Intergeneracional del Conflicto en Colombia*. Ariel recently served as an adviser to Bogotá's Centre for Memory Peace and Reconciliation, in charge of the design and initial implementation of the capital's memory and reconciliation strategies. He has been a consultant for UNICEF and the Colombian Administrative Department for Public Service on topics related to peace pedagogies. Ariel currently works as an analyst and coordinator of the Restorative Justice team for Colombia's Peace Tribunal (Jurisdicción Especial para la Paz) and among his recent publications is a chapter in the edited volume *Truth, Justice and Reconciliation in Colombia* (Routledge, 2018).

Marc Simon Thomas is a legal anthropologist, trained in law and in cultural anthropology, and has specialized in empirical research on dispute settlement. Currently he is assistant professor in the School of Law at Utrecht University in the Netherlands, and a researcher in the Montaigne Centre for Rule of Law and Judicial Administration where he conducts research on alternative dispute resolution (ADR) in the Netherlands. For his PhD dissertation, he combined his law and cultural anthropology background and analyzed how internal conflicts among indigenous inhabitants of the Ecuadorian highlands are settled within the context of formal legal pluralism. His dissertation *The Challenge of Legal Pluralism: Local Dispute Settlement and the Indian-state Relationship in Ecuador* was published by Routledge in 2017.

Eva van Roekel is assistant professor at VU Amsterdam at the Department of Social and Cultural Anthropology. She has lived and worked for more than a decade in Latin America. She has carried out ethnographic field research on poverty, adolescence, and political violence in Venezuela. Her PhD at Utrecht University focused on the reopened trials for crimes against humanity committed during the military regime in Argentina (1976-1983) from both a victims' and perpetrators' perspective. This resulted in the monograph *Phenomenal Justice: Violence, Trauma, and Time in Argentina* published by Rutgers University Press (forthcoming 2019). She has published articles and book chapters on themes such as empathy, emotion, humor, temporality, and trauma and violence and has also completed three documentaries and a short story for a wider audience. Her current research focuses on military subjectivity, mental health and transnationalism in Cyprus and Argentina. For further details, see: www.dokumento.org.

Monique Sonnevelt holds an MA in cultural anthropology (Utrecht University) and carried out extensive field research in Guatemala and Mexico, publishing several articles based on her ethnographic studies. She is also a board member of Los Cachorros, a foundation that provides a haven for children and teenagers in Ayacucho, Peru.

Ralph Sprenkels is lecturer in the Centre for Conflict Studies at Utrecht University. His work focuses on the aftermath of violent conflict in Latin America. With a background in philosophy and history, he obtained an MA degree (cum laude) in Latin American studies at the University of Amsterdam (in 2004) and a PhD degree in social science at Utrecht University (in 2014). Co-founder of Salvadoran human rights group Asociación Pro-Búsqueda de Niñas y Niños Desaparecidos, Ralph Sprenkels has extensive work experience in the field of human rights research and activism. His publications include books and articles about El Salvador's civil war, the legacies of human rights abuses, social movements, memory politics and post-insurgency. An updated and revised version of his PhD thesis was published by the University of Notre Dame Press in 2018, titled *After Insurgency: Revolution and Electoral Politics in El Salvador*.

Floortje Toll has an MA in international relations (University of Groningen) and an MSc in Latin American studies (Utrecht University). She has worked as an analyst for the Dutch Ministry of Foreign Affairs and as a teacher at the Utrecht University Department of Cultural Anthropology. On two occasions she worked for the Mission to Support the Peace Process in Colombia of the Organization of American States (MAPP/OEA) monitoring conditions of security, peacebuilding, and transitional justice in different parts of the Colombian territory, first in the aftermath of the paramilitary demobilization (2009-2011), and from 2015 onward during the peace agreement with the FARC-EP. Her ongoing PhD project concerns the implementation of transitional justice mechanisms in remote conflict-affected areas in Colombia.

Nikkie Wiegink is assistant professor in the Department of Cultural Anthropology at Utrecht University. She defended her PhD thesis titled *Beyond Fighting and Returning: Social Navigations of Former Combatants in Central Mozambique* in 2014. Her book *Former Combatants in Mozambique* is forthcoming with the University of Pennsylvania Press. She previously worked as a disarmament, demobilization, and reintegration expert for the Bonn International Center for Conversion (BICC) in Khartoum, Sudan. Her current research project is called "Enacting the Coal Enclave: Corporate Sovereignty in Central Mozambique" and focuses on issues of conflict, power and governance surrounding extractive investment projects. It is financed by the Netherlands Organisation for Scientific Research (NWO).